*The Black Soldiers
Who Built the
Alaska Highway*

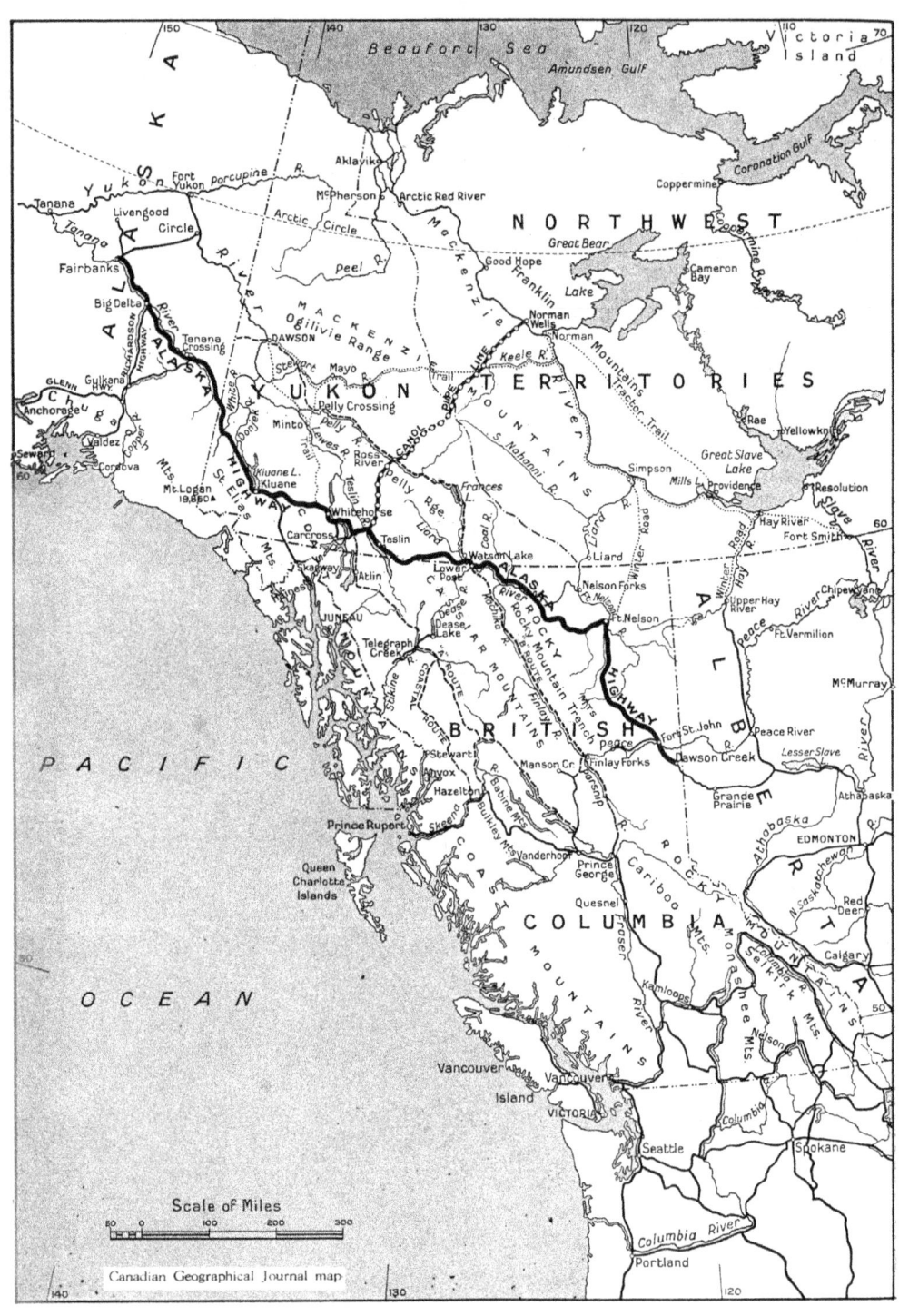

The Black Soldiers Who Built the Alaska Highway

A History of Four U.S. Army Regiments in the North, 1942–1943

JOHN VIRTUE

Foreword by Monte Irvin

McFarland & Company, Inc., Publishers
Jefferson, North Carolina, and London

ALSO BY JOHN VIRTUE
South of the Color Barrier: How Jorge Pasquel and the Mexican League Pushed Baseball Toward Racial Integration (McFarland, 2008)

Frontispiece: Alaska and Canada's Northwest (courtesy *Canadian Geographical Journal*).

LIBRARY OF CONGRESS CATALOGUING-IN-PUBLICATION DATA

Virtue, John.
The Black soldiers who built the Alaska highway : a history of four U.S. Army regiments in the north, 1942–1943 / John Virtue ; foreword by Monte Irvin.
    p.   cm.
Includes bibliographical references and index.

ISBN 978-0-7864-7117-1
softcover : acid free paper ∞

1. Alaska Highway — History — 20th century.
2. United States. Army — African American troops — History — 20th century.
3. African American soldiers — Alaska — History — 20th century.
4. World War, 1939–1945 — Regimental histories — United States.
I. Title.
TE24.A4V57 2013   940.54'1273—dc23   2012044142

BRITISH LIBRARY CATALOGUING DATA ARE AVAILABLE

© 2013 John Virtue. All rights reserved

No part of this book may be reproduced or transmitted in any form or by any means, electronic or mechanical, including photocopying or recording, or by any information storage and retrieval system, without permission in writing from the publisher.

On the cover: Members of the 95th Regiment, which bet white soldiers their paychecks that they could build a bridge across the Sikanni Chief River in fewer than five days, carry logs for the construction (courtesy Office of History Collection, U.S. Army Corps of Engineers); background map of Alaska (© 2013 Shutterstock)

Manufactured in the United States of America

*McFarland & Company, Inc., Publishers
Box 611, Jefferson, North Carolina 28640
www.mcfarlandpub.com*

For Madeline Gene and Samantha Rose,
who love books

Contents

Foreword by Monte Irvin	1
Preface	4
Introduction	6
1 — Pondering a Pathway to Alaska	9
2 — Highway and Pipeline Approved	14
3 — The Second Emancipation Order	25
4 — Blacks Rush to Enlist	33
5 — Black Soldiers Voice Their Complaints	48
6 — Army Reluctantly Assigns Black Regiments	55
7 — Heading North	60
8 — Japanese Attack Justifies the Alcan Highway	72
9 — The 93rd and the 95th Start Off with Picks and Shovels	83
10 — The 97th Completes the Highway	96
11 — The 388th Does the Heavy Lifting	109
12 — An Unexpectedly Severe Winter	127
13 — Surviving Isolation	141
14 — The Highway Is Praised, the Pipeline Criticized	155
15 — Identifying Problems	166
16 — News Coverage of Black Troops Suppressed	179
Epilogue	185
Chapter Notes	195
Bibliography	211
Index	217

Foreword by Monte Irvin

World War II was over by the time I learned about the black regiments that had served in Alaska and Canada's northern territories. They helped build the Alaskan Highway and install the Canol pipeline, but it was generally unknown that those guys were up there. When I later heard accounts about how badly they were treated, it was no surprise to me because I experienced it firsthand in my own outfit.

In 1941—before we got into the war—the Negro National League owners had decided that I would be the one to break the color line when the time came. After the season, I was playing winter ball in Puerto Rico when it was announced over the loudspeaker that the Japanese had bombed Pearl Harbor and the United States had declared war on them. The fans all started cheering. I thought, "Don't they realize what this means?" At that time I didn't know how it would affect me or what role I would play in the war.

When Uncle Sam needed me, I was just coming off a fantastic season in the Mexican League, where I led the league in both batting average and home runs and only missed the triple crown by a couple of RBIs. I was in my baseball prime and loving the game more than ever, but I swapped my baseball colors for Army khaki.

Making the transition from Mexico, where I was treated the same as anybody else and could come and go anywhere I pleased, to the rigidly segregated military was a big change.

I was in the 1313th Battalion, General Service Engineers, from March 1943 through September 1, 1945, and it was the same old discrimination pattern throughout the U.S. Armed Forces. The scuttlebutt was that our military leaders decided to put white Southern officers in charge of black units because it was believed that they knew best how to handle black soldiers. They let us know that we were not going to be treated as well as other troops. I don't think many people know just how bad it was for black soldiers.

When they were billeting troops in England, President Franklin Delano Roosevelt said, "We'll just handle it the same way we do in the U.S." My outfit was all black and we had one commissioned officer, a white first lieutenant from Texarkana, Arkansas, and the other officers were black non-coms under him. Soon after we arrived in Red Ruth, England, he addressed us and said, "Men, I understand that there has been some integration and fraternization with local families. I want it to stop." What he meant was that he didn't want us to interact with the English populace in any form or fashion.

Afterward, a black chaplain, who was a captain, addressed us and said, "You're members of the U.S. Armed Forces. If anyone invites you to their homes or anywhere else, by all means, you go. You have the right to go any place you're invited." Then he said, "I assure you that the lieutenant will not be with us much longer." Within a week he was gone and we were glad. We all wondered how he could be so insensitive.

If anything, those units working up north in Canada were probably treated worse than we were in my outfit because they were among the first black regiments formed — mainly in 1941 before the United States entered World War II — and their officers would not have been skilled in race relations and probably had received even less training about commanding black troops than the white officers that we had initially.

After I came back home and met some of the fellows who were in those outfits, they confirmed the accounts that I had heard previously and validated my personal assessment. Any black serviceman will tell you the same thing — we were treated terribly. We were assigned to road building and other menial jobs. It was totally unfair how black troops were treated, but that's the way it was at that time. All we wanted was to be treated the same as any other American soldier.

We could march, train and fight just like anyone else. We wanted to fight, too. In those instances when we were given the chance, we performed just as well as any other soldier. During the Japanese attack at Pearl Harbor, a black cook manned a machine gun and was decorated for his actions.

Look at the Tuskegee Airmen and what they did. They escorted those B-29 bombers and never lost a plane, but when they got back to England they couldn't even have a cup of coffee with the men they saved.

The Red Ball Express hauled ammunition and fuel from France to Germany and risked their lives in so doing, sometimes driving over roads that had not been completely cleared of mines or driving through sniper fire intended to ignite the trucks.

During the Normandy invasion the black 818th Amphibian Battalion earned praise for bringing ammunition ashore at Utah and Omaha beaches. Leon Day, my teammate with the Newark Eagles both before and after the war, was a member of that outfit and one of the soldiers who drove the amphibian "ducks" loaded with ammunition.

My unit arrived about two months later, and by the time we landed at Omaha Beach, it had been cleared. We built bridges and roads, and guarded German POWs at Mailly Le Camp. They were mostly either very young or very old and all of them were completely defeated and glad to be out of the war and safe behind the lines. They didn't want to be there any more than we did.

When U.S. units got in trouble in Belgium during the Battle of the Bulge, General Patton called back to his black artillery battalion and they said, "We heard you were in trouble. You didn't have to call us. You trained us well and we're already on the way."

My unit packed up and moved to Rheims to guard a big gasoline depot. If Bastogne had not held, Rheims would have been the next big city in France that the Germans would have hit because of the fuel dumps located throughout the city. We were issued rifles and bandoliers of ammunition and readied for the Germans should they break through. Before that our leaders wouldn't even give us ammunition. That was the nearest we came to combat. We were just glad that we were able to survive and come back in one piece.

When the subject came up about the conditions that existed for black soldiers during those years, I just thought that the world in general didn't know how badly the black troops were treated, although they still performed very well under adverse conditions. They finished their work in great fashion and I think that their contributions should be recognized.

The U.S. military didn't know what to do with us and they didn't use us properly. All I want to say is that I just wish we had been appreciated and treated more fairly. But that was the tone of the country at that time. Based on my experiences, much progress has been made in race relations. They are much better now, but they could have been better way back then. Maybe everyone should know just what we endured.

We also need to remember that freedom is not free. Although my baseball career suffered due to my military service, the three-year interruption, along with the discrimination and unfair treatment that I experienced in the Army, was a part of the personal price that I paid. However, I salute President Harry S Truman for integrating the armed services in 1948. Many other Americans paid a much higher price for the freedom that we have in our country.

I commend John Virtue for writing this book, which will bring about a more complete understanding of the existing conditions that black regiments faced, while also honoring the contributions of those who participated in building the Alaska Highway.

Monte Irvin, who once said he was a .300 hitter before going overseas in World War II and a .200 hitter when he returned home, was a five-time All-Star with the New York Giants. He served 17 years as a public relations specialist in the office of the baseball commissioner and he was elected to the Hall of Fame in 1973.

Preface

The person who suggested I write this book was Monte Irvin, a former New York Giant and a member of baseball's Hall of Fame who had served in a black service unit in Europe during World War II. I had just published *South of the Color Barrier*, my book on the role of the Mexican League in the desegregation of baseball, when Monte, who had played in Mexico, asked me what my next project would be. I told him I was thinking of writing a fictionalized memoir of my maternal grandmother. "Why don't you write a book instead about the black soldiers who helped build the Alaska Highway during the war?" asked Monte, whose wartime service interrupted his baseball career.

I was intrigued by Monte's suggestion since I knew more than most people about the Alaska Highway, having been raised in Edmonton, Alberta, the jumping-off point for the road. Yet I had never heard of black soldiers working there. My father had cooked at a construction camp on the Alaska Highway during the war and an uncle had driven a truck there. Both would later regale people about what they did and saw up north. Neither mentioned seeing any black soldiers there; that was because the American Army had forbidden them to go into settlements in Alaska or northern Canada for fear they would father a "mongrel" race.

After my initial research turned up the name of Lael Morgan, currently on the journalism faculty of the University of Texas, I became convinced of the need for a book about the achievements of the black soldiers up north in the face of racial discrimination. A writer-photographer, Lael and her husband had driven from Maine to Alaska in 1959 and settled there. As the 1992 fiftieth anniversary of completion of the highway approached, *National Geographic* hired her to write a story. She located, photographed, and interviewed about thirty black veterans who had been involved. When she wanted to make them a focus of her story, the magazine relieved her of the writing assignment and gave it to another journalist. Consequently, she put together a traveling museum show of photos, helped by the Alaska Humanities Forum and University of Alaska, where she then taught. The exhibition was shown in Alaska, northwestern Canada and eventually at the Pentagon, thanks to Colin Powell, the first black chairman of the Joint Chiefs of Staff.

I want to thank Lael for giving me access to her archival material at the University of Alaska in Fairbanks and for encouraging me to write this book, the first one about the 5,000 black soldiers who labored on the highway and the companion Canol pipeline project in northern Canada.

Preface

Research took me twice to the National Archives at College Park, Maryland, and to the Corps of Engineers in Alexandria, Virginia; the U.S. Army Military History Institute in Carlisle Barracks, Pennsylvania; the Black Archives Research Center at Florida A&M in Tallahassee; the University of Washington in Seattle; the University of Alaska in Fairbanks and Anchorage; Archives Canada in Ottawa; the University of Alberta in Edmonton; and the Yukon Archives, MacBride Museum and Public Library in Whitehorse, Yukon Territory. Librarian Ana Cabrera at Florida International University in Miami also obtained more than one hundred books and articles for me.

Two people in particular went out of their way to help me: Michael J. Brodhead at the Corps of Engineers and Peggy D'Orsay at the Yukon Archives. Mike was the go-to person for over a year as he fielded my queries; Peggy mentioned my research on a local website that resulted in several productive responses.

Most importantly for the book, my wife Anna, a former reporter-researcher at the *Los Angeles Times*, managed to locate fourteen surviving black soldiers whom I interviewed, some multiple times, plus wartime interviews with others published in the mainstream and black media. She was helped by former colleague John Beckham.

The late William E. Griggs not only agreed to an interview but also arranged for two other black veterans, John A. Bollin and Otis E. Lee, to meet with me at his home in Baltimore. He also gave me permission to use the photographs he had taken as photographer for the 97th Regiment in Alaska.

As occurred with four of my previous books, Lawrence and Lucile Finsten critiqued the manuscript, fact-checked and edited it.

And a special recognition goes to the late Michael McQueen, former faculty colleague at Florida International University. Although suffering from cancer, Mike agreed to read the manuscript for political correctness. I will always remember his generosity.

Introduction

During the spring of 1942, when frost was still on the ground, the American Army reluctantly sent nearly 5,000 black soldiers to Alaska and Canada's Northwest to work on two of the biggest construction projects of World War II: the 1,650-mile-long Alaska Highway that linked the then territory to the lower forty-eight states and the Canol pipeline that supplied Canadian oil to the U.S. military in Alaska. Many, if not most, of the soldiers were farm boys from the Deep South who had never before seen snow. When they left their Southern training camps aboard troop trains, they had no idea of their final destination (such was the secrecy surrounding the two projects), or of how they would be treated after they arrived.

The soldiers were members of four segregated Engineer General Service Regiments, the 93rd, 95th, 97th and 388th, the first black units to be sent abroad during World War II. The first two regiments were deployed in northern British Columbia and the Yukon Territory, the 97th in Alaska and the 388th in northern Alberta and the Northwest Territories. The nearly two hundred officers who commanded them were white; the only black officers were regimental chaplains.

Four days after leaving Camp Livingston, Louisiana, the train carrying the first of 1,240 enlisted members of the 93rd Regiment stopped in Seattle, Washington, leading its officers to believe they were going to board a ship for the Pacific theater in the Far East. Instead, the train continued north into Canada. "Whenever we stopped, the local Canadians gathered around and stared at us," reported one officer. "I don't think many of them had ever seen black boys before. The young Canadian girls were particularly intrigued and loved to talk to the boys."[1] The members of the 93rd were surprised when, after disembarking in Prince Rupert, British Columbia, they were taken dockside to board the CSS *Prince George*, a Canadian Steamship Lines luxury cruise liner not yet converted to a troop carrier. For their last good meals for more than two years, the black soldiers sat at tables set with linen, fine chinaware and silver utensils; they ordered from a menu.

When the regiment reached Skagway, Alaska, after a two-day cruise up the Inner Passage, the cabins onboard ship gave way to tents and the courteous service of Filipino waiters gave way to gibes from local residents, who asked the black soldiers if they had tails. Tired of the questioning, one of the soldiers dropped his pants and mooned his audience. "That's the kind of tail we got," he told them.[2]

The 95th Regiment's 1,225 enlisted men traveled by train from Fort Bragg, North

Carolina, to Dawson Creek, British Columbia, known as "Mile Zero" on the Alaska Highway. As had happened with the 93rd, the 95th was greeted at railroad stations along the way. "We were on the train six days before we got to Dawson Creek and [at] all the little towns along the way the people came out to greet us," reported one black master sergeant. "It made us feel pretty good."[3] But a welcome was thwarted when the train pulled into Dawson Creek, by then an outpost of the American Army on Canadian soil. Another enlisted black soldier said Canadian girls met their train and wanted to give them cookies and candies but were prevented from doing so by white officers with drawn revolvers who patrolled the platform. "We were treated more like convicts than members of the United States Army," he said.[4] The girls had wanted to treat the black soldiers the same way they had treated white soldiers who had arrived earlier.

The 1,185 enlisted men of the 97th Regiment traveled on two trains from Pensacola, Florida, to Seattle, where they boarded the SS *David W. Branch*, an Army transport ship, for Valdez, Alaska. On open sea, a Navy warship escorted the slow-moving vessel while soldiers with rifles patrolled the deck, scanning the skies for Japanese warplanes. When the residents of Fairbanks learned that black troops were in Alaska, they circulated a petition asking that the soldiers be transferred to a "country and climate more closely resembling their natural habitat."[5] A section of the Alaska Highway on which the 97th worked became known as "The Negro Road" to residents of Fairbanks.[6]

When the 388th Regiment arrived in Waterways, Alberta, from Camp Claiborne, Louisiana, its 1,218 enlisted men made up fully half of the troops on the Canol project. The other Army units were white battalions or platoons. Many of the black soldiers temporarily bivouacked in an area the local called Nigger Rock, a term said to have originated with white officers.[7]

That the black enlisted men should be ill treated upon arrival was not surprising, since no one in the Army had wanted to send them north in the first place. They ended up on the highway and pipeline projects because the Army had run out of white soldiers for non-combat missions.

The Japanese surprise attack on Pearl Harbor on December 7, 1941, had exposed the "Achilles' heel" of America's defense: Alaska.[8] Oil and war matériel could only be supplied by ships passing through waters subject to enemy attack; airplane service was risky since airports were scarce and radio contact problematic due to magnetic disturbances.

The solution: build a highway to connect Alaska with the contiguous U.S. states and lay a pipeline to bring oil from one of the world's most northern oil fields to a refinery on the highway. The Army Corps of Engineers assigned four white regiments to build the highway, in conjunction with civilian workers from the Public Roads Administration. When the Corps of Engineers realized it could not complete the project within a year as planned unless it had additional troops, it turned to the black recruits.

The War Department had recently reaffirmed its policy of racial segregation in the Army in the belief that morale would be adversely affected if white and black soldiers served alongside each other. It was also thought that black soldiers, especially those from the Deep South, would be unable to withstand the cold — the temperature could drop to lower than seventy below zero — in the Far North.

Army policy wasn't the only obstacle. The commanding general in charge of the defense of Alaska claimed there'd be an "astonishingly objectionable race of mongrels" if black soldiers were to meet up with Indian or Eskimo ladies.[9] His superior, the commanding general of the Western Defense Command based in San Francisco, agreed. The American secretary of war and the governor of Alaska also opposed sending black troops to the Far North.

But the need for additional road builders was such that the Army reluctantly approved sending the hastily assembled black regiments. To win the support of the top general in Alaska, the Corps of Engineers agreed that the black soldiers would not be allowed to go into any settlements, even in Canada.

The Army believed that Canada and Newfoundland — a British colony destined to become Canada's tenth province after the war — would recognize the need for American troops, regardless of color, being posted within their territory. "No serious difficulties are anticipated with regard to the presence of Negro troops on the soil of either of these two countries," said the War Department's intelligence division.[10] But Canadian authorities were expected to keep the black soldiers out of Canadian settlements. The famed Royal Canadian Mounted Police appear to have sometimes been the enablers of American racial policy in Canada's Northwest.

The three black regiments played a key role in completing the highway in record time, but received scant mention in the mainstream American press, as opposed to the four white regiments. While the Alaska Highway became a famous thoroughfare, the Canol pipeline in Canada's Northwest soon faded from memory.[11] Nothing remains of it except graveyards of rusted trucks and machinery; the refinery and pipeline were dismantled and shipped elsewhere. The highway cost $138 million to build and the pipeline $134 million, almost $2 billion each in today's dollars. The totals do not include the paying, feeding, clothing, housing and transporting of more than 12,000 soldiers, white and black, on the two projects.

The building of the Alaska Highway has been compared to the construction of the Panama Canal in the early 1900s.[12] One knowledgeable Army consultant went further, saying that the highway and the Canol pipeline together represented the "biggest construction program in the history of the world."[13]

Because the four black regiments were the first deployed abroad, their success earned greater acceptance for all black troops in the U.S. Army. When the Army sought volunteers from black service units to fight as part of white combat units in the final months of World War II, members of two of the regiments then posted to Europe signed up. The seeds were planted for a presidential study that in 1948 led to the desegregation of the Armed Forces in the United States for the first time since the War of Independence. In 2005 the U.S. Congress recognized the work of the four regiments up north and their contribution to breaking the color barrier.

1

Pondering a Pathway to Alaska

*"The construction of this highway now appears
desirable as a long range defense measure."*

The 1897-1898 Klondike Gold Rush in Canada's Yukon Territory prompted public interest for the first time in an overland route from the continental United States to Alaska. An estimated 100,000 people headed for the Klondike with dreams of finding gold. Most of them went from Seattle to Skagway by sea and then covered the remaining 600 miles on foot, by dogteam and by boat. Fewer than 40,000 reached the hub of the gold rush, Dawson City.[1]

Gold was discovered on August 17, 1896, on Rabbit Creek, soon given the more glamorous name of Bonanza Creek. Several people were credited with the initial find, including Skokum Jim Mason, a member of Canada's Carcross-Tagish tribe. There was probably a touch of racism involved when Skokum Jim's Californian brother-in-law, George Carmack, opted to file the claim in his own name.

Almost a year passed before news of the find reached the outside world with the docking in Seattle of the first ship laden with gold. By then, the United States was mired in a financial recession. Among the resulting unemployed were many white-collar workers — doctors, bankers, teachers — who headed north to try their luck, although they were inexperienced in rugged outdoor life. Americans made up two-thirds of the prospectors.

The gold seekers included more than one hundred blacks, mainly from the southern United States.[2] But one of them was *not* the successful American prospector known as James ("Nigger Jim") Daugherty. He was a tall blond from Missouri who was given his nickname because of his twang and the fact he liked to sing Negro spirituals, accompanying himself on a banjo. His claim on what became known as Nigger Jim's Gulch was worth $360,000.[3] But Nigger Jim died penniless in the Yukon, his fortune spent on women and the dance halls he bought.

One of the successful black prospectors was Charles Hunter from Alabama, who took his pregnant, teenaged bride, Lucile, to the Klondike. After his death, Lucile learned in 1942 that American troops were in the Yukon, so she moved to the town of Whitehorse with a granddaughter. There she opened a laundry for the troops and civilian workers, doing the washing herself while her granddaughter did the pickups and deliveries.

Not all of the blacks in the Yukon became prospectors. Charles Bennett ended up

A land route to the lower forty-eight states was first talked about during the Klondike Gold Rush of 1897 when prospectors had to ascend on foot the 3,500-foot-high Chilkoot Pass from Alaska to British Columbia (courtesy University of Washington Libraries, Special Collections, Hegg 97).

in the service industry, cooking in a restaurant. After three years in Dawson City he committed suicide. An acquaintance said, "His color had relegated him to an inferior position to that he thought he should occupy in society."[4] Several black women, among them "Black Kitty" of Circle City, "Black Alice" of Nome and "Snake Hips Lil" of Dawson City, worked the mining camps.[5] And the first black soldiers stationed in Alaska were members of Company "L" of the 24th Infantry who were sent north to maintain order among those heading for the gold fields.[6]

If the War Department in Washington wanted assurance that black troops could function in extreme cold, the experience of the black prospectors could have provided proof. So could that of Matthew Henson, a black from Charles County in Maryland who rose from cabin boy to member of Admiral Robert E. Peary's party that reached the North Pole a decade after the Klondike Gold Rush. It was Henson who planted the American flag, but he received scant recognition until World War II, when Congress awarded him a silver medal, a duplicate of the one given Peary years earlier.

1—Pondering a Pathway to Alaska

When the American prospectors crossed from Alaska into the Yukon during the gold rush, the Royal Northwest Mounted Police (as the Royal Canadian Mounted Police were then known) met them at the border. To the surprise of the Americans, the Mounties relieved the new arrivals of their handguns. This was in keeping with the Mounties' role in the settlement of the Canadian West: preceding the settlers and establishing the rule of law. An American general will face the Mounties over *his* personal handgun.

There was a secondary reason for the Mounties to be on guard in the Yukon. The Canadian government was a bit leery of the intentions of the United States, whose citizens were flooding the Yukon during the gold rush. Did the Americans want to take over the Yukon and add it to Alaska, purchased from Russia for $7,200,000 thirty years earlier? During World War II, when Americans were returning to the north in great numbers, a future governor-general of Canada would likewise question the purpose of their presence.[7]

Given the gold rush, American railroad magnate E.H. Harriman proposed building a railroad from Chicago to Alaska, where it would link up on the other side of the Bering Sea with a railroad to be constructed by Russia. The only railroad eventually built was the White Pass and Yukon Railroad, financed mainly by British investments. It ran from Skagway 325 miles to Whitehorse, following the Klondike Trail taken by the prospectors. By the time the railroad opened in 1900, the gold rush was dying out, but the line survived as a mover of goods and people to and from the Yukon. During World War II, the White Pass and Yukon would have a renewed life. For much of the first thirty years of the twentieth century, there were rumors that some company was going to build a railroad from Edmonton, Alberta, to the Yukon. Slowly, the idea of a railroad was replaced by talk of a vehicular road to Fairbanks, Alaska, and the emphasis shifted from a prairie route to a west coast route.

The first concrete move occurred almost simultaneously with the establishment in early 1929 of two highway associations, one in Fairbanks and the other in Dawson City, then the capital of the Yukon. Their common goal was a highway crossing through the Yukon and linking Alaska with the lower forty-eight. The Alaska Legislature on April 17, 1929, approved construction of such a highway and asked for congressional support. A month later, Congress urged President Herbert Hoover to appoint a commission to seek an agreement with Canada. Hoover duly appointed a three-man International Highway Commission, but when the commission recommended in 1933 that the government negotiate a treaty with Canada for construction of a highway, Franklin D. Roosevelt was president and the Great Depression was at its peak. British Columbia's newly elected premier, Thomas J. Pattullo, became Canada's leading proponent of establishing a highway. Since the province already had over 600 miles of road to Hazelton in northern British Columbia, he thought a highway would boost tourism. But he failed to gain the support of Canadian Prime Minister Mackenzie King, who only reluctantly agreed to a highway after the United States had entered World War II.

Competing needs of the Great Depression scuttled the highway project in 1933.

The outcome might have been different had the commission cited a military justification for a highway. The War Department, which had not been asked its opinion, said later it could still depend almost exclusively on a sea route to furnish Alaska with troops and materiel.[8] That changed in 1937 when Japan invaded China, a harbinger of its territorial ambitions in the Pacific.

After President Roosevelt appointed a second International Highway Commission in 1938, the Japanese government protested that it would consider construction of a highway inimical to its interests.[9] The Japanese consul in Vancouver was ordered to travel to Whitehorse and report on highway plans. The Tokyo newspaper *Hochi Shimbun* warned of the military nature of a highway: "American measures in this direction will be regarded as a continuation of the horseshoe-shaped encirclement of Japan by the Washington government. Military bases of the United States would thus be strategic from Singapore, via Australia, the Philippines, Hawaii and the United States to Canada."[10]

The new commission consisted of five members, chaired by Congressman Warren G. Magnuson of Washington, who felt Seattle should be the southern jumping-off point for the highway; it also included Governor Ernest Gruening of Alaska. Four months later, Prime Minister King appointed a parallel Canadian commission called, to be different, the British Columbia–Yukon–Alaska Highway Commission. It was headed by Charles Stewart, a former premier of Alberta.

The two commissions met twice in Canada, on July 24, 1939, in Victoria, British Columbia, and January 24–25, 1940, in Ottawa. They reached different conclusions concerning the route. The Americans favored a coastal "A" route that British Columbia Premier Pattullo initially recommended: it would start at Hazelton, B.C., and go to Whitehorse and Dawson City in the Yukon, then due west to Fairbanks. That was the route favored by Donald MacDonald, often called the Father of the Alaska Highway since he had been urging a land route since the 1920s when he was chief engineer of the Alaska Road Commission. He was also a member of President Hoover's highway commission.

MacDonald used showmanship to promote his vision. He had Alaskan adventurer Clyde ("Slim") Williams drive his dogteam from Fairbanks to Seattle in late 1932, a trek that took five and a half months and followed MacDonald's route. Williams put booties on the dogs in Seattle and continued on to Chicago for the 1933 World's Fair, where he and his team were star attractions. He met later that year with President Roosevelt, pitching MacDonald's route. At age fifty-seven, Williams repeated the Fairbanks–Seattle route in 1939 by motorcycle, crossing rivers on improvised rafts. After six and a half months of travel, he and a companion, John Logan, reached Seattle, where they were feted as the first men to motor the proposed highway.[11] MacDonald's route was put to a third test in January 1941 by a twenty-four-year-old University of Alaska student from Hot Springs, Montana, named Elden Borders. Supplied with a map by MacDonald, Borders set out with a fifty-pound backpack and a pair of skis. It was thirty below in Fairbanks when he got a lift in a mail truck for the first stage. After that, he walked or skied. From Whitehorse he followed the Klondike Trail of '97 south through Telegraph Creek, British Columbia. He reached Hazelton ninety-one days after leaving Fairbanks.[12]

The Canadians, however, favored a more easterly "B" route starting at Prince George, B.C., bypassing Whitehorse en route to Dawson City and Fairbanks. The "A" and "B" routes would be of similar length, 1,344 and 1,306 miles, respectively. Washington State, Oregon and Alaska favored route "A," while British Columbia and the Yukon favored route "B." Montana, North Dakota and Alberta joined forces to suggest a "C" route that would go through Alberta to Fort Grahame in northwest British Columbia. Then there was route "D" recommended by Arctic explorer Vilhjalmur Stefansson, a special consultant to the War Department. Born William Stephenson in Canada, he changed his name to a more exotic Icelandic version after his family moved to the United States. By early 1941, the War Department was considering a highway, so Army Chief of Staff Gen. George C. Marshall called in Stefansson to explain his route, which was partly on water. From the end of the rail at Waterways in northern Alberta, 300 miles north of Edmonton, the route crossed Great Slave Lake in the Northwest Territories and went down the Mackenzie River to Norman Wells, where oil had been discovered twenty years earlier, and then by land across the Mackenzie Mountains to Dawson City and Fairbanks.

The civilians failed to agree on a route, which was fine with Canada's prime minister. Although Canada had been active in World War II since September 1939, Mackenzie King told Parliament that a highway, if built, would be a tourist attraction but would also open up potentially rich mineral areas in the nation's northwest.[13]

While the civilians were trying to determine the route of a possible highway to Alaska, military leaders from the United States and Canada were meeting to consider joint policy toward the Axis nations even though the United States was not yet a combatant in World War II. The venue was the Permanent Joint Board on Defense, which grew out of a meeting between President Roosevelt and Prime Minister King held on August 18, 1940, in Ogdensburg, New York. This was the first time that two nations not joined together by an alliance set up a permanent board to discuss defense problems.[14]

The following month, Germany, Italy and Japan signed a tripartite military alliance. Now the defense of Alaska moved up on the agenda of the joint American-Canadian board. The Americans were especially interested in the pioneering efforts in far north aviation by Canada's intrepid bush pilots. The phrase "Great Circle Route" had not become common until 1935, when the Canadian government financed a survey to find an airway over the top of the continent to Japan, China and Siberia. As a result, Canada had ordered the construction of airfields between Edmonton and Whitehorse in the Yukon. Once the Americans learned about Canada's activities in the north, the joint defense board recommended on November 12, 1940, that the primitive runways at the northern airfields be paved and lighted, navigation equipment installed, weather stations built and intermediary strips constructed for emergency use on flights from Edmonton to Fairbanks. Canada agreed to pay for the improvements in Alberta, British Columbia and the Yukon for what was named the Northwest Staging Route.

The improvements were relatively easy at airstrips at Grand Prairie, Alberta; Fort St. John, British Columbia; and Whitehorse in the Yukon, because they were accessible by road or rail. But Fort Nelson and Watson Lake, where Canadian aviation pioneer Grant McConachie had built rudimentary airstrips, presented problems that were a precursor of those faced by the Army regiments which would build the Alaska Highway. During the winter of 1940-1941, two tractor trains carrying construction material, equipment and supplies left, one heading to Fort Nelson and the other to Watson Lake. The first was led by a bulldozer that knocked down trees and created a winter trail from the railhead at Dawson Creek 300 miles north to Fort Nelson. The second left from Wrangell, Alaska, on the coast and traveled by barge and over land 400 miles to Watson Lake. By the fall all five airstrips were operational for daytime flights, but another year would pass before they could handle nighttime flights.

On June 22, 1941, Germany attacked the Soviet Union, with which it had signed a non-aggression pact just two years earlier. Now the Allies had a new ally and President Roosevelt approved the shipment of aircraft to the Soviet Union under the Lend-Lease Act. By the end of the war, nearly 8,000 American fighters and bombers were ferried to Alaska via the Northwest Staging Route for delivery to Soviet pilots waiting at Ladd Field just east of Fairbanks.

The German attack on the Soviet Union came as Congress was discussing a resolution proposed by Anthony J. Dimond, delegate from Alaska in the House of Representatives, for the construction of a highway. On October 6, 1941, Secretary of War Henry L. Stimson told Congress, "From an evaluation of the trend in international affairs, the construction of this highway now appears desirable as a long range defense measure."[15]

Two months later Japan made the highway a certainty by launching a surprise attack against the United States.

2

Highway and Pipeline Approved

"Alaska is wide-open to attack and we're in no position to defend it."

On January 16, 1942, President Roosevelt and his cabinet discussed whether the sneak attack on Pearl Harbor six weeks earlier might be a prelude to a Japanese invasion of Alaska. The Japanese had sunk four battleships, destroyed 188 aircraft and killed 2,402 at Pearl Harbor. The possibility that Japan might target Alaska was made apparent when a Japanese broadcast heard there on the day of the attack on U.S. facilities on Hawaii told of 3,000 killed in a raid on Anchorage and stated that American military facilities on Dutch Harbor and Kodiak were in flames. The broadcast had anticipated an attack from a Japanese aircraft carrier that bad weather was believed to have prevented.[1] Convinced that Alaska was vulnerable, Roosevelt named a three-man cabinet committee, consisting of the secretaries of war, navy and the interior, to study the immediate construction of an overland route to Alaska. Alaskan roads engineer Donald MacDonald, who had long promoted a highway, was in an I-told-you-so mood. "I don't know who taught people to place all their reliance on Pearl Harbor, but I know their blind faith is not shared in Alaska," he said. "We can't afford to let Alaska remain a naval liability, which is exactly what it will be as long as she has no overland connection with the United States."[2]

Not only had the defense of Alaska become a major issue, but American military leaders also anticipated using bases in the territory for an air attack on Japan now that the United States had entered World War II. Pearl Harbor had coincided with a simultaneous attack on the British fleet in the Indian Ocean, temporarily eliminating Allied sea power in the Pacific. Lt. Gen. John L. DeWitt, head of the Western Defense Command, cautioned the War Department that Japan could easily impose a sea blockade on Alaska, making it dependent upon air transportation. Japanese submarines and warships had been detected in waters off the Pacific coast, including Alaska, forty-one times during a three-week period following Pearl Harbor.[3] The general in charge of Alaska's defense, Brig. Gen. Simon Bolivar Buckner, Jr., urged immediate improvement of Northwest Staging Route airfields.

There were only six combat-ready planes in Alaska at the time of Pearl Harbor.[4] Anxious to reinforce the territory's defenses, the War Department made its first major use of the Northwest Staging Route a month later. The experience was not encouraging. Flown by young pilots unfamiliar with the northern territory, thirteen B-26 bombers and twenty-five P-40 fighters took off from Boise, Idaho, for Fairbanks. Only twenty-one of the thirty-eight planes arrived. Three of them crashed in a remote valley in the Yukon dubbed "Million Dollar Valley" for the value of the lost planes. Blame was divided between the pilots (none of whom even had any winter gear or clothing) and the weather, the distance between airfields and inadequate navigational aids.

The crashes occurred before the January 16 cabinet meeting, prompting a discussion of less risky ways of getting planes to Alaska. Interior Secretary Harold Ickes suggested reviving plans for a highway that would make improvement of the airstrips easier. The War Department had already done an aerial survey of a possible link to the end of the rail at Prince Rupert, British Columbia, 1,500 miles to the south, but the laying of tracks would take longer than building a highway.[5]

Brig. Gen. Robert W. Crawford and Col. James K. Tully, Army engineers assigned to the War Plans Division, were given the job of recommending a route for the highway. They rejected overland coastal routes "A" and "B," offered by the American-Canadian highway commission, on the grounds that they would be susceptible to Japanese attack from the Pacific. "C," proposed by Alberta, Montana and North Dakota, was attractive, but not the Fort Grahame starting point. "D," championed by Vilhjalmur Stefansson, was too dependent on seasonal river traffic. At the request of William J. Donovan, director of the OSS (the Office of Strategic Services, a precursor of the CIA), Stefansson had touted the advantages of his route just two days after Pearl Harbor. But Stefansson probably planted the seed for the creation of the Canol project to tap the oil at Norman Wells.

Crawford and Tully came up with a fifth route, influenced by the early January plane crashes: start the highway at the end of the rail at Dawson Creek, British Columbia, and follow the path of the Canadian airstrips on the Northwest Staging Route. This represented a modification of the route "C" proposal and included the last 500 miles in Alaska covered by route "A." "It is desired to have a road as a trace for our airmen to fly along," explained Tully.[6] They estimated that a two-lane gravel highway could be built in two years at a cost of $50,000 to $60,000 per mile, $700,000 to $800,000 in today's dollars. Although 70 percent of the highway would be in Canada, the Alaska-Canadian Highway was selected as its name, soon shortened to Alcan, a combination of Alaska and Canada. But the name was destined to be changed.

The cabinet committee accepted the two engineers' recommendation. Roosevelt approved the route on February 11, 1942, allocating $10 million from his war emergency fund for a survey. Washington State Congressman — later Senator — Warren Magnuson, chairman of the International Highway Commission, never forgave the Roosevelt administration for not selecting route "A," which would have meant a key role for Seattle, rather than Edmonton. He criticized the highway until the end of the war. Had the highway been built in peacetime, the coastal route favored by Magnuson undoubtedly would have been selected. As it was, there was solid support in the military for a highway that could be used to supply troops and the airstrips of the Northwest Staging Route, as well as serving as a visual guide for pilots.

2—Highway and Pipeline Approved

Less than ten weeks after the Pearl Harbor attack, the United States had approved a pathway to Alaska, ending almost half a century of debate.

The day after the president gave his approval, Brig. Gen. Clarence L. Sturdevant, assistant chief of the Corps of Engineers, summoned Col. William M. Hoge, a veteran Army roadbuilder, to Washington. "He told me I had been selected to carry out a reconnaissance by going up there to figure out the logistics of building a road through unfamiliar wilderness," Hoge said.[7] At forty-eight, Hoge, soon to be promoted to brigadier general, was a lanky, broad-shouldered, gruff officer like those portrayed by John Wayne in war movies. A native of Boonville, Missouri, he attended West Point and later earned an engineering degree from the Massachusetts Institute of Technology. He was awarded the Distinguished Service Medal for having built pontoon bridges under German shellfire in World War I. Between wars he commanded a battalion that built roads and bridges in the jungles of the Bataan peninsula in the Philippines. He was based at the Engineer Replacement Training Center at Fort Belvoir, Virginia, when tapped for the Alcan project. His superiors thought his experience under tough conditions in the Philippines made him the ideal commander for the equally challenging northern highway.

On February 19, before the Canadian government had even been officially advised of plans to build the highway, Hoge flew to Edmonton. He was accompanied by Lt. Col. E.A. Mueller of the Army's Quartermaster Corps, Lt. Col. Robert Ingalls of the Corps of Engineers and engineer Fred Capes of the U.S. Public Works Administration. "Our job was to pick the brains of every Canadian who knew anything about the North to assess the feasibility of construction," Hoge said.[8] Among those he met were Grant McConachie, general manager of the Canadian Pacific Air Lines, and James McArthur, general manager of the Northern Alberta Railway. "Alaska is wide-open to attack and we're in no position to defend it. That's where you and your fliers can be of enormous help to us," Hoge said, a nod to McConachie. "It hasn't been announced yet, gentlemen, but our government, with the cooperation of yours, will build a military road from the end of steel at Dawson Creek through to Fairbanks."[9] Hoge would lease planes from McConachie and use the railroad to carry troops and freight north. "At first I could hardly credit my ears," said McArthur. "I realized what all this might mean for us, but I wanted to make sure. I checked the credentials, consulted the proper sources, and was convinced."[10]

The same day that Hoge flew to Edmonton, Brig. Gen. Clarence Sturdevant was in Ottawa to brief Canadian officials about the highway. Returning to Washington, Sturdevant was called before a Senate Foreign Relations subcommittee to explain why a coastal route was *not* selected for the highway. He told the senators the inland route was chosen because planes could more safely fly where there were already existing operational airfields.

Following his Edmonton meeting, Hoge and his party left by train on the 500-mile trip to Dawson Creek. From there they were driven by an old northern hand,

Homer Keith, to Fort St. John, crossing the ice on the frozen Peace River, for there was no bridge, a surprise to Hoge. He realized then he'd have to get his troops and their heavy equipment across the river before the breakup of the ice if the highway was to be completed in a year.

While Hoge was making his way back from Canada, Japan made its first attack on the U.S. mainland. A submarine shelled an oil refinery at Ellwood, California, confirming to the military the need for the Alcan Highway. On February 25–26, Hoge met in New York with War and Navy Department officials and with the U.S.-Canadian Joint Board of Defense, briefing them on what he had learned. The joint board seconded an immediate start on the highway, although it made no recommendation on the route, except that it should parallel the chain of airports built by Canada.[11]

On March 1, McArthur received a telegram from Washington saying that freight cars were already en route to Edmonton to hook up with his Northern Alberta Railway for the run to Dawson Creek. Five days later Canada's War Cabinet approved the highway project. The following day, Prime Minister King informed Parliament.

Once Canada had approved the project, General Sturdevant officially named Hoge to oversee construction of the highway. Plans called for the troops to build a pioneer or access road from Dawson Creek to Delta, Alaska, where a 100-mile-long highway to Fairbanks already existed. The Public Roads Administration (PRA) was to hire private contractors who would use the access road to carry equipment and workers for construction of a parallel finished highway. "The pioneer road will be pushed to completion with all speed within the physical capacity of the troops," Sturdevant stated. "The objective is to complete the entire route at the earliest practicable date to a standard sufficient for the supply of troops engaged on the work."[12] But by mid–1942 plans for a parallel highway would be abandoned.

The formal agreement between the United States and Canada took effect on March 17, 1942, through an exchange of notes between J. Pierrepont Moffat, the U.S. minister to Canada, and Prime Minister King, who doubled as Canada's secretary of state for external affairs. Under the accord, the United States agreed to pay for building and maintaining the Canadian portion of the highway, turning it over to Canada within six months of the end of the war. For its part, Canada agreed to provide the rights of way for the highway, and to waive duties on imported building supplies and equipment and sales taxes on local purchases, plus facilitating the admission of American workers. On June 26, Canada's War Cabinet issued an Order-in-Council allowing the presence of American troops in its Northwest.

Said American minister Moffat: "Can you cite me another instance where one country has asked its neighbor to let its army and road administration construct a great public work on and across its territory, and have agreement reached in principle within seven days and in detail within a month?"[13]

By this time, Japan had seized the oil fields of the Dutch East Indies in the Pacific. It had triumphed in Manila, Singapore, Rangoon, Java, Guam, Wake Island and in the

Battle of Java Sea. German Field Marshal Erwin Rommel's *Afrika Korps* was threatening Middle East oil fields. German submarines were sinking tankers bringing oil to the United States from Mexican and Venezuelan fields. The tanker *Potrero del Llano*, carrying 50,000 barrels of Mexican crude, was torpedoed off Miami Beach with a loss of fourteen lives. When Mexico demanded an explanation, Germany responded by sinking a second tanker. This prompted Mexico to declare war on Germany, Italy and Japan on May 23.

The possibility of tapping the Norman Wells oil field in Canada's Northwest Territories had been briefly mentioned at the January cabinet meeting that discussed construction of the highway. Given the Axis drive to obtain oil and attacks on U.S.-bound tankers, now was the time to rethink northern oil sources. Secretary Ickes, who was also the wartime petroleum administrator, urged the cabinet at a meeting on April 2 to order exploration of oil in Alaska. President Roosevelt agreed and told Ickes and Secretary of War Stimson, both members of the committee that recommended the Alcan Highway, to study the question of Alaskan oil. When Stimson brought up the subject with the Army, he was told of Vilhjalmur Stefansson's recommendation of the already-producing field in northern Canada. Consideration of Alaskan oil was dropped.

The officer assigned to investigate Norman Wells oil was the man who most needed it: Maj. Gen. Brehon B. Somervell, commander of the Army Service Forces, the Army's logistical arm. As such, he was responsible for the supply of fuel for military units in Alaska and along the highway. Somervell in turn asked his civilian assistant for transportation, James H. Graham, on leave as dean of the School of Engineering at the University of Kentucky, to make a feasibility study of Norman Wells oil produced by Imperial Oil, the Canadian subsidiary of what was to become ExxonMobil. The discovery of oil at Norman Wells in 1920 had been serendipitous. The team of oxen hauling the rig to a pre-selected site for a test hole had become too exhausted to continue further. The driller decided to try his luck where the oxen stood, bringing forth a gusher of oil. Later drilling at the intended site came up dry.[14]

Oil men present at an April 26 meeting with Sturdevant agreed that a pipeline could be installed to deliver the oil to the Alcan Highway, but that it would not be easy. As soon as the meeting ended, Graham wrote a memo to Somervell recommending that at least nine more wells be drilled and in production by September and that a refinery be dismantled, moved to Whitehorse and installed and operating a month later. Somervell agreed and immediately sent a letter of intent to Imperial Oil. He later regretted the speed with which he made the decision. "I knew it couldn't be done," he conceded.[15]

Once the United States organized the Northwest Staging Route using existing Canadian fields, the need for fuel became apparent. Trucks carrying it by road would consume the equivalent of half their load just making the delivery, so a more cost-efficient supply was needed. Hence what would become known as the Canol project, an acronym for either Canadian American Norman Oil Line or just Canadian Oil.[16] A consortium of three American companies—W.A. Bechtel, H.C. Price and W.W.

Callahan Construction—signed a cost-plus, fixed-fee contract to lay a 595-mile-long pipeline to Whitehorse and install a refinery there. The Army Corps of Engineers was given orders to get the pipe, equipment and supplies to the Norman Wells field.

The Canadian government had reservations about the pipeline and the fact that the U.S. military would now be moving into the Northwest Territories' Mackenzie District, an area twice the size of Texas. Its 5,000 inhabitants, including 800 whites, would be dwarfed by the number of American troops and civilians. After some hesitation, Canada gave formal approval on June 29, by which time thousands of Americans had already arrived and started work.

The emergency created by Pearl Harbor provided the War Department with a rationale for maintaining racial segregation in the Armed Forces: wartime is not when the military should undergo dramatic social change. However, the United States' victory in its War of Independence was achieved by black and white soldiers fighting alongside each other. Blacks were present at the start of the revolution. The very first person to fall before British bullets was a black named Crispus Attucks, probably a runaway slave. He was part of a protest in Boston against British taxes on March 5, 1770, when he was shot, dying two days later of his wounds. After hostilities started, Gen. George Washington, an owner of slaves like seven of his successors in the presidency, issued orders barring all blacks, slaves and freemen alike, from serving in his Continental Army. He changed his mind after the British offered freedom to any slave who joined their army; 200 blacks accepted the offer and served in what became known as the British army's Ethiopian Regiment. When Washington started competing for black recruits, more than 5,000 enlisted; at the time, 20 percent of the colonial population of 2.5 million was black. Two black soldiers accompanied Washington when he crossed the Delaware River at night on Christmas Day 1776. Once the British were defeated, however, the Army discharged all the black soldiers, returning the slaves to their owners.[17]

During the Civil War, President Abraham Lincoln was also initially reluctant to recruit blacks. When he issued the Emancipation Proclamation on New Year's Day 1863, he included the right to serve in the Union Army. By then the war was in its second year and the Army badly needed the additional manpower. Lincoln realized that the North would fail if it didn't use black soldiers. In addition, black leaders and abolitionists were urging the Army to accept blacks, many of whom were volunteering. The Confederate Army also accepted blacks. However, neither army allowed blacks and whites to fight alongside each other as they had in the War of Independence. Eventually the Union Army had 187,000 soldiers—"black warriors," Lincoln called them—in 154 all-black regiments, usually commanded by white officers. Nearly 40,000 black Union soldiers died in the Civil War, and twenty-five Congressional Medals of Honor were awarded to black soldiers. Ironically, the war that ended slavery introduced racial segregation in the Armed Forces of the United States. Still, black soldiers died with General Custer at the Battle of the Little Big Horn (fourteen medals were awarded during the Indian wars) and charged up San Juan Hill in Cuba with Teddy Roosevelt during the Spanish-American War (during which six Congressional Medals of Honor were awarded to black soldiers).

More than 200,000 blacks served in the Army during World War I, but most of them were in non-combat engineer or quartermaster regiments. However, one black regiment that did see action was the 369th, a National Guard unit from New York composed of Harlem volunteers. It was the only volunteer American regiment that served in France, where it fought as part of the French Army. For obvious reasons, the French called them *Les Enfants Perdus*— The Lost Children — as they appeared to have been abandoned by their parents. They saw 191 days of combat, the most of any American unit. The first American soldiers to receive France's *Croix de Guerre*, bestowed for acts of heroism in combat, were members of the 369th, Henry Johnson and Needham Roberts.[18] The United States itself only awarded one Congressional Medal of Honor to a black soldier for gallantry and bravery beyond the call of duty during World War I.

By 1940, America's peacetime Army numbered half a million men, but only 3,640 were black, serving in six segregated regiments.[19] Why so few blacks? There were several reasons. Many whites joined the peacetime Armed Forces during the Great Depression in order to get a paycheck. Blacks would have liked the paychecks too, but only the Army accepted them; the Army Air Forces and the Marines barred them, while the Navy limited them to mess duties.[20] Most of the blacks came from the South, where schools were poor and nutritious food not as plentiful as for whites, so they faced educational and physical disadvantages when they applied to the Army. As well, top echelons of the Army generally had a low opinion of blacks. This is what the U.S. Army War College said in a report prepared by senior officers on the eve of World War II:

> As an individual the Negro is docile, tractable, lighthearted, care free and good natured. If unjustly treated he is likely to become surly and stubborn, though this is usually a temporary phase. He is careless, shiftless, irresponsible and secretive. He resents censure and is best handled with praise and by ridicule. He is unmoral, untruthful, and his sense of right doing is relatively inferior. Crimes and convictions involving moral turpitude are nearly five to one as compared to convictions of whites on similar charges.
> On the other hand the Negro is cheerful, loyal and usually uncomplaining if reasonably well fed. He has a musical nature and a marked sense of rhythm. His art is primitive. He is religious. With proper direction in mass, Negroes are industrious. They are emotional and can be stirred to a high state of enthusiasm. Their emotions are unstable and their reactions uncertain. Bad leadership in particular is easily communicated to them.[21]

The Army in 1940 only had five black officers: three were chaplains and the other two a father-and-son duo: Col. Benjamin O. Davis, Sr., and Lt. Benjamin O. Davis, Jr. Secretary of War Henry L. Stimson, a native New Yorker who served in France as an officer in World War I, had an explanation for there being so few black officers. Writing in his diary in 1941, he said, "Leadership is not imbedded in the Negro race yet and to try to make commissioned officers to lead the men into battle — colored men — is to work disaster to both. Colored troops do very well under white officers but every time we try to lift them a little bit beyond where they can go, disaster and confusion follows. In the draft, we are preparing to give Negroes a fair shot in every service, however, even in aviation where I doubt if they will not produce disaster there. Nevertheless, they are going to have a try, but I hope to Heaven's sake they won't mix the white and the colored troops together in the same units for then we shall certainly have trouble."[22]

As the Armed Forces mobilized in 1940, the role of blacks in the military became an issue in that fall's general election. Said Ulysses Grant Lee, Jr., a black officer with a Ph.D. who was serving as an Army education specialist in Washington: "Up to the beginning of World War II the impression was widely held that the Army probably had no concrete plans for the use of Negro troops other than a grudging admission that in time of war they would be useful primarily as laborers and that they must be kept completely segregated from white troops."[23] Since the Civil War, those blacks who could vote had supported the Republican Party as it was the party of Lincoln. But because of the Great Depression that brought Roosevelt to power, black voters abandoned the Republican Party in 1936. A major reason was the New Deal's Emergency Relief Administration, which provided aid to the unemployed and their families. At the time of the 1936 election, an estimated 30 percent of blacks depended on the government's welfare program.[24] But other New Deal programs left out blacks, such as the Agricultural Adjustment Administration, which supported white farmers and workers, and the National Recovery Administration, which failed to protect black workers from discrimination.[25]

Seeking an unprecedented third term in 1940, Roosevelt had to perform a juggling act. His coalition consisted, on the one hand, of the "Southern plantation elite" that sent the so-called Dixiecrats to Congress, who, because of seniority, held the chairmanships of most key committees. On the other hand were northern industrial workers, ethnic minorities, and the urban poor, including many blacks who had moved north.[26] Nearly 80 percent of the black population still lived in the South, where poll taxes, literacy tests and other restrictive measures prevented all but a handful from voting. The nascent civil rights movement realized that the war presented it with an opportunity to seek more equitable treatment of blacks, especially in the military and the burgeoning defense industries. Roosevelt dropped some of his New Deal programs to appease Southerners and declined to support civil rights in 1940. The Republican Party included a strong civil rights plank in its platform and its presidential candidate, Wendell Wilkie, received the endorsement of leading black newspapers, such as the *Pittsburgh Courier* and the *Afro American* in Baltimore.

Until Germany invaded France in May of 1940, the American military had depended on volunteers for the Armed Forces. That summer Congress passed the Selective Service Act, under which draftees would serve for one year. To ensure there would be no racial discrimination in the selection process, the legislation made clear that blacks would be drafted in proportion to their percentage of the population, then about 10 percent. The two key clauses of the legislation said:

3 (a) That within the limits of the quota determined — for the subdivision in which he resides, any person, regardless of race or color, between the ages of eighteen and forty-five, shall be afforded an opportunity to volunteer for induction into the land or naval forces of the United States for the training and service prescribed....

4 (a) In the selection and training of men under this Act, and in the interpretation and execution of the provisions of this Act, there shall be no discrimination against any person on account of race or color.

However, the legislation also stipulated that all draftees would have to meet mental and physical standards and that adequate housing and other facilities would have to be available. Given the fact that the military was segregated, the availability of housing appeared to be a loophole that could be used to limit black participation.

The National Negro Congress (NNC) opposed the Selective Service legislation on the grounds that it would "increase the influence of the anti–Negro Army forces" in determining government policy,[27] and it passed a resolution urging young blacks to refuse to fight for democracy abroad if they continued to be the target of discrimination at home.[28] The NNC, formed with Communist backing in 1936, had elected as its first president A. Philip Randolph, head of the Brotherhood of Sleeping Car Porters. The most important black union leader in the United States, he quit the NNC in 1940 because of its stand on the war. Eventually Roosevelt, wary of the questioning by black leaders of the Selective Service Act, invited Randolph and other leaders, including Walter White, executive secretary of the National Association for the Advancement of Colored People (NAACP), to the White House on September 27, 1940. Randolph and the others wanted an end to segregation in the Armed Forces, greater use of black troops in combat units and an end to discriminatory hiring in defense industries. Said Randolph, "I thought I might say on the part of the Negro people, they feel they are not wanted in the Armed Forces of the country, and they feel they have earned their rights to participate in every phase of the government by virtue of their record in past wars since the Revolution."[29] Undersecretary of War Robert P. Patterson sounded amenable to considering desegregation in the future, but Secretary of the Navy Frank Knox said he'd resign first.[30]

On October 9, 1940, the War Department had announced its policy toward blacks in the military:

- "The policy of the War Department is not to intermingle colored and white enlisted personnel in the same regimental organizations. This policy has proven satisfactory over a long period of years and to make changes would produce situations destructive to morale and detrimental to the preparation for national defense."
- "The intermingling of the races in messing and housing would not only be a variation from well-established policies of the Department but it does not accord with the existing customs of the country as a whole."
- "Superiors are forbidden to injure those under their authority by tyrannical or capricious conduct or by abusive language."

- "The use of any epithet deemed insulting to a racial group should be carefully avoided."
- "While maintaining discipline and the thorough and prompt performance of military duty, all officers, in dealing with enlisted men, will bear in mind the absolute necessity of so treating them as to preserve their self-respect."
- "Commanders should avoid all practices tending to give the colored soldier cause to feel that the Army makes any differentiation between him and any other soldier."
- "The strength of the Negro personnel of the Army will be maintained on the general basis of proportion of the Negro population of the country."

The announcement said that problems in commanding black troops were due almost exclusively to a "lack of knack" on the part of the white officers assigned to the black units. "Officers must be selected with the primary requirement the ability to handle Negroes," it said.[31]

The NAACP immediately sent a telegram to Roosevelt: "We are inexpressibly shocked that a president of the United States at a time of national peril should surrender so completely to enemies of democracy who would destroy national unity by advocating segregation. Official approval by the Commander in Chief of the Army and Navy of such discrimination is a stab in the back of democracy ... [and a] blow at the patriotism of twelve million Negro citizens."[32] The NAACP was blunter in its magazine, *The Crisis*: "WHITE HOUSE BLESSES JIM CROW" was its headline on the story of the War Department announcement.[33] (Jim Crow was the stage name used by a white performer who used blackface in minstrel shows in the nineteenth century. Segregation laws and other restrictions, usually enacted and enforced in the South after the Civil War, were named after him.) This was at a time when separate air-raid shelters in Washington were being considered for blacks and whites.[34] The presidential press secretary, Steven Early, didn't help Roosevelt's relations with the black community. He struck a black policeman in New York as he broke through a police cordon to catch the presidential train, a most newsworthy incident.[35]

The election would challenge Roosevelt do to something to win over black voters, while the Army wrestled with the role to be played by black troops in the war.

3

The Second Emancipation Order

"We are suffering from the persistent legacy of the original crime of slavery."

On November 5, 1940, President Roosevelt won his third election to the presidency, capturing thirty-eight of the forty-eight states. Two weeks earlier, he had sought to appease black voters with two acts of tokenism: he named Judge William H. Hastie, dean of the law school at Howard University, a traditional black institution, as civilian aide to Secretary Stimson, and he promoted Col. Benjamin Davis to brigadier general, the first black officer to achieve that rank, and appointed him to head a special section of the Inspector General's Department dealing with racial issues involving troops.

Born in Washington in 1877, Davis was a Howard graduate who had helped organize one of the black companies that fought in Cuba during the Spanish-American War. As he rose through the ranks, he was never assigned to command white troops — only black troops. He had been a military attaché at the American Embassy in Liberia, had taught at Wilberforce University and at the Tuskegee Institute, and was an instructor to National Guard units. His son would command the black Tuskegee pilots during World War II and would become a general himself. Nearly 500 black pilots saw action during the war, taking part in bombing missions in North Africa and Europe.

As for Hastie, he had been raised on a chicken farm outside of Knoxville, Tennessee. He had graduated from Harvard Law School and had been appointed a federal judge by Roosevelt in 1937, thus becoming the first black to hold that office. Hastie explained why he agreed to become Stimson's aide: "I have always been constantly opposed to any policy of discrimination and segregation in the Armed Forces of this country. I am assuming this post in the hope that I will be able to work effectively toward the integration of the Negro into the Army and to facilitate his placement, training, and promotion."[1] Stimson also appointed an eight-member committee to advise him on black troop policy.

The appointments of Davis and Hastie served their purpose. But the New Year would bring increased efforts by the NAACP and others to change War Department policy. As soon as Roosevelt was inaugurated for his third term as president, he was threatened with a March on Washington unless he did something to address racial discrimination in the military and in the defense industries. Three key black figures joined forces to press their demands: union leader A. Philip Randolph; Judge Hastie, aide to Secretary of War Stimson; and NAACP leader William White. Randolph distributed a flier titled "Why Should We March?" in which he stated, "American Negroes, involved as we are in the general issues of the conflict, are confronted not with a choice but with the challenge both to win democracy for ourselves at home and to help win the war for democracy the world over."

Hastie wanted an end to segregation in the Armed Forces and, barring that, black officers commanding only black units. Stimson had given Hastie the following mandate, but whether the secretary knew how far his aide would go was another thing:

> I hope that you will be able to assist us in the development of and improvements in the War Department's plans for the organization of Negro units in each major branch of the service, and for the utilization of Negro reserve officers, candidates for commissions, and aviation cadets. I also hope that you will be of assistance to us in connection with policies involving the employment of Negroes on civilian status at army establishments and by army contractors. It will be part of your duties to investigate complaints concerning the treatment of Negroes in the military service or in civilian employment in the War Department. In this connection, I hope it will be possible for you to spend time visiting camps, posts and stations for the purpose of observing and reporting to me upon matters of Negro participation in the national defense.[2]

Especially galling for Randolph and White were factories that assembled aircraft, tanks and armaments for the Allies. Jobless whites had found employment in these factories as World War II brought an end to the Great Depression, while blacks were mainly left out. Black unemployment was twice that of whites and the average pay of blacks, when they found work, was only half that of whites. The federal government itself later pointed out the discrepancy in employment. A January–March 1942 report by the Social Security Board noted that "there is little evidence that employers are hiring Negroes" even though there was a shortage of skilled and semi-skilled workers in the defense industries.[3] Many companies placed help-wanted ads in out-of-town newspapers rather than hire available local blacks.[4] Randolph and White met with Roosevelt early in 1941 to tell him of the planned March on Washington. "How many people do you plan to bring?" asked Roosevelt. "One hundred thousand, Mr. President," replied Randolph. The president then asked the same question of White and received the same answer. "You can't bring 100,000 Negroes to Washington," the president told them. "Somebody might get killed." Randolph told Roosevelt there would be no violence if he, the president, spoke at the event. "Call it off and we'll talk again," Roosevelt said.[5]

Randolph, by then head of the organizing committee, announced on May 1 plans for what he said would be a peaceful march. "An 'all out' thundering March on Washington, ending in a monster and huge demonstration at Lincoln's Monument will shake up white America," he predicted.[6] He sent letters to Roosevelt and his wife, Eleanor, as well as Stimson, seeking their support for the march. Hastie told Stimson that he or some other representative of the War Department should speak to the marchers about segregation in the Armed Forces and job opportunities in the war industries.

Worried about how the march might affect the image of the United States abroad, Roosevelt enlisted the help of his wife to derail it. Eleanor Roosevelt, who was raised in a Southern household and whose ancestors were slave owners, was much beloved by blacks, whose rights she often supported, both publicly and privately with her husband. Mrs. Roosevelt was known as an idealist while the president was a pragmatist who favored a go-slow policy on race.[7] Now he asked her to consult with Undersecretary of War Robert P. Patterson about how to prevent the march. Patterson suggested that Maj. Gen. Edwin M. Watson, the president's military aide and secretary, try to persuade Randolph and Hastie to call it off. She and Watson dutifully met with Randolph, who was unmoved. He said the march would proceed if the president didn't issue an executive order banning segregation and discrimination.[8]

After setting July 1, 1941, as the date for the march, Randolph was summoned to the office of New York mayor Fiorello LaGuardia. There, to his surprise, he found Eleanor Roosevelt. She told him, "I am opposed to the march on Washington because I fear the consequences to Negroes if thousands of them march there in protest against job discrimination in national defense industries."[9] Still unmoved, Randolph was summoned the following week to the White House for a meeting with the president, Secretary of War Stimson and Secretary of the Navy Frank Knox. Randolph said he'd call off the march if Roosevelt signed an executive order "with teeth in it" that would ban discrimination in the defense industries and the government itself, meaning the Armed Forces as well.[10] The president replied that he wouldn't sign such an order until there had been a study that recommended such an action.

Days before the proposed march date, Randolph was again summoned to Washington to meet with LaGuardia. "I must tell you, Phil, it looks bad about the executive order," the mayor said. "Those Southern congressmen are sore about this thing already and the Negroes will certainly lose many of their 'good white friends' if you go through with the march."[11] After some arm-twisting with the White House on the part of Randolph and the mayor, the march was called off. The president gave in on June 25, 1941, signing Executive Order 8802, which said in part:

> I do hereby reaffirm the policy of the United States that there shall be no discrimination in the employment of workers in defense industries or government because of race, creed, color, or national origin, and I do hereby declare that it is the duty of employers and of labor organizations, in furtherance of said policy and of this order, to provide for the full and equitable participation of all workers in defense industries, without discrimination because of race, creed, color, or national origin.

As part of the agreement with Randolph, the president also established the Fair Employment Practices Committee to oversee compliance with the executive order. However, the door to employment in the defense industries would only be opened a crack for black workers and segregation remained in the Armed Forces, in which more than a million blacks would serve during World War II.

Black newspapers hailed the executive order as the second Emancipation Proclamation, following the one freeing the slaves during the Civil War. *Fortune* magazine noted it was only the second presidential executive order to directly affect blacks.[12]

On September 22, 1941, Judge Hastie sent Secretary of War Stimson a 30-page report recommending desegregation of the Armed Forces — if necessary with white and black volunteers on an experimental basis — and an end to discrimination against black personnel. Titled "The Integration of the Negro Soldier into the Army," the report said in part:

> Whenever the Army Command shall demonstrate to its personnel that it intends for every man in uniform to be accorded the same treatment as every other man in uniform, there will be a great improvement in the morale of colored troops. Today, the use of the epithets "Nigger" and "boy" by white officers are all too frequent. Men who have bullied and browbeaten Negroes in civilian life are bringing the same practices into the Army. There has been no impressive manifestation that the higher authorities strongly disapprove such practices and will deal sternly with offenders.[13]

Stimson accepted only one of Hastie's recommendations — the curbing of demeaning language by white officers. Three months after receiving the report, Stimson issued the following order:

> Superiors are forbidden to injure those under their authority by tyrannical or capricious conduct or by abusive language. While maintaining discipline and the thorough and prompt performance of military duty, all officers, in dealing with enlisted men, will bear in mind the absolute necessity of so treating them as to preserve their self-respect. A grave duty rests on all officers and particularly upon organization commanders in this respect. In this connection the use of any epithet deemed insulting to a racial group should be carefully avoided. Similarly, commanders should avoid all practices tending to give the colored soldier cause to feel that the Army makes any differentiation between him and any other soldier.[14]

Hastie also fought against another type of segregation suffered by the black soldier: his blood. Initially, the Red Cross refused to accept blood from black donors. Once the United States entered World War II, it adopted a policy of blood segregation: "Blood will be processed separately so that those receiving transfusions may be given plasma from blood of their own race."[15] Ironically, blood plasma was developed for the Red Cross by a black doctor, Charles R. Drew, a native of Washington. He was put in charge of America's Blood for Britain Project in 1940. Drew, among others, opposed the segregation of blood. The executive secretary of the NAACP, Walter White, wrote, "The Red Cross has agreed to accept the blood of Negro donors, but it is segregating the Negro blood on orders from the Army and Navy. This is true despite the fact that every scientist worthy of the name has asserted that there is no difference whatsoever in plasma made from the blood of persons of different races."[16]

Judge Hastie appealed to his boss, Secretary of War Stimson, to change the blood policy. "All blacks were insulted by policy made in deference to those who insist that our country treat the Negro as a loathsome being even as all non–Aryans are regarded under the ideology which we are fighting to the finish with force of arms," he wrote Stimson. "Even the saving of the lives of soldiers is weighed against the appeasement of the sentiments most alien to our professions, and found to be wanting."[17]

Col. Joseph S. Leonard, who had commanded the black 366th Infantry Regiment, was supportive of black troops as secretary of the Advisory Committee on Negro Troop Policies. This was reflected in a memo he wrote to the assistant secretary of war, John J. McCloy, on blood policy: "Objection to this practice fits into the pattern of opposition to all types of segregation. While this is a matter of small importance, it provides a cause for agitation."[18] But the surgeon general, Maj. Gen. James C. Magee, opposed any change in blood policy. "For reasons not biologically convincing but which are commonly recognized as psychologically important in America," he said, "it is not deemed advisable to collect and mix Caucasian and Negro blood indiscriminately for later administration to members of the military forces."[19] Finally, the War Department decided that if a mistake had been made in publishing the blood policy, a change during the war would create another fuss. But the belief was strong among many people that black and white blood should not be mixed.

Ernie Hatfield, a black sergeant, told what happened to a white couple over the issue of mixed blood. "One incident that occurred at Tuskegee involved a white pilot who crashed his plane and was severely injured. He needed a blood transfusion and the only two who matched his blood type were black officers," the sergeant said. "While all were in the operating room, the injured pilot's wife burst in and announced, 'Don't put none of that Nigger blood in my husband.' They gave the pilot the black officer's blood and saved his life. It was learned that soon thereafter the pilot's wife divorced him."[20]

The Red Cross worked closely with the Armed Forces during World War II, both in the United States and abroad. Red Cross crews met troop trains and served refreshments to the servicemen. But in the South, the Red Cross was said to follow local customs when troops were transferred by train, serving white troops first and often running out of supplies by the time workers reached the segregated black coaches.[21] Over 200 blacks served overseas with the Red Cross during the war, but almost all were assigned to black service clubs.

Judge Hastie also recommended that the Army use black newspapers in its recruiting campaign. Largely unknown by an incurious white establishment, the black press played a central role in black communities. This was reflected in weekly circulation: *Pittsburgh Courier*— 350,000 copies sold; *Chicago Defender*— 230,000; Baltimore's *Afro American*—170,000; and *Norfolk Journal and Guide*—100,000.[22] Gen. H.B. Lewis, the acting adjutant general, told Hastie the War Department had developed an advertising campaign in 1939 and it didn't contemplate the use of black newspapers to recruit black enlisted men.[23] Fortunately, as it turned out, word of mouth would be sufficient to recruit blacks.

Following Roosevelt's executive order, the black press concentrated its criticism on segregation in the military and the relegation of black troops to non-combat roles, such as those in the engineering and quartermaster units. "Wherever there is work to be done in the Army, you may expect to find Negro troops predominantly," said the

Pittsburgh Courier. "Wherever there is fighting to be done, white soldiers will be in the forefront. The choice doesn't belong to the Negro soldier. It is a difference based on color, which embitters him."[24] Despite making up only 10 percent of the Army as whole, black troops made up over 40 percent of the Corps of Engineers, charged with building, and over 30 percent of quartermaster units, those responsible for food, housing and transportation. As mobilization was underway, a distribution of black enlisted personnel in the Army showed the following:

Infantry	11,766
Cavalry	2,516
Field artillery	1,968
Coast artillery	1,865
Engineers	12,416
Quartermaster	14,206
Total	44,737

At a time when the War Department was considering the assignment of black regiments up north, it admitted it had a problem with the placement of such troops. Its Operations and Training Division, in a memo prepared for Brig. Gen. H.R. Bull, acting assistant chief of staff, said:

> World War history confirms the opinion that Negro combat units are less efficient than white. A basic reason for this lower efficiency is indicated by the markedly lower intelligence and specialist qualification ratings obtained by colored personnel from the intelligence and classification tests given to all selectees at the time of their induction.
>
> Innumerable objections from members of Congress and citizens have been received to the stationing of colored personnel in their communities. Colored units have had to be moved in several cases to other stations because of objections to their presence in certain communities.
>
> Separate recreation facilities must be provided at a considerable cost to the Government at all stations where colored personnel is stationed. There have been sporadic outbreaks of trouble at posts and in adjoining communities between white and colored personnel. These incidents amply demonstrate the necessity for segregated assignments and provision of separate recreation facilities.[26]

While the Army's leadership questioned the ability — if not the willingness — of black soldiers to fight in battle, commanders in the service sector cast doubts on their contribution to the war in non-combat roles. Lt. Col. J.C. Christensen of the Corps of Engineers said black troops were not as good as white troops because they lacked imagination and initiative. He told a conference that few skilled blacks were found in construction in civilian life, ignoring the fact that racial discrimination limited their access to such jobs. Gen. Henry Dorsey Munnikhuysen said at the same conference that similar problems existed in the Quartermaster Corps. "Every unit requires certain specialists and experience to date has been that such specialists are difficult to train from Negro personnel," he said. "This is particularly true in the case of the mechanical trades. It has been difficult to find or train three competent motor maintenance specialists in the average truck company."[27] By 1944, however, the Army would concede that black troops weren't entirely to blame for their lack of certain skills. "The performance of Negro soldiers on mechanical-aptitude tests is on the average markedly inferior to that of white soldiers," it said in a booklet of advice for white officers. "This is to be expected, since Negroes as a whole have not had opportunities nearly equal to those available to white men to gain mechanical experience."[28]

The Adjutant General's Office criticized Judge Hastie and his recommendations to Secretary of War Stimson in language so blunt that it was eliminated from the final memo. Among the excised language was the following: "Those Negro leaders who seek to prove discrimination because of color employ special pleading for a race which as a class has not as yet the attained mental equipment to be employed in military functions other than those where brawn is prerequisite."[29] This comment, from Lt. Col. James W. Boyer, Jr., did make it into print: "Judge Hastie considers himself a representative of the National Association for the Advancement of Colored People first, and a representative of the War Department second. I do not believe that he has helped solve any problem of significance but has created them."[30]

Ten weeks after Hastie had submitted his recommendations, Chief of Staff George C. Marshall told Secretary of War Stimson what he thought of them: "A solution of many of the issues presented by Judge Hastie in his memorandum to you on 'The Integration of the Negro Soldier into the Army,' September 22, would be tantamount to solving a social problem which has perplexed the American people throughout the history of this nation. The Army cannot accomplish such a solution."[31] Marshall decided the War Department should directly face its critics, so invitations were extended to the editors and publishers of the leading black newspapers for a briefing on military policy toward blacks. The chosen date was December 8, 1941, which happened to be the day after the Pearl Harbor attack.

The officer selected to make the presentation was Col. Eugene R. Householder of the adjutant general's staff. "The Army is made up of individual citizens of the United States who have pronounced views with respect to the Negro just as they have individual ideas with respect to other matters in their daily walk of life," he said, adding:

> The Army then cannot be made the means of engendering conflict among the mass of people because of a stand with respect to Negroes, which is not compatible with the position attained by the Negro in civilian life. This principle must necessarily govern the Army not only with this subject of contention but with respect to other dogma be it religious, political, or economic. The Army is not a sociological laboratory; to be effective it must be organized and trained according to the principles which will insure success. Experiments, to meet the wishes and demands of the champions of every race and creed for the solution of their problems, are a danger to efficiency, discipline and morale and would result in ultimate defeats.[32]

Ulysses Grant Lee, Jr., the black education specialist for the Army, heard Householder's remarks. He said the editors and publishers were "appalled" by them. "They contended that current practices extended segregation and prejudices to sections of the country where such patterns had not formerly existed," he said. "They took Col. Householder's statement to mean that the Army had no intention of modifying its racial practices."[33]

Increasingly, Judge Hastie found that he was not being invited to War Department meetings that involved policy toward black troops. He submitted his resignation in February 1943 after just over two years in government service. "As you know, I have believed for some time that my presence in the War Department is no longer essential to the maintenance of the several substantial gains made during the past two years in the handling of racial issues and particular problems of Negro military and civilian personnel," he said in his letter of resignation to Secretary of War Stimson. "Therefore, it has seemed to me that my present and future usefulness is greater as a private citizen who can express himself freely and publicly upon such issues than as a member of the War Department under obligation to refrain from such public expression."[34]

Secretary of War Stimson, the man who brought Hastie into the government, described himself in his memoirs as a northern conservative Republican born in the abolitionist tradition who believed in full freedom, political and economic, for men of all colors.[35] Shortly after receiving Hastie's letter of resignation, Stimson wrote in the privacy of his diary something he was probably not prepared to voice in public, especially to the military's top echelon: "We are suffering from the persistent legacy of the original crime of slavery."[36]

Many of the young black men who would go north to work on the highway and the pipeline, however, didn't pay much attention to the legacy of slavery: they just welcomed the opportunity to join the Army and earn some money.

4

Blacks Rush to Enlist

"We did anything we could, anything the white man had for us."

The two young men in Army uniforms were home on leave in the black Titanville neighborhood of Lafayette, Louisiana, that June day in 1941 when they ran into a teenaged friend named Bobby Lee Mouton. They'd put on weight since he'd last seen them because, as they explained, they had plenty to eat in the Army, as well as free uniforms and room and board. Why, you could even send home a monthly allotment of twenty dollars. The youngest of eight children of a single mother, Bobby Lee was forced to quit school in the eighth grade to help support the family. A bright student, he had loved the classes at St. Paul's, an all-black Catholic school run by nuns from the black Sisters of the Holy Family order in New Orleans. Hearing about Army life from his friends, he decided he'd be better off joining them than continuing his job of delivering groceries on his bicycle. Underage at seventeen, he asked his mother to sign a release allowing him to enlist. She did and he convinced two other friends, Murphy Haskins and Joseph Anderson, to join as well. The trio was soon heading by train to Camp Livingston, eighty miles away, where they joined hundreds of other black recruits from Louisiana who were destined to work in Alaska and Canada's Northwest.

"We were poor," Mouton said. "We didn't have enough to eat. Sometimes when my mother made *couscous*, a cornmeal mush you ate with milk, she wouldn't have enough money to buy milk — it was ten cents a quart — so we ate it with sugared water instead. Sometimes she didn't have enough money to pay the one dollar monthly rent. I didn't even own a coat until I got in the Army. I joined up because we were poor."[1]

The Army took one look at Bobby Lee, five-four, 123 pounds and looking younger than seventeen, and decided he was not husky enough to do the pick-and-shovel work required by the Corps of Engineers. He was assigned to the 93rd Regiment as a supply clerk, and would grow two inches over the next four years.

Mouton's given name was really Anthony. Bobby Lee was the name of his cat, which an older brother had applied to the pet's master as well. He became Anthony in the Army and Tony once back in civilian life.

Another recruit from Fayetteville was also a friend of Mouton's — Joseph Prejean, the illiterate son of tenant farmers. When he told his landlord that he planned to enlist, the man said he'd be killed in action. "I told him I just couldn't make it on a dollar fifty a week," Prejean said of the laboring job he then had. Prejean learned to read from a buddy who was dating a teacher and was admitted to the Army's cooking school. After the war, he became a famous chef in New Orleans.²

The decision by Prejean and Mouton to enlist was common among young blacks, who saw the Army as a path out of poverty, especially in peacetime. The Army estimated annual pay to a recruit was worth between $2,000 and $2,600, factoring in accommodations, food, clothing, and dental and medical attention. At the outbreak of war, the average annual income of blacks in the United States was less than $400, compared to the national average of almost $1,000 for all Americans.³

Passage by Congress of the Selective Service Act in 1940 made the enlistment process simple — on paper — as the Army and Navy were actively seeking recruits while war raged in Europe. All a black person aged eighteen to thirty-six had to do was go to a local draft board and volunteer for one year of service. This was new for the Army. Before 1940 there were no vacancies in the Army's "colored" regiments, so almost all volunteers were automatically rejected. The Navy and the Marines initially did not use the Selective Service for recruiting since they were the glamour services and received more than enough volunteers. The Army was uncomfortable with the restrictions placed on recruiting by the Selective Service Act and sought ways to thwart those encouraging black enlistment. First Army Headquarters, for instance, sent secret orders to draft boards in Massachusetts, Connecticut, Maine, New Hampshire, Vermont and Rhode Island that no blacks should be accepted.⁴ Of 25,000 national draft board members, there were virtually no black representatives in the South and just 450 in the North.⁵ Some white recruiting officers purposely failed to send induction notices advising blacks classified A-1 that they should report to the draft board. Most of those rejected — black and white, but mainly black — failed to pass literacy tests, tests that Secretary of War Henry L. Stimson admit-

Anthony Mouton (courtesy Lavern Mouton).

ted were primarily aimed at blacks. "The Army had adopted rigid requirements for literacy mainly to keep down the number of colored troops and this is reacting badly in preventing us from getting in some very good but illiterate [white] recruits from the southern mountain states," Stimson said.[6]

One of the top candidates rejected was John Hope Franklin, the preeminent black historian who later counseled Martin Luther King and Justice Thurgood Marshall. A native of Rentiesville, Oklahoma, he tried to enlist in the Army in 1941. He thought his background in education and ability to take shorthand and write, plus the fact that he had a Ph.D. from Harvard, might earn him a desk job. "You're perfect except for the color," he was told by the recruiter.[7]

At the other end of the classification scale, the number of blacks judged IV-F was considered shocking. Almost one million were in the lowest classification, percentagewise twice the rate of whites. A contemporary report stated:

> The overwhelming number of rejections, both white and Negro, startled the nation out of its complacency concerning its living standards. The greatly disproportionate number of Negro rejections was a serious indictment of our social system.... The nation was surprised to learn that, in one southern state, one out of every thirteen white residents lacked the fourth grade education, which was needed for an understanding of simple Army orders. But four out of every five Negroes had not completed the fourth grade in some sections of our country.[8]

The Army itself admitted that blacks were ill served by the school system. "Differences in the educational achievement of groups of people in the United States appear to be directly proportional to the amount and nature of their educational facilities," said an Army report. "In the South, for example, the educational opportunities afforded Negro children are inferior to those provided for white children, and it is in the South that such a relatively high proportion of Negro adults are classed as illiterate." The report noted that the average yearly amount spent to educate a black pupil in nine Southern states was $18.82 in 1939–1940, while the average for a white pupil was more than three times as great—$58.69. Both, however, lagged behind the national average of $88.09.[9] Inadequate schooling for blacks was a legacy of the Civil War and Reconstruction in the South, where many whites felt that educated blacks threatened their way of life.[10] The burning of black schools was a common occurrence in the nineteenth century, but one black serviceman said that the Ku Klux Klan burned down his school in Georgia in the 1930s.[11] The educational disadvantages of Southern blacks led the Army to place a disproportionate number of them in pick-and-shovel units, preferring Northern blacks for technical and combat units.

After Pearl Harbor, the American Army faced a severe manpower shortage, so it lowered literacy requirements and began remedial educational courses for blacks and whites. For periods of two to three months, those assigned to these courses spent eighteen hours a week on reading, language and math skills. The rest of the time was spent on military subjects. Besides teaching skills, the instructors were selected for their ability to teach slow learners. Blacks taught blacks, but sometimes there were integrated classes taught by whites. Once the recruits could read at a fourth-grade level, they were reassigned to regular basic training camps.

The results showed that, given an equal opportunity, black recruits could perform as well as — or even better than — white recruits. Nearly 150,000 blacks received literacy training during the Second World War. Some months up to 45 percent of new inductees were assigned to literacy training units. There were 250 such units spread across the nation. Of the blacks assigned, 85.1 percent completed the training. Of the 160,000 whites assigned, 81.7 percent did. A postwar report published by the Defense Department (the renamed War Department) stated, "The percentage of Negroes who successfully completed the training course was a shattering blow at racists. The units had provided an ideal experiment: thousands of men of various colors and creeds were assembled from all sections of the country and subjected to an absolutely uniform period of training. The experiment proved that, given a comparable learning situation, Negroes did as well as whites."[12] The success of the literacy training even won over Secretary of War Stimson. He said in his memoirs, written in the third person, "Stimson's early distrust of the use of the Army as an agency of social reform dissolved under the impact of the manpower shortage, and was turned into enthusiasm by direct observation of the accomplishments of soldiers in attacking illiteracy among Negroes (and whites) at Fort Benning."[13]

Even before the literacy training, Army recruiters must have looked the other way at times as far as the non-combat black regiments were concerned. The four regiments that went to the Far North had many illiterate Southerners, especially from Louisiana and Mississippi. When the 93rd Regiment, based at Camp Livingston, Louisiana, was trying to get up to strength, its officers would go into New Orleans to recruit.[14] Many of the new recruits came from Louisiana plantations and spoke French rather than English, a barrier to passing Army literacy tests. "The large number of illiterates and mentally handicapped enlisted men assigned to this regiment during its initial phase of organization created a serious problem and had a detrimental effect on the progress made by other soldiers who were not so handicapped," said Lt. Col. James L. Lewis of the 93rd Regiment.[15]

The problem wasn't limited to the 93rd, but the handicaps of the enlisted men could be misleading. "A lot of the boys come from the plantations couldn't count money when they first went into the Army because they got paid in due bills," said Lee Young, a black sergeant with the 97th Regiment from Engelhard, North Carolina, referring to the system of tokens used by the workers for purchases at company stores. "The best engineers that we got were from the South. Some of them had high IQs. They had no formal education, but they were anxious to learn."[16] At least one white officer who served in Alaska with the 97th would have agreed with Young's assessment. "Many of them could not read and write," said Walter Parsons, a lieutenant from Palestine, Texas. "It wasn't a handicap for some. Those boys who couldn't read and write listened well and retained what they heard."[17]

The Selective Service Act sought a population balance in the Army: blacks would be recruited in accordance with their share of the population (then 10 percent). However, so many blacks were enlisting that the percentage reached 16 percent, or 38,538 recruits, as of 30 September 1941. This was a number especially disturbing to Southern congressmen, many of whom feared blacks from their districts would become more worldly after service abroad and would seek improvement in their civil rights once back home. Most blacks still lived in the South and the black enlistees were overwhelmingly from Southern states, especially Louisiana, like Bobby Lee Mouton.

Fewer blacks would have joined the Army if the defense industries had been more open to them. Congress passed legislation providing $60 million for 4,630 training courses for applicants seeking work in the war plants, but only 194 courses were open to blacks.[18] The United States Employment Service in January 1942 asked defense industries with large military contracts if they would hire black workers. Just over half said they did not and never would, while a quarter said they might under certain conditions.[19] This was six months after President Roosevelt had issued Executive Order 8802 barring racial discrimination in defense industry hiring.

Not only were company executives opposed to hiring blacks, but so were their white workers. When twelve black workers at the Alabama Dry Dock and Ship Builders Company in Mobile, Alabama, sought a status upgrade to welder, 20,000 white workers walked off the job.[20] At the Packard Motor plant in Detroit, production of bomber engines was halted when 25,000 white workers struck in protest over the promotion of three black workers. "I'd rather see Hitler and Hirohito win than work next to a Nigger," said one white worker, justifying the walkout.[21] Even though war plants were short of workers, many jobs were ruled off limits to blacks, usually because of racial bias by management and the workforce: 37,659 of 64,859 jobs in the aircraft industry; 5,561 of 8,083 in chemicals; 20,397 of 33,230 in iron and steel; and 10,346 of 20,792 in electrical machinery. The exception was shipbuilding, where fewer than a third of 64,000 jobs were closed to blacks.[22] As a result of workplace discrimination, more blacks were available for the Armed Forces because fewer worked in the defense industries and had the industrial and technical skills that warranted a deferred draft classification.

Lee Young was cleaning potatoes for seventy-five cents a day on a farm in North Carolina when he decided to enlist in the U.S. Army. "We did anything we could, anything the white man had for us," he said. "The doors were closed to the blacks. Roosevelt opened them." Young finished high school while in the Army and rose to become first sergeant. "I was glad to get in the Army," he said.[23]

Nathaniel ("Nate") Dulin was eighteen and working on a project of the Civilian Conservation Corps, one of the most popular New Deal programs during the Depression as it targeted the unemployed. When the United States entered the Second World War, Congress cancelled the program. A high school dropout, he was unable to find work. "Nobody would have me," he said. "My father was a miner in the West Kentucky coal fields and he wanted me to join him. His father took *him* out of school when he was twelve and took *him* to the coal mine with him."24 Dulin enlisted in the Army instead and was assigned to the 95th Regiment.

Fred Spencer was an eighteen-year-old from Grande Ridge, Florida, who was "looking for adventure" when he decided to enlist in the Army in 1941. "I'd been working on a tobacco farm," he explained. He was assigned to the 93rd.25

Like Bobby Lee Mouton, Joseph Haskin was from Lafayette, Louisiana. "Four of us went to the recruiting office and volunteered," he said. "If you volunteered, you could go to the camp you wanted. So in 1941 we chose Camp Livingston. We were greenhorns. We were assigned to the Engineers and thought we were going to be on locomotives. I said, 'What a mistake we've made.' I was in the medics, so I didn't have to do hard work."26 He also was assigned to the 93rd Regiment.

Nolan Hamilton was accepted at a recruiting office in New Orleans. "I volunteered because I thought I would be drafted," he said.27 He was likewise assigned to the 93rd.

Jesse Balthazar, born in McIntosh, Louisiana, had just started work as a substitute letter carrier in Texas. "A co-worker had told me we wouldn't be drafted because we were government employees," he said. "Two of us from the Post Office were drafted and we went to training thinking we wouldn't be kept."28 He was assigned to the 97th.

Otis E. Lee, a native of Virginia, volunteered in May 1941 when recruits signed

Sgt. Jesse Balthazar (courtesy William E. Griggs).

up for just one year. "I wanted to get it over with so I could get on with my life," he said. "But Pearl Harbor came and it ended up being almost five years."[29] Lee was assigned to the 95th Regiment.

John E. Bollin, a native of Virginia, wanted to further his education. "I enlisted in August 1941 hoping to save some money so I could go to university," he said. "I didn't realize the pay was only twenty-one dollars a month."[30] He was assigned to the 93rd and never did go to university.

James F. Jones of Whitesboro, New Jersey, enlisted on 18 March 1942. "I thought I'd get some education," he said. A high school graduate, he was assigned to the 95th as a company clerk.[31]

Wansley Hill was in his second year of agriculture at Alcorn A & M College in Mississippi in 1941, enjoying his studies and playing the trumpet in the school band, when Army recruiters showed up on campus. "I said to myself, 'If I'm going to go into the service, rather than being drafted, and they could send me any place, I would go to Camp Livingston where they promised to send me for a year.'"[32] Hill enlisted and ended up with the 388th Regiment.

Sgt. Reginald Beverly (courtesy Reginald Beverly).

Reginald Beverly of Ruther Glen, Virginia, was a rarity — a black recruit with a university degree. "I was drafted December 5, 1941, two days before Pearl Harbor," he said. "I was a high school math teacher. I went to school, called the roll and bid them goodbye and went two miles to Bowling Green to catch the bus to go to Fort Meade. I was twenty-six years old."[33] Beverly had received a Bachelor of Science degree from Virginia State University, the first fully state-supported, four-year institution of higher learning for blacks in America. He was assigned to the 95th Regiment.

Hayward Oubre, Jr., son of a New Orleans mail clerk, was studying in Tuskegee, Alabama, when his draft board contacted him in April of 1941. "They told me I'd be jailed if I didn't show up in New Orleans the next day," he said.[34] He showed up in time and was assigned to the 97th Regiment at Camp Blanding,

Florida. A graduate of Dillard College in New Orleans, he was attached to the headquarters' intelligence unit as a draftsman and special design person.

Nehemiah Atkinson, one of ten children of a New Orleans preacher, was in his second year at the Louisiana Normal School when he was drafted in 1941. He was trained to be a medical corpsman with the 97th Regiment.

Tommie L. Walker, born in Helena, Arkansas, but raised in Chicago, also attended Virginia State. He graduated with a degree in chemistry and was subsequently drafted.

Irving Smith was born in Darlington, Maryland, but raised by an aunt in Philadelphia. A high school graduate, he wanted to be a mechanic but was drafted in April 1941 and made a supply clerk with the 95th Regiment.

James Taylor, from suburban Washington, D.C., was drafted out of college and made a personnel clerk with the 95th. "They figured, 'No point putting this boy out there to do this [manual labor]. Let him stay in here to handle this kind of stuff.'"[35]

Richard E. Trent was a member of the only black family — eleven boys and seven girls — in Crafton, a town of 7,000 four miles west of Pittsburgh, Pennsylvania. Three of his brothers graduated from university (one of them as a medical doctor), but their coal-miner father died when Richard was a teenager, so he ended up working on a farm. When he was twenty, he and his best friend, Ernie, decided to join the Army Air Forces in 1941, so they went together to the draft board in Pittsburgh. Ernie was accepted but Richard was rejected because the Air Forces did not accept blacks. "I almost cried," he said. He went back to the draft board the next month and enlisted in the Army. Because he was "one of the Trent boys," the townspeople gave him a going-away dinner. The mayor spoke about him going to a Southern camp. "You might get involved in something you can't handle," the mayor said in his remarks. "What could I get into that I can't anywhere else?" he thought. The mayor clarified the point after the dinner. "He told me that blacks in the South weren't allowed to do this or that," said Trent. "That's something we'd never talked about." He was assigned to the 95th Regiment, then at Fort Belvoir, Virginia, and later Fort Bragg, North Carolina.[36]

That blacks were willing to fight was reflected in the draft-dodging rate. "It is believed that only a few hundred individuals among nearly three million Negro registrants have been indicted for evasion of the Selective Service Act," the Army reported. "Some of these men were accused of such offenses as failure to register, falsifying questionnaire returns, failure to return questionnaire, and using incorrect name and address on registration card. The small number of cases indicates that evasion of the Selective Service Law is not a serious problem among Negroes."[37]

Several blacks told their draft boards they'd only serve in non-segregated units. "Unless I am assured that I can serve in a mixed regiment and that I will not be compelled to serve in a unit undemocratically selected as a Negro group, I will refuse to report for induction," Winfred W. Lynn of Jamaica, New York, wrote.[38] He was arrested for draft evasion, but joined the Army and challenged its segregation policy. An appeal against lower court judgments was refused by the U.S. Supreme Court because he was then overseas and outside the court's jurisdiction. Ernest Calloway, the educational director of the Chicago local of the United Transport Employees of America, wrote to his draft board in January 1941, "I can't accept the responsibility of taking the oath upon induction into military service under the present anti-democratic structure of the United States Army and ask to be exempted from military training until such time that my contribution and participation in the defense of my country be made on a basis of complete equality."[39] He lost his case and was sentenced to prison.

For many of the blacks, especially those from the Deep South, life in the Army represented an improvement in their standard of living. "These men had grown up with very little on farms and so forth, very poor economic circumstances," said Lt. Walter Mason from Roanoke, Virginia. "Times were still hard in the South. It was a step up for these men to be in the Army. Not only that, they were given something definite to do and they were increasing their skills."[40]

But many found that the racial discrimination they encountered in civilian life followed them into the Army. The members of the four black regiments destined to be posted to Alaska and Canada's Northwest faced two sources of racial discrimination when they joined the Army: from some of the white officers assigned to their units and, since the camps where they trained were in the South, from local police and residents whenever they ventured into neighboring towns. Training in the South was especially difficult for the minority of black soldiers who were Northerners. They were not accustomed to the everyday Jim Crow laws of the South, such as being forced to ride in the back of buses. Some of the Northern enlistees would rebel against these restrictions.

Among those picked up by police in Alabama were two well-known black soldiers: world heavyweight champion Joe Louis, a sergeant from Detroit, and future welterweight and middleweight champion Sugar Ray Robinson, a corporal from New York. They opted to wait in the white waiting room at a bus depot, rather than in the black one. When the pair challenged orders from police to move, they were placed in a patrol car and taken to a nearby training camp where they had performed for the troops.[41] On January 9, 1942, Louis had fought Buddy Baer in a Navy Relief Society benefit fight before a sellout crowd of 16,689 at Madison Square Garden in New York. The referee stopped the fight in the first round after Louis had floored Baer for the third time. "The only way I could have beaten Joe that night was with a baseball bat," Baer said after the fight.[42] Louis donated his $100,000 purse to the victims of Pearl Harbor. "Ain't fighting for nothing," Louis said to explain his loss of income, "I'm fighting for my country."[43] Two days after the fight he enlisted in the Army.

The War Department decided in 1940 to build the majority of the training camps in the South for a simple reason: they offered outdoor training year-round. The large, wooded areas permitted realistic Army maneuvers, and costly heating equipment and insulation were not needed in newly constructed buildings. The proximity of nearby towns with black neighborhoods where soldiers could entertain themselves was also prized. As the Army mobilized, it limited black units at all training camps to battalion size except at Fort Huachuca, Arizona, where a black infantry division was allowed. The Army thought that the smaller units would allay fears of those living near the camps. The Army structure was as follows:

    Squad — 9–10 men led by a sergeant
    Platoon — 16–44 men commanded by a lieutenant
    Company — 62–190 men commanded by a captain
    Battalion — 300–1,000 men commanded by a lieutenant colonel
    Regiment — 1,000–3,000 men commanded by a colonel
    Brigade — 3,000–5,000 men commanded by a brigadier general or colonel
    Division — 10,000–15,000 men commanded by a major general

This meant that a black unit assigned to a white post had to make do with the leftover space, usually on the perimeter of the facility. A reporter for the *Pittsburgh Courier* visited training camps in 1941. "It was observed that the Negro area, in nine cases out of ten, was in the most inaccessible section of the camp," he reported. "Negro soldiers were quartered next to the woods (the last area to be cleared) or across the railroad tracks or highway from the main camp."[44]

Sgt. William E. Griggs (courtesy William E. Griggs).

When Baltimore native William E. Griggs and the 97th Battalion (soon to become a regiment) were moved to Eglin Field in Florida, the troops had to build their own barracks and other facilities, including a movie theater. "A member of the 97th would wait outside the white theater and be given the reel to take over to the black theater," Griggs said. "I don't recall ever being to the main post at Eglin."[45] Griggs's father, a high school principal in Baltimore, ran a photo studio — Oreo Photo Shop — on the side, so it was natural that his son Bill would become the 97th's photographer.

While at Eglin, the 97th Regiment built an airfield for the 99th Pursuit Squadron, whose members were the first black pilots, later known as the Tuskegee Airmen. The unit had been formed in March 1941, three months before the 97th arrived. "I don't think white engineers would have served the 99th the way we did," said Sgt. Lee Young, who drove a bulldozer during construction of the airfield. "I was glad I had that experience, digging up stumps and moving things around."[46] That experience would serve him well on the Alcan Highway construction.

Southern states and even some western and northern places — such as Spokane, Washington — wanted blacks barred or restricted in number. Wrote official black military historian Ulysses Lee: "Negro troops, according to the post commanders, would be resented at five out of six Northern posts, over half of the Southern posts, and practically all of the southwestern and western posts. Nearly all commanders of Southern posts indicated that Northern troops would produce greater resentment than Southern Negro troops. Post commanders felt that large numbers of Negroes should not be stationed at any one post and that in no case should more Negro than white troops be placed on a post."[47]

When the mayor of a town near Camp Swift, Texas (probably Bastrop, nine miles away), heard that 3,000 black troops might be assigned to the training center, he "asked his Congressman to inform the President that he would personally shoot the first one who came into town."[48] Editorialized the *Dallas Morning News*: "The federal government apparently has never learned that it cannot without unfortunate consequences billet ... Negro troops in the South. Until it does learn that axiomatic fact, there will continue to be trouble."[49] Because of past racial incidents, the War Department had decided to never again train black troops in Texas, but it rescinded the policy in 1937. However, the policy remained *de facto* until the needs of wartime required use of Texas camps to train black recruits. Southern governors meeting at Hot Springs, Arkansas, voted not to allow black military police jurisdiction over disobedient white soldiers and that Southern blacks be trained in the South and Northern blacks in the North.[50] The *Pittsburgh Courier* had its own take: *all* blacks, not only Northerners, should be trained in the more tolerant North.[51]

Those few Southern blacks who were transferred to Northern camps met with cultural changes nearly as great as those seen by the Northerners trained in the South. Said a contemporary report: "Northern-born Negroes are appalled at meeting Jim Crow on his home ground for the first time, and as a rule the northern whites are also shocked. But Southern Negroes crossing the Mason-Dixon Line for the first time are confused by the comparative freedom of conditions in the North and West; it is claimed that they become demoralized. Southern white officers and trainees coming North often turn into rabid missionaries for 'keeping the Niggers in their place.'"[52] President Roosevelt, however, did not make any public comment about racial incidents because of the upcoming 1942 congressional elections and his dependence on Southern Democrats.[53]

Lt. Alton Post of Zumbrota, Minnesota — he would eventually become a major general — was surprised at the treatment of blacks when he was assigned to Camp McCain, Mississippi, with the 4070th Quartermaster Truck Regiment (Colored). Once he had to take his platoon to Camp Shelby, Mississippi, to pick up some trucks. "When we stopped at the first restaurant on the way back and I started to take my troops in, I was barred at the door," he said. "'You can't come in here,' I was told. 'We can give you some stuff out the back door.'" He told his sergeant to lead them to the black part of town where they could be served. "I was certainly an object of curiosity in that place," he said. "I was with my platoon and I think they appreciated that."[54] Cpl. Horace Evans of the black 761st Tank Battalion complained that white officers had iced water to cool themselves during maneuvers in the Texas heat while black recruits sweated. "It was these little petty things that really burned you and made you know just what a vicious, scheming character [the white officer] was."[55]

The Social Science Institute at Fisk University in Nashville, Tennessee, reported that there were 242 racial clashes in forty-seven American cities in 1941,[56] although it did not break down those involving black soldiers and those involving black civilians. The black press noted nineteen cases of racial violence that year, all but two involving soldiers. One was the lynching of a black soldier outside the Fort Benning, Georgia, training camp. His body was found hanging from a tree, hands bound behind his back.

Transportation between Southern training camps and neighboring towns was often the source of problems that could escalate into violence and even death. If the black soldiers were obliged to use public transportation, they were subject to segregated buses. When seats were needed for white passengers, they were forced to give up their seat in the back of the bus. Master Sgt. Warren Bryant of the 812th Aviation Engineers said that "overt segregation was a new experience" for him at McDill Field outside of Tampa, Florida, since he had been born in Cincinnati and raised in Detroit. "When we got a chance to go to town we had to wait until all of the white soldiers who wished to go had been taken to their destinations," he said. "Then we were crowded like sardines into a couple of buses and driven directly to the colored section of the nearby town."[57] Train travel could include a wait of twelve hours before the ticket agent would attend a black soldier. Because whites boarded first, all the seats might be taken anyway and the soldier left on the platform as the train pulled out. White taxi drivers wouldn't pick up black fares even if the soldier was in uniform. If the soldier ventured out of the black district, bars and other white establishments would refuse to serve him.

A black private named Booker T. Spicely, who had worked in the business department of the Tuskegee Institute before joining the Army, was shot and killed in Durham, North Carolina, by a white bus driver who ordered him to move. As the disgruntled soldier disembarked, he allegedly said, "If you weren't a lousy IV-F, you wouldn't be driving a bus."[58] The bus driver followed Spicely and shot him. A jury acquitted him of second-degree murder. Baltimore's *Afro American* proved to be prescient when it nicknamed Fayetteville, North Carolina, "Uncle Sam's Powder Keg" because of the hostility local residents felt toward the black soldiers from nearby Fort Bragg, the nation's largest Army post. Six months before Pearl Harbor, the last bus was taking only blacks back to Fort Bragg when a dispute broke out between the driver and soldiers over the fare. Four white military policemen (MPs) boarded the bus with nightsticks swinging to stop the subsequent pushing and shoving. A black private named Ned Thurman grabbed an MP's .45 caliber pistol, allegedly shouted, "I'm gonna break up you MPs beating us colored soldiers," and shot and killed one of them. Thurman was killed and seven other black soldiers wounded.[59]

A fight broke out in Centerville, Mississippi, between a white MP and a black soldier whom he chastised for lacking a button on his sleeve. When the black soldier started to get the best of it, the MP yelled at the local sheriff, who was watching the fight, "Shoot the Nigger." He did and asked the MP, "Any more Niggers you wanted killed?"[60]

When a black sentry at a Louisiana training camp refused a state trooper's order to move from his post, he was shot and killed. The trooper was given a one-day suspension.[61] In addition, a city policeman clubbed and shot a black soldier in Beaumont, Texas,[62] and a black Army nurse was beaten and jailed in Montgomery, Alabama, after refusing to move to the back of the bus.[63]

William Walker, a black private, was shot and killed during a fight with white MPs and local police at Camp Van Dorn in Mississippi. His buddies seized rifles and attempted to leave the camp to find those who shot Walker. They were stopped by black MPs.[64]

Alexandria, Louisiana, was a town of 25,000, dwarfed by four nearby Army posts with 75,000 soldiers, 16,000 of them black. Since the town's colored district just consisted of four blocks, black soldiers would occasionally saunter into the white area. On the night of January 10, 1942, a white MP from Camp Livingston tried to arrest a drunken black soldier outside a movie theater. As the soldier resisted, his buddies tried to rescue him. Reinforcements were called, including state and local police, and what became a riot ensued for the next hour. Thirty unarmed black soldiers were wounded, most by gunshot. Back in the black district, Joseph Haskin and some buddies from the 93rd Regiment were looking for a drink. "We went to a place on lower Third. When we got there, they were closing the place. 'Don't you know there's a riot going on?' we were asked. State troopers told us we couldn't leave, that our commanding officers were coming to get us and take us back to base."[65]

The way to avoid trouble for many of the black soldiers was to reluctantly accept the local reality. "I could go into town, but I knew what segregation was," said John E. Bollin of the 93rd. "I stayed in the black neighborhood. The mentality in Alexandria was, 'Don't cross this line.' I didn't try to change anything. You stayed in the back of the bus if you were black, the front if you were white. You're accepted as a slave, then accepted in a segregated society, and then that segregated society has to go to war, we don't exist. We didn't exist before the war, and we don't exist now in a war."[66]

Reports of black soldiers being attacked by whites were so common in black newspapers that the rumor of a soldier being killed by a policeman in New York's Harlem sparked a riot on August 2, 1943, in which six people were killed and 185 injured. A black soldier was shot and *wounded* by a white policeman. The soldier had objected to the language the policeman directed toward a woman with whom he was arguing. He punched the officer, who fired; the woman shouted he had been killed, and the riot erupted. Two months earlier, thirty-four people were killed in Detroit when a series of scuffles on a hot, humid day erupted into a riot, fulfilling rumors that one was taking place.

At one point, Gen. George C. Marshall, the chief of staff of the U.S. Army, felt obliged to send a memo about racial disturbances to all commanding generals. It said in part:

> All of the reported disturbances follow a fairly definite pattern. Unrest and disaffection begin with real or fancied incidents of discrimination and segregation. No positive action is taken to overcome the causes of irritation or unrest. Gossip or rumor of a nature designed to excite the men circulates among the units and a minor incident brings on a general outbreak....
>
> Under no circumstances can there be a command attitude which makes allowances for the improper conduct of either white or Negro soldiers, among themselves or towards each other. Improper conduct cannot be justified on the basis of relative average intelligence....
>
> These instructions will be transmitted to the proper elements of your command and the necessary supervision established to insure a rigid compliance therewith.[67]

But the Army emphasized it could not effect any changes in racial behavior in the towns visited by soldiers: "Soldiers, Negro and white, should be instructed that the Army has no authority to alter in any direction the existing community pattern as a matter of social reform, and that it will expect the soldier, when in the community, to abide by its laws."[68]

When the 93rd was assigned to build bridges over several rivers and creeks in Louisiana, the soldiers would sometimes ask permission to swim after a hot day of work. Lt. Robert Platt Boyd, Jr., would give his approval and the men would strip and dive naked into the water. Trouble came when they found a tree that leaned over the water and allowed them to do some high diving. A farmer complained to Army authorities that his daughters were mortified by the sight of nude black men. "I had noticed that his teenaged daughters, who had stopped on a bridge downstream from the leaning tree, had a pair of field glasses to help them watch my soldiers," said Boyd, a native of Huntsville, Alabama.[69]

Secretary of War Stimson had second thoughts about his department's decision to concentrate the training camps in the South. In his memoirs he wrote the following: "Most training camps were in the South, and the South had feelings which seemed wholly wrong to the northern Secretary. Still more disturbing were its actions. A Negro in the Army was a United States soldier, and Stimson was deeply angered when it proved impossible to bring to justice southern police who murdered a colored MP. Southern bus companies enforced the peculiar rules of the region in serving Army camps; as often happens under these rules, insufficient space was provided for Negroes. Stimson insisted to his deputies that this sort of blatant unfairness must be stopped."[70]

Could the Army have done more to protect the black soldiers training in the South? "The record of the War and Justice Departments was one of constant evasion of their democratic responsibilities and surrender to southern racial patterns," said a report commissioned by the NAACP. "The Army refused to stand up for its colored soldiers in controversies with local authorities. It is inconceivable that wanton slayings of white personnel would have been ignored by the federal government as they were ignored in the case of Negro troops."[71]

The soldiers soon found a way to make their complaints public: write letters to the hometown black newspapers.

5

Black Soldiers Voice Their Complaints

"I was shocked to have someone tell me they didn't know how to read and write."

Writing letters, especially to hometown black newspapers, was one way the soldiers could vent their frustrations over discrimination in the Army. Many of those who came from Southern plantations were illiterate, so colleagues (often from more northerly states) would write letters for them or encourage them to learn how to do so themselves. Writing in the letters to the editor section of the *Atlanta Daily World*, an unnamed soldier asked, "I would like to know if your paper approves of a General calling his soldiers 'Nigger' to their face? I think that we are in this war to fight for the rights of all minority races; the morale of this organization will be low if our soldiers are not addressed in the right manner."[1]

The use of racial epithets by white officers when referring to black recruits was one of the first signs of racial discrimination in the Southern training camps. Alerted by complaints from the troops, future Supreme Court justice Thurgood Marshall and Judge William H. Hastie, former aide to Secretary of War Stimson, submitted a paper on racial discrimination in the military to the National Lawyers' Guild:

> To address a Negro soldier as "Nigger" is such a commonplace in the average southern community that little is said about it. But the mounting rage of the soldier himself is far from commonplace. He may not express his feelings when he must wait until all the white passengers are accommodated before he can get transportation. He may even hold his tongue when he is forced to get out of the bus in which he is seated in order to make room for white passengers. But it is of such stuff that bitterness and hatred are made. In such a climate resentments grow until they burst forth in violent and unreasonable reprisal.[2]

There is no record of the lawyers' guild acting on the complaint.

One private, Jus Hill, told his hometown newspaper, the *Pittsburgh Courier*, that black soldiers at Randolph Field in Texas were assigned to clean up the quarters of white officers: "They started us cleaning the white officers' rooms, making us they [*sic*] dirty beds and cleaning the latrine and are still doing that right at the present."[3]

Pfc. N. Lyles, a native of Ohio, told the *Call and Post* of Cleveland what it was like for a Northerner in a Southern training camp (Keesler Field in Mississippi in his case). "The northern Negro feels most keenly about his being stationed in the South, as on the whole he has been accustomed to greater freedom of movement and security of person in his home community," he said. "Specifically, he has generally not suffered definite segregation in public conveyances, public eating places, and in theaters."[4]

Another soldier told of his experience going to Biloxi, the town nearest to Keesler Field. "I went into the city one night on a pass and was walking down that street in the Negro section where there were no sidewalks," he wrote. "This may sound fantastic but the police tried to run over me! I mean they veered across the street in their police car and if I hadn't leaped across a ditch they would have deliberately run me down. If they were trying to tell me something, I got the message. I got back to Keesler Field fast and I never returned to Biloxi."[5] Another soldier stationed at Keesler Field told the *Afro American* of Baltimore about the feelings of his Army colleagues. "I would like for you to picture the position I, or any other Negro officer, holds here at Keesler Field," he wrote. "I have heard it expressed openly, hundreds of times by Negro soldiers, that they would just as soon give their life fighting the injustices inflicted upon them right here in the United States than to fight to correct the injustices of other people they know nothing about on foreign soil."[6]

A tradesman in civilian life complained to the *Pittsburgh Courier* of demeaning work assignments only given to black recruits: "Most of us got trades of our own to help win this war. But instead we are servants and dig ditches and we want better, if it ever been slavery, it is now, please help us because we want better."[7]

One private, Charles Wilson, wrote directly to President Roosevelt: "The picture in our country is marred by one of the strangest paradoxes in our whole fight against world fascism. The United States Armed Forces, to fight for World Democracy, is within itself undemocratic. The undemocratic policy of Jim Crow and segregation is practiced by our Armed Forces against its Negro members."[8]

A group of black soldiers who signed themselves as "Negro Slaves" had a complaint about treatment at Fort Leonard Wood, Missouri: a black corporal was obliged to show newly promoted white sergeants how to do their job, but never got promoted himself. "In the personnel office they have one white corporal, who can barely read and write, four white sergeants, one of whom was tutored in his job by a Negro youth, one white staff sergeant and one white master sergeant," they wrote. "Whenever a white sergeant is transferred another white is told that he will be made sergeant provided he consents to go to work in the Seventh Group personnel. A Negro does not know enough to be placed in the vacancy created by the transfer of his superior non-commissioned officer. The Negro corporal is then forced to tutor this incumbent sergeant. It is quite obvious what the outcome of this is — the Negro is still corporal and the white boy is now sergeant."[9]

Black enlisted men training at Fort Leonard Wood were not free from local discrimination. While training there in early 1943 before being sent to Dawson Creek as a replacement in the 95th, Pvt. Henry Easter and two buddies went to an off-post bar. "I see you darkies are in town tonight," was the welcome given them by one of the patrons.[10]

A black sergeant, Edward ("Eddie") Donald, reported on discrimination at Camp Claiborne, Louisiana, where the 93rd Regiment was based: "Black soldiers were quartered on the back side of the grounds in what I would call swampland, the most undesirable area of the whole camp. White soldiers were at the other end of the camp, on good ground with the highway nearby and bus facilities to take them to town. We were not allowed in the white area and they were not allowed in ours. When we went into town we had to go to the ghetto. We learned, with some difficulty, to accept this.... While there, I noticed that a number of German prisoners were in the camp in a special area, not swampland. They were given freedom of movement and had access to facilities denied black American soldiers. They were given passes to town when black soldiers were confined to the area and did not have their privileges. This was one of the most repugnant things I can recall of the many things that happened to Negro servicemen."[11]

Anthony (formerly Bobby Lee) Mouton recalled what happened to members of the 93rd Regiment, back from deployment up north, when they were assigned to guard German prisoners being transferred to a prison in Louisiana. "They stopped at some little town to feed the prisoners. They let the prisoners go inside and eat but they wouldn't let the black soldiers go into the restaurant to get sandwiches to bring out for themselves."[12] On another occasion, black soldiers and German prisoners found themselves on a mixed-troop train traveling through Texas. When it came time to dine, a curtain was hung at one end of the dining car, behind which the black soldiers were served. The German prisoners were seated in the main body of the dining car along with the white soldiers.[13]

Ulysses S. Keys, a black lawyer and former soldier, blamed the Army itself for imposing segregation throughout the country. He wrote, "Even in places where Negroes had never before been discriminated against, the Army set up discriminatory systems. In Cheyenne, Wyoming, where I was stationed, the few Negroes of the town were quite free to go about as they pleased. But when the Army moved in signs appeared all over town barring Negro troops from certain bars, hotels, and movies."[14]

The Japanese government was aware of racial strife in the United States and used it for propaganda purposes. In late January 1942, Radio Tokyo noted on its Far East broadcast news that a black man had been dragged from jail by a mob and burned to death in Sikeston, Missouri. The man, Cleo Wright, had been arrested for the rape and stabbing of a white woman. (The federal government reported that from 1889, when it started keeping statistics, through 1940, there had been 3,842 lynchings of blacks in the United States.) On another occasion, Radio Tokyo said, "It is a singular fact that supposedly civilized Americans in these times deny the Negroes the opportunity to engage in respectable jobs, the right of access to restaurants, theaters or the same train accommodations as themselves, and periodically will run amuck to lynch Negroes individually or to slaughter them wholesale — old men, women, and children alike — in race wars like the present one."[15] Three months later, another broadcast from Tokyo said, "Democracy, as preached by the Anglo-Americans, may be an ideal and noble system of life, but democracy as practiced by Anglo-Americans is stained with the bloody guilt of racial persecution and exploitation."[16]

German propaganda also tried to lure blacks: "A specifically conditioned anti–Semitism has made certain inroads into Harlem; but so far the Nazis seem to realize how little chance the author of *Mein Kampf* has to be accepted as a savior of Negroes and they do not address them openly."[17]

One man who sought to improve the lot of the black troops was Benjamin O. Davis, Sr., the nation's first black general. A member of the War Department's Advisory Committee on Negro Troop Policies, he visited Fort Huachuca in Arizona, and Forts Bliss and Clark in Texas. Among his findings was that of a white officer who objected to a black chaplain and his wife dining in a privately run restaurant on one of the posts. Davis was also told of a white lieutenant beating and injuring a drunken black enlisted man.[18] After another tour, Davis reported to the Committee, "In a tour I found the morale of the Negroes in the North good, while it was poor in the South. Negroes feel badly about Jim Crow practices. The War Department can control where it has jurisdiction. Jim Crow has been introduced where it didn't exist. I think there should be a follow-up."[19] Minutes of the meeting indicate no action was taken.

One of the units Davis inspected was the 93rd, a regiment destined for work on the Alcan Highway. At the inspection in the mess hall, the sergeant on duty, surprised at seeing a black general, saluted and said, "Sir, Company 'C' mess hall is ready for — Sir! You looks just like my uncle!" Nonplussed, Davis returned the salute and asked the sergeant who was his uncle, whereupon the man went into a long story. Before leaving, Davis told the commanding colonel and lieutenant that no disciplinary action was to be taken against the sergeant. Then he added that he was sure the sergeant had a "good looking" uncle.[20] Said Master Sgt. George A. Owens, a sharecropper's son from Bolton, Mississippi, with a degree in economics from Tougaloo College in Mississippi, "We felt proud that one of us was being saluted first."[21] When Davis visited the 95th at Fort Belvoir, the reception wasn't as warm. The commanding colonel refused to salute the general and was consequently demoted to major. "He has hated colored ever since," said Henry Roberts, an enlisted member of the 95th who later served under this officer in the Yukon.[22] Roberts was drafted in mid–1941 after finishing his first year at Lehigh University in Bethlehem, Pennsylvania.

The engineering recruits underwent twelve weeks of training. The program for the first two weeks was for all recruits, regardless of specialty: calisthenics, drills, military discipline, hygiene and sanitation, and care and maintenance of equipment. Over the next six weeks the men learned how to shoot a rifle and pistol, but, most importantly, they also learned carpentry and welding and the use of hand tools. The final four weeks they worked in the squads and platoons to which they were assigned. Some with aptitude were sent for special training, as was the case of Reginald Beverly, who had taught high school math. "They needed surveyors, so after basic training at Fort Meade, Maryland, I was sent to surveyors school at Fort Belvoir," he said.[23]

Lt. Robert Platt Boyd, Jr., of "C" Company was a rarity in the 93rd Regiment—one of only a handful of officers who had actually studied civil engineering. He'd done so at the Alabama Polytechnic Institute, now Auburn University. "They were a bunch of young, somewhat frightened, boys who had not the first idea how to march in formation," he said of his charges. "Most of the men (boys really 17–20 years old) were from the cotton and corn fields of southern Mississippi, or from the rice and cane fields and the Bayou Country of southern Louisiana. Very few of them had much education, and I subsequently discovered that some Bayou Boys spoke very little English, but a sort of French Patois that was their native language."[24] When it came time for the men to sign for their twenty-one-dollar monthly pay, Boyd discovered that twenty-seven members of "C" Company couldn't write their own names. Since no signature meant no pay, Boyd wrote each man's name in large letters and had him trace and practice the signature, gradually reducing it to normal size. "That's how he taught me to write," said his daughter, Winnie.[25] By the following payday, all the recruits could sign their names.

While Boyd's system worked for "C" Company, Col. Walter Dudrow sought another solution for the enlisted men of the 93rd Regiment who couldn't sign their names. "We recruited some boys from Tuskegee Institute so they could teach the others," he explained. "They learned fast."[26] Recruiters were also sent to Tougaloo College in Jackson, Mississippi, and Grambling College in Grambling, Louisiana, recruiting twenty and sixteen men, respectively. Some had finished their junior years, while others were in the graduating class; most quickly rose to become sergeants.

A surveyor from the 93rd Regiment helps select the route of the Alcan Highway in the Yukon Territory (courtesy Office of History Collection, U.S. Army Corps of Engineers).

One Southerner wasn't prepared for the educational level he found in the Deep South. "I was shocked, being twenty-one, to have someone tell me they didn't know how to read and write," said John A. Bollin of the 93rd. "I was from Virginia and had graduated from high school and knew how to write and talk. It hadn't dawned on me there existed people who didn't know how to do those things. I wrote the letters for most of the soldiers in my company. I wrote letters to sweethearts and mothers. They'd come up and ask me to write letters. I'd ask them what they wanted me to tell their mothers. They'd say to tell them the same thing I told my mother. I'd write the letters as if I was them. I'd sign the letters. They couldn't."[27] Another member of the 93rd, Nolan Hamilton, a college graduate from Louisiana, did likewise. "Most of the fellows could hardly read or write and I would spend many evenings writing letters home for them," he said.[28] It was common for the better-educated blacks, especially those from up north, to help their Southern brethren. "I met a lot of guys from New York and Virginia," said Louisiana native Anthony Mouton. "We spoke French, Creole and broken English. Those guys were speaking pretty good English. I thought it was so fantastic to hear a black man speak pretty correct English."[29] Mouton had

Sgt. John Bollin recalled, "I wrote the letters for most of the soldiers in my company" (courtesy Lois J. Bollin).

learned French from his illiterate mother, whose English was scant. One of the New Yorkers who befriended him was Paul E. Sandiford, who took young Anthony under his wing. "I idolized him," said Mouton. "I used to ask him what such-and-such a word meant. He helped me write letters to my girl, to use correct English. My father having left home when I was seven or eight, I didn't have a male figure to teach me anything about being a man. All the older guys in the Army helped me."[30] After the war, Sandiford became a high school principal and his sister a judge in New York.

One of the reasons the 93rd had to recruit new members was because so many seasoned men were transferred to the 388th, then being formed. It would be sent to Canada's Northwest Territories to work on the hush-hush Canol pipeline project. "We did not know at the time that the 388th was being created," said Sergeant Bollin. "Nobody knew anything about the 388th when we were in Louisiana. It was obviously a secret maneuver so they could get them on the Canol without anybody knowing."[31] "Quite a few of us moved from the 93rd, maybe over a hundred," said Wansley Hill, who was promoted to first sergeant and became a cadre member setting up his new company. "There might have been some from other regiments as well, but we had enough men for a battalion."[32] The battalion was redesignated a regiment before going north to Canada. Hill was from Mississippi but there were also enlisted men from New Jersey, Ohio and Michigan.

The 95th was the only one of the four black regiments deployed in Alaska and Canada that had participated in the Carolina Maneuvers, war games that ran from October 6 to November 30, 1941. However, all four regiments were involved in actual construction projects. While stationed at Eglin Field with the 97th Regiment, Clifton B. Monk, a farm boy from Newton Grove, North Carolina, learned to operate heavy equipment and helped build a bridge and six miles of road near the post.[33] The 93rd built several miles of road and buildings at Camp Livingston and Camp Claiborne.

The 388th was formed January 10, 1942. The others had been redesignated from battalions a year earlier: the 93rd Engineer Regiment (Separate) at Camp Livingston, Louisiana, February 10, 1941; the 97th Engineer Regiment (Separate) at Eglin Field, Florida, February 22; the 95th Engineer Regiment (Separate) at Fort Belvoir, Virginia, February 28. The designation "Separate" or "Colored" was needed to alert officers that these were *not* white regiments.

Their assignments weren't determined until Brig. Gen. William M. Hoge, put in charge of the construction of the Alaska Highway, returned from a trip to northern Canada. Once there, he realized that he had not been given enough manpower to build the Alcan Highway on schedule.

6

Army Reluctantly Assigns Black Regiments

"We have enough racial problems here and elsewhere already."

During the planning stage, no one knew how long it would take to construct the Alcan Highway. Northern old-timers, who scoffed at the idea of the highway, predicted that just a survey would take a year.[1] The International Highway Commission, which disapproved of the route, said construction would take five to six years.[2] Canadian journalist and Arctic expert Richard Finnie, hired by the Army as an advisor on the project, predicted two years.[3] Secretary of the Interior Harold L. Ickes, a member of President Roosevelt's three-man highway cabinet committee, anticipated completion within a year.[4] General Hoge, the man entrusted with overseeing construction, originally predicted the survey alone would take a year, but he subsequently also settled on a one-year target.[5]

Even the enemy had a prediction. When Germany and the Soviet Union were allies, the Geopolitical Institute in Berlin had drawn up an "Alaska Plan" that contemplated an invasion of Alaska via Siberia.[6] Now the German magazine *Signal*, aligned with propaganda minister Joseph Goebbels, called the highway "The Ice Road" and asked, "Who could build such a road? Who could take care of it? And who could keep it open to traffic? In Alaska, you would not find enough Indians and Eskimos to clear the road from snow every morning. We estimate that the construction of the road will take ten years. In ten years the first truck with promised help arrives … when the guns have been silent for a long while and after the present war has paved the way for a New World Order."[7]

One man who was delighted with the prospect of a road, no matter how long it took to build, was a native Canadian named George Johnston. After a good trapping season in 1933 he had bought a car and had it shipped by rail and water to Teslin Bay in the Yukon. Only then did he realize he needed a road. He cleared three miles of bush himself and charged people for a ride in his newfangled contraption.[8]

General Hoge had initially thought that the highway could be built with just 3,000 Army engineers, barely three regiments.[9] As a military man experienced in roadbuilding, he favored using troops for construction rather than civilians. Troops were more reliable; civilians could quit at any time, as many of them did on the Alcan and Canol projects.

In addition, Army engineers could be mobilized quickly while civilians took months to be assembled.

After arriving in Fort St. John as the spring thaw was approaching, Hoge realized that the project was going to fall behind schedule even if he got his troops and equipment across the Peace River to start work before the breakup of ice: he just didn't have enough Army engineers to do the job. "Somebody got looking at a map and realized that this was an impossible task," said one officer assigned to the project.[10]

Hoge asked the War Department in early March for reinforcements and to have the Army, instead of the Public Roads Administration, build the Alaska portion. All available white engineer regiments had been assigned to the Pacific and European theaters. The shortage of engineer units was such that two of the white regiments assigned to the highway, the 18th and the 35th, were actually combat engineer regiments that normally followed combat troops into battle, building roads under fire and demolishing obstacles. That just left the black regiments being trained at Southern camps, but there was a consensus among the military's high command that their use on important projects should be avoided, if at all possible. "Perhaps the most frequently heard reason for opposing the use of black troops was that they were not as intelligent as whites," said Ulysses Lee, black military historian. "One did not have to be a racist; there were simply test scores, which proved scientifically the superior intelligence of whites, the claim went."[11] But Lee said the Army General Classification Test was culturally biased because it did not take into consideration the fact that 80 percent of black recruits were from the South and most had only a grade-school education in segregated schools. "A few officers recognized that the AGCT was not a good indicator of performance," Lee noted. "'I have come to the fixed opinion that the AGCT is not worth a damn with colored troops,' said one white commander of black troops."[12]

The chief of the Corps of Engineers, Maj. Gen. Eugene Reybold, recommended on March 14 that the 93rd and 97th Regiments be added to the Alcan project, the former in Canada and the latter in Alaska. The War Department gave its approval the following week. This marked the first time during the war that black engineers were assigned to work in an overwhelmingly white foreign country. Two other black engineering regiments, the 41st and the 45th, were scheduled to leave at the same time for the African nation of Liberia.

The use of black troops up North met immediate opposition from Brig. Gen. Simon Bolivar Buckner, Jr., commander in charge of the defense of Alaska. He was supported by his superior officer, Lt. Gen. John L. DeWitt, commanding general of the Western Defense Command based in San Francisco, and also by Alaska governor Ernest Gruening. DeWitt, who did not look sympathetically on non-whites, was the officer charged with the forced relocation and internment of Japanese Americans following Pearl Harbor. "A Jap's a Jap," he had told a congressional subcommittee. "I don't want any of them here."[13] Regarding the black troops, a memo dated March 25 from the War Plans Division of the War Department to Chief of Staff George C. Marshall said, "DeWitt stated informally that colored troops could not be used in Alaska. Governor Gruening stated informally that he was unfavorably inclined to the assignment of colored troops to Alaska as he feels that the mixture of the colored race with the native Indian and Eskimo stock is highly undesirable. Colored Engineer construction troops must be used temporarily in connection with the construction of the Alaska Highway, but they will be withdrawn by winter."[14] Discrimination against Alaska's natives was not unknown during the war. The Alaska Native Brotherhood on December 30, 1941, complained in a letter to Governor Gruening that there was a sign reading "No Natives Allowed" affixed to the entrance of the Douglas Inn on Douglas Island in southeast Alaska. "In view of the present emergency, when unity is being stressed, don't you think that it is very Un-American?" asked Brotherhood president Roy Peratrovich.[15]

Secretary of War Stimson initially said no black troops should be sent to where they were not welcomed.[16] He also had insisted that no black troops be assigned to the Far North because the Army believed they could not function in cold weather.[17] Now, because there were no available white units and the Alcan Highway had become a top priority, Stimson relented, overrode the opposition and authorized the use of the black troops.

Brig. Gen. Clarence L. Sturdevant, assistant chief of the Corps of Engineers, wrote General Buckner on April 2 to advise him that two black regiments would be sent north—the 93rd assigned to work in the Yukon, and 97th to Alaska. Buckner was a tall, "hard driving, bourbon drinking Southern aristocrat" raised in rural Kentucky.[18] His father and namesake, Simon Bolivar Buckner, was a Confederate general who agreed, against his wishes, to the unconditional surrender of his troops to his West Point classmate, Gen. Ulysses S. Grant, following the Battle of Fort Donelson during the Civil War. The relationship between Buckner and Sturdevant was on a "Dear Buck," "Dear Sturdy" basis. Wrote Sturdevant in his letter:

> I have heard that you object to having colored troops in Alaska and we have attempted to avoid sending them. However, we have been forced to use two colored regiments and it seems unwise for diplomatic reasons to use them both in Canada since the Canadians also prefer whites. I hope, therefore, that you will not protest this action since I believe it would only cause delay, with no different result, because the urgency of the project prevents reduction of the force and all remaining white regiments are assigned to task forces. We are now organizing two of the white regiments especially for this job. We cannot organize two others due to limitations of time, containment space, and output of training centers.
>
> It is planned to have the two colored regiments return to warmer stations south of latitude 49 next fall. They will be hard at work in two reliefs on a 20-hour schedule in out-of-the-way places and I cannot see how they can cause any great trouble.[19]

Buckner said in his reply:

> I appreciate your consideration of my views concerning Negro troops in Alaska. The thing which I have opposed principally has been their establishment as point troops for the

unloading of transports at our docks. The very high wages offered to unskilled labor here would attract a large number of them and cause them to remain and settle after the war, with the natural result that they could interbreed with the Indian and Eskimos and produce an astonishingly objectionable race of mongrels which could be a problem here from now on. We have enough racial problems here and elsewhere already. I have no objections whatever to your employing them on the roads if they are kept far enough away from the settlements and kept busy and then sent home as soon as possible. I hope, however, that none of them will be placed at the points of entry, since here is where our principal problem will arise.[20]

Buckner said elsewhere, "Certainly the Army has a responsibility in not further complicating the population characteristics of the Territory by leaving a trail of new racial mixtures."[21] He also barred native women from going to USO clubs in Alaska, to "protect their virtue," he said.[22] Governor Gruening flew to Washington and personally obtained President Roosevelt's rescinding of Buckner's USO ban. "Although a product of the border state of Kentucky, Buckner had the color prejudice of the Deep South and held it strongly," said Gruening.[23]

Said Walter Mason, then a lieutenant with the 97th Regiment, "When we came up here, the junior officers — and maybe even higher up — didn't know the attitude of the top brass in Alaska or that General Marshall himself didn't believe in sending black troops to the northern country."[24] The 95th regiment was later added to Hoge's highway roster, giving the general a military workforce of 10,607 men.

When authorities in Edmonton learned that black troops had been assigned to work in northern Canada, they voiced their opposition to any of these soldiers spending time in the city. The U.S. Army assured the local authorities that the black regiments would just be passing through Edmonton.[25] The 95th regiment would be going by train en route to Dawson Creek, British Columbia, and the 388th to Waterways, Alberta. However, residents recalled seeing black soldiers riding in the back of Army trucks on Edmonton streets.[26]

The chief of staff of the Canadian Army, Lt. Gen. Kenneth Stuart, did complain informally to the American deputy chief of staff, Lt. Gen. Joseph T. McNarney, about the stationing of black antiaircraft troops in Canada to help defend the canal locks at Sault Ste. Marie, Ontario. According to Ulysses Lee, "General McNarney persuaded the Canadian general of the necessity of leaving these troops in Canada, but the objection was another indication of the general feeling toward the use of Negroes in foreign areas."[27]

Although there were very few blacks in the province of Alberta, the reaction in Edmonton reflected an opposition dating back to the arrival of the first black settlers from the United States thirty-five years earlier. Mainly from Oklahoma and numbering about a thousand, they settled in rural areas, where they were accepted. But the reaction in the towns and cities was different. Business and women's groups protested. Residents of Edmonton sent a petition in 1911 to Prime Minister Robert Borden asking for a ban on black immigration. "We, the undersigned residents of the city of Edmonton, respectfully urge upon your attention and upon that of the Government of which you are the head, the serious menace to the future welfare of a large portion of Western Canada, by reason of the alarming influx of Negro settlers," the petition said. "Already this season nearly three hundred have arrived, and the statement is made, both to these arrivals and by press dispatches, that these are but the advent of such Negroes as are now here was most unfortunate for the country, and that further arrivals in large numbers would be disastrous."[28] A member of Parliament from Lethbridge, Alberta, C.E. Simmons, joined the debate, saying the immigration of "Dark Spots" had to be stopped. The prime minister issued an Order-in-Council banning the immigration of blacks, but shortly thereafter rescinded it for fear of damaging Canada's image.[29] Blacks were barred from Edmonton's parks and swimming pools in 1924, a ban later overturned by the city council.[30] Between the two world wars, minstrel shows featuring white actors in blackface were popular in Calgary, Alberta; one group calling itself the "Crazy Coons" was the top-billed entertainment at social events of the Calgary Rotary Club.[31]

While there were virtually no blacks seen in Edmonton in 1942, there were 33,000 white Americans, most of them in the military.[32] One Canadian just returned from England said he saw more American uniforms on the streets of Edmonton (population 120,000) than he did in London.[33] Housing was so scarce in Edmonton that local residents rented out their spare bedrooms. The city was not only the shipping center for supplies for the highway and the pipeline, but also the hub of the Northwest Staging Route for which the highway and pipeline projects were undertaken. The U.S. Army's 1,500-acre Edmonton railhead was called "Little Chicago" because it was built for a quartermaster unit from Chicago. American military police patrolled the city's streets, a welcome addition as the Edmonton police force was depleted because so many of its officers were serving overseas in Canada's armed services. The American MPs would arrest errant Canadians and turn them over to the local police.

The city's beer parlors, restaurants, social clubs and dance halls were popular among the Americans. The military kept an ever-changing list of which places were off-limits for its personnel. Edmonton residents joked that the Americans took to heart "Drink Canada Dry," a slogan for the ginger ale company. The post office made an effort to deliver letters mailed from the United States and addressed to individuals at "Edmonton, Alaska," while an American team joined Edmonton's semi-professional baseball league. The American military also popularized an item of clothing: the parka. All the soldiers were issued one but the garments were then just becoming generally worn in Canada.

More so than their white colleagues, the black soldiers who were to traverse Edmonton on their way north would need their parkas, as most had never been exposed to cold weather or even seen snow.

7

Heading North

"Those Niggers just looked at all that snow..."

Master Sgt. George H. Burke learned that the 95th Regiment was going to northern Canada when he was instructed to have "Dawson Creek, B.C." stenciled on boxcars waiting to be loaded. Burke, who had spent two years studying electrical engineering at Howard University, decided to investigate. "I was in charge of freight loading at Fort Bragg," he said. "I had never heard of the place before and when I looked at the map I had it confused with Dawson City."[1] It was a common mistake as Dawson City, the hub of the Klondike Gold Rush, was the capital of the Yukon Territory, whereas Dawson Creek was a frontier town in northeastern British Columbia with a population of 500 (which would soar to 10,000 within the coming weeks).

Ironically, the Canadian public knew more about what was about to happen up north than did Americans, whose taxpayer dollars were going to finance the construction. It was virtually impossible to hide the magnitude and importance of the Alcan Highway project following the visit to Dawson Creek in February by Brig. Gen. William M. Hoge and Lt. Col. E.A. Mueller of the Quartermaster Corps. The two officers hired one hundred drivers and their trucks to carry tanks of gasoline from the end of the rail at Dawson Creek to Fort Nelson.[2] They also rented the town's former "Five to a Dollar" store for use as Army headquarters and contracted for the immediate construction of six eighty-foot-long platforms at the railroad station for the unloading of equipment and supplies.[3]

While in Canada, the two Army officers made no attempt to keep their presence or the purpose of their trip secret. Hoge even took a young reporter from the *Edmonton Journal*, Peter Elliott, into his confidence. "Much to my surprise, Hoge seemed quite willing to talk about what he was doing, where he was going and why he was there," said Elliott. "This was a new experience for me because, having been on the military beat, I had been drilled for months to be careful about what I wrote."[4] Hoge even promised Elliott he'd call him when he came back from Dawson Creek, which he did, telling the reporter it was "entirely feasible" to build the highway.[5] That was the lead story on the front page of the evening newspaper on February 25, 1942: "ALASKA ROAD VIA CITY GETS U.S. ARMY O.K.," in inch-high type. As indicated by the headline, local residents always considered that any highway to Alaska would start in Edmonton, not Dawson Creek in neighboring British Columbia.

Another reporter in the southern Alberta city of Lethbridge, George Yakulic, decided to check rumors he had heard. He went to the Unemployment Insurance Commission, where manager W.E. McCutcheon showed him a telegram from the War Department asking him to "hire as many men as possible" to work on construction of the highway. Yakulic then wrote a story the Associated Press picked up. "We all laughed like hell that a whistle stop like Lethbridge had scooped all the big American papers on their own story," he said. "Washington had imposed a news blackout on the story—then I broke it."[6]

It wasn't until March 7 that Prime Minister King told Parliament that the highway was to be built. Under parliamentary procedures, he was regularly questioned about the highway, but official pronouncements rarely came from Washington, especially about troop movements. "There was undue secrecy used on this project," said Walter Mason, then a lieutenant with the 97th Regiment. He also mentioned that part of the reason for the secrecy was to train officers and men for future operations in a combat zone.[7]

The first lesson in northern construction was provided in Dawson Creek. The quartermaster battalion that arrived at 1 A.M. on March 9 initially set up the first camp near the railroad station. Since the soldiers were unable to drive pegs into the frozen ground they ended up securing their tents by stringing ropes to trees. As the temperature was thirty below zero, stoves were installed in the tents to warm the soldiers. By dawn, everyone was sinking in mud because heat from the stoves had melted the frozen topsoil. The camp was moved to higher ground a mile away by the time the first engineer regiments arrived. Pvt. Clyde Young, Jr., of Frederick, Maryland, a member of the white 35th Regiment, told his parents what it was like. "It was nothing but an open place in the woods with a big patch of sawdust here and there on the ice and snow for us to lie on," he wrote. "We got in our sleeping bags after undressing in the open and a snow storm came in about two o'clock in the morning and when we got up at seven o'clock everything was covered with snow."[8]

The most eye-catching buildings in Dawson Creek were the five reddish Alberta Wheat Pool grain elevators that stored the wheat grown in the Peace River region. Completion of the Northern Alberta Railway line in 1931 drew to the area prairie farmers weary of the Depression and crop failures. "There are very few automobiles here, and horses are a very popular mode of transportation," said one contemporary report. "There is a hitching post in front of every business establishment. These towns would make an ideal movie set for a western thriller."[9] Befitting a town in the Old West, there were soon three brothels doing a brisk trade. The town likewise boasted four hotels—the Dawson, Red Apple, Dew Drop and Ritz—several restaurants, a Canadian Bank of Commerce branch, an all-purpose dry goods store, a hardware store, a livery stable, a drug store, a lumber yard, a library, a doctor's office, a dentist's office, a pool hall and a movie house that doubled as a community center. Two of the hotels had beer parlors, or taverns. Water was delivered from a nearby town in a horse-drawn wooden cistern. As a young man, John Ireland witnessed the arrival of the troops. "Rumor got around that they were coming, so we expected them, but nothing like we did get," he said. "There were trainloads and trainloads."[10] As the regiments arrived, the *Peace River Block News* headline read: "UNITED STATES TROOPS INVADE DAWSON CREEK TO BUILD ALASKA ROAD."[11]

Since the 95th was a late addition, it was the last regiment to arrive in Dawson Creek for work on the highway. It left Fort Bragg, North Carolina, in late May in four trains and reached Dawson Creek on June 1. As the trains wended their way northwest through the United States, the troops were often paraded before curious citizens who had seldom seen blacks. "We'd stop every, I'd say, fifteen hours, more or less, get out and march around the city," said Eugene Long, a supply sergeant. "I guess they knew ahead of time 'cause most of the people would be out there watching."[12] Said another sergeant, Henry Roberts, a native of Washington: "In North Dakota or South Dakota, they got all the black soldiers out, had us stand in line and wanted us to sing 'Carry Me Back to Old Virginny.'"[13] Their stay in the camp outside of Dawson Creek was brief, consistent with War Department policy to keep the black soldiers away from settlements. "When we arrived, we were taken from the train station to a cattle field," said Pfc. Nate Dulin. "We set up our pup tents, two men to a tent, but we weren't there long. We had to stay on base. We weren't allowed to go to town."[14]

Many black soldiers were convinced that white officers told tales about them to townspeople so they wouldn't be welcomed even if they chanced to go into a town or settlement. "There was a lot of ignorance concerning the Negro, the black," said Capt. Edward G. Carroll (chaplain, and the only black officer assigned to the 95th). "There were vicious stories people told, that black people grew tails and so forth."[15] Private Dulin said this was certainly the case of the lieutenant who commanded Company "A" of the 95th: "He told people that we had a disease, that once you got it, you couldn't get rid of it. He said that so the people wouldn't have anything do with us."[16]

Although American officers kept local girls from greeting the black soldiers at the train station, town fathers issued an official proclamation to the U.S. Army: "Dawson Creek on behalf of the forces of democracy welcomes you."[17] Unlike the members of the 95th, the arriving white engineers partook of the few delights the town had to offer. News reports said the taverns did a "roaring business" and that among those who crowded the sidewalks there were some blacks (later identified as porters from the Northern Alberta Railway).[18] However, the following year members of the 95th would return to play an important role as tragedy hit Dawson Creek.

Units of the 93rd started departing Camp Livingston by train on April 7, 1942, their destination unknown by those onboard. The train on which Anthony Mouton traveled had two cars of troops — one with black soldiers, the other with white. The train stopped in a small Arkansas town for an hour. "There were some white ladies who gave doughnuts to the soldiers as they came through," said Mouton. "They let the white soldiers get off the car but wouldn't let us off."[19] The car carrying the white troops was dropped off before the black troops reached Montana, where some young girls had come out with cookies, expecting to give them to white troops. They handed them out instead to members of the 93rd. Not even the regimental commander, Col. Frank M.S. Johnson, knew where his troops were headed. When they reached Washington State's Camp Murray, a staging area for overseas embarkations, the officers thought the 93rd was going to be sent to the Pacific theater. There was even time for some R&R in Seattle. "Most of the fellows were from Louisiana and that area and were amazed at the city of Seattle," said Sgt. John A. Bollin. "The hospitality at that particular time was overwhelming. The restaurants weren't segregated. When we were in the Yukon, everybody talked about Seattle, about the good times we had there. I think many of the boys from Louisiana settled there after the war."[20] Instead of boarding a troop ship, the men boarded another train and headed north to Vancouver, British Columbia, and eventually to the port of Prince Rupert, where they boarded a luxury cruise ship for Skagway, Alaska, arriving on April 16.

Skagway was the lawless town through which almost all the participants in the Klondike Gold Rush passed on their way to the Yukon. Now it was almost a ghost town, its population shrunken from as high as a floating 20,000. "We found the town itself almost empty of local citizens, a total of forty-three hardy individuals remaining from the 240 or so who had been living there when the war began," reported one officer from the 93rd.[21] Gone were Soapy Smith's Parlor, the Silver Bar and other dance halls, gambling dens and places of ill repute. But instead of scaling the steep Chilkoot Pass to get to the Yukon Territory, as the gold seekers had done, the troops could now take the narrow gauge White Pass and Yukon Railway, which carried passengers and freight as far as Whitehorse.

The 93rd had traveled like tourists on the cruise ship, but their construction equipment did not accompany them. Army trucks were waiting to take them to their camp areas. All but Company "F" pitched their tents near the airport ten miles outside of Skagway; Company "F" was posted to a mountainside area where it guarded the railroad roundhouse. To put in time while waiting for their equipment to arrive, the other companies of the 93rd were loaned equipment and put to work repairing streets in Skagway and doing maintenance on the railway, which the Army would soon lease. This was when members of the 93rd first heard local people inquire about their tails. As with the 95th, white officers were blamed for spreading the rumors. "The Southern white officers would go ahead of us," said Joseph Haskin. "When they got to these small towns they went in and spread the word that we were black monkeys with tails."[22] According to Anthony Mouton, "We had white officers who probably told them we had tails so they wouldn't mingle with us. Prejudice was very violent at that time."[23] Percival L. Prattis, editor of the *Pittsburgh Courier*, said, "Every Negro newspaper office has reports concerning white officers who have gone into Northern, Western and Canadian communities and have told tradesmen and townsfolk to treat Negroes of their commands as inferiors."[24]

The demonizing of black troops was not confined to the Army in Alaska and

Canada. One researcher said the turning of local people against black troops was done worldwide during the war. "One of their many means of accomplishing this objective was to poison the mind of the British, the Italians, the Australians and many other nationalities against the Negro Americans," this researcher wrote. "In dozens of countries, the people were told that all Negroes were savages who would rape every woman who came in sight. They were also told that Negroes had tails which they concealed inside their uniforms and that they could only bark, not talk."[25]

A rape did occur in Skagway when the 93rd was in transit there. A private from "C" Company was found guilty of raping a sixty-three-year-old woman; the soldier was easily followed back to camp by the woman's trapper husband, a professional tracker who found the man's dog tags caught on a bush where he had jumped an embankment. "He had slipped away and gone for a walk up the mountain," said Robert Platt Boyd, Jr., commander of "C" Company, a career officer who was promoted to captain before heading north and would retire as a full colonel. "He had knocked on the door and requested a drink of water ... the lady invited him in and he proceeded with his dirty work. The lady resisted and whooped and hollered, but the soldier accomplished what he had set out to do. He became scared for the lady was still yelling, so he'd rushed out of the house and headed for the airfield. He did not follow the road but came directly down the mountain through the woods."[26] Found guilty, the soldier was sentenced to forty years in prison. The case might have been hushed up because several members of the 93rd who were in Skagway at that time said they were unaware of the rape and questioned whether it had taken place.[27] The Corps of Engineers, in its history of the Whitehorse Section (which consisted of Alaska and the Yukon Territory), noted the rape: "With the exception of one incident which occurred in Skagway at the time the 93rd Engineers were stationed there, there was no difficulty between the soldiers and civilian population."[28]

If amends needed to be made to the local civilians, they might have been offered by the chaplain of the 93rd, who took some of the regiment's best singers to the town of Haines, fifteen minutes by boat from Skagway. "The chaplain brought his singers and his sermon to the church on at least one occasion, affording both the minister and his choir some relief," reported an employee of the Public Roads Administration, Willis R. Grafe.[29] Not waiting for all its equipment to arrive, the 93rd traveled by train in early May from Skagway to Carcross in the Yukon, where it started work.

William E. Griggs of the 97th Regiment was on leave in his hometown of Baltimore to marry his longtime girlfriend, Rebecca, on April 6, 1942. Before they could start their honeymoon, Griggs received a telegram from headquarters: "You will return to your station at once."[30] He kissed his bride goodbye and left immediately for Eglin Field in Florida to join his departing unit. "I had mixed emotions about going to Alaska," said Griggs, who was drafted in the fall of 1941. "I didn't even spend the night with my bride."[31]

There was a snowstorm when the second of two troop trains was passing through

7—Heading North

Members of the 97th Regiment ride in a Pullman sleeping car for the first time (courtesy William E. Griggs).

the Rocky Mountains. One of the soldiers awakened at 2 A.M., saw the snow and shouted to the others. "They opened all the windows they could and let the snow blow in," said Lt. Walter Parsons, commander of the train. "They had snowball fights. It was the first time some of these boys had seen snow. They were mainly from Florida, Georgia and Alabama. They didn't realize they were going to see plenty of snow."[32] Lt. Walter Mason, commander of the lead train, said the Army feared there might be desertions as the trains crossed the country because the troops didn't know where they were headed. "There were none," he said.[33]

"We had no idea where we were going until we got on the ship in Seattle. It was like that then," said Sgt. Hayward L. Oubre. "We got to Valdez, we had our parkas on, and I said to myself, 'My God, this is the most beautiful landscape.'"[34]

Local residents literally heard the 97th arrive in Valdez. There was no harbor tug available, so the captain of the SS *David W. Branch*, the Army troop ship carrying the regiment, decided to make an unassisted docking. The bow sheared off the end of the dock, and the noise brought townspeople rushing down to see what had happened.

"I remember up there when we got that regiment," said Hoge, the commander in charge of building the Alcan Highway. "Those Niggers just looked at all that snow — it was all white ... they had to go across the mountains up through that pass and get over into the valley beyond ... and they got worried about whether they were going to get out of there.... I told them.... The only way you're going to get home — back to Alabama or Georgia — is to work down south. Head down south and keep working ... because they took all the ships out behind them."[35]

The 388th Regiment departed from Camp Claiborne, Louisiana, in such a hurry in late May that Sgt. Wansley Hill was almost left behind. "I was on my way from the guest house where a friend had visited and I saw my company get on the train," he said. "I was so surprised. I was the First Sergeant and didn't know anything about it. I didn't even have time to count the number of my men before boarding the train. They didn't tell us anything there about the movement of troops."[36] He managed to dash to his tent and pick up his belongings. The troops had been assigned to work on the Canol project in Canada's Northwest Territories. The only stop the troops made before reaching Waterways, Alberta, on June 7 was in Montana, where the men were allowed to get off at the station. "The local people came out to see the troops," said Sergeant Hill. "I don't think they'd seen black troops before. It was quite amazing to them to see us."[37]

The 1,218 members were soon spread throughout northern Alberta and the Northwest Territories' Mackenzie District. As occurred with the other three black regiments, rumors about the black troops soon could be heard wherever they were assigned. "When reaching our destination our officers spread rumors among the people that we colored soldiers were no good, and everything they could think of to make things hard for us, they tried to make the people believe we were not even humans," said Pfc. Howard G. Conley. "Of course the people themselves knew nothing of us."[38] Residents of Fort Fitzgerald reported hearing negative comments.[39] Following the lead of the Army, the Royal Canadian Mounted Police also discouraged intermingling of the races. It reported "no mixing in any way with the local natives" in Fort Smith.[40] But the role of the 388th did not lend itself to isolation as was the case on the Alcan Highway, where the black regiments were assigned construction in remote areas. The members of the 388th were mainly involved in stevedoring, so they worked at riverside docks, which were invariably near towns.

The four black regiments had just settled in up north when the War Department issued a memo on how such units should be used in a country such as Canada:

> A thorough survey of conditions prevailing in strategically important friendly foreign territories indicates that American Negro troops should in general only be used overseas under certain specific limitations. These limitations are as follows:
> Negro troops should be subjected to a rigid discipline.
> Negro units should in general be officered by white men....
> The military situation alone should decide whether Negro troops should be accepted in any specific area.[41]

7 — Heading North

When General Hoge set about determining the detailed route the soldier-engineers were to follow, he had to depend on maps that originated in the *National Geographic* magazine. Such was the lack of information and the remoteness of the area; people had never set foot on much of it. The only way to judge suitability for a road was from the passenger seat of an airplane — and the Army didn't have one of its own this far north. Hoge had to lease one, along with the pilot. Fortunately, Les Cook, a Canadian bush pilot who lived in Whitehorse, was available. But Cook didn't have a passenger seat for Hoge the first time he took him up in his Norseman monoplane; the general had to sit on a gasoline drum. "This Canadian bush pilot was just a crackerjack," said Hoge. "He's the one that showed me the route to follow because when I first went up there I didn't have any plane. You were just helpless because there were no roads and there was no transportation."[42]

The initial challenge Hoge faced was finding a feasible route from Fort Nelson through the Rocky Mountains to Whitehorse, 640 miles to the northwest. The first route he came up with crossed the mountains at the 6,000-foot level. When he pointed it out on a map, Cook told him there was a lower, shorter route through heavy forest growth that he had flown over many times in taking supplies and equipment to a Canadian contractor building the airstrip at Watson Lake. "It came through the mountains in a pass that was less than 3,500 feet," Hoge said. "Henceforth we always called the pass he showed us Cook Pass. Had Cook not been on the job we would have had to make the highway 500 miles longer than the final route."[43] Miles were not the only thing saved. Had the pass been at 6,000 feet, there would have been more snow, which would have made the highway often impassable. Cook, who was killed in a plane crash in 1944 at age thirty-four, was posthumously awarded the U.S. Air Medal for his role on the Alcan Highway.

Hoge had met Cook shortly after setting up his Whitehorse headquarters in a former barracks the Army leased from the Royal Canadian Mounted Police. The general's initial contact with his landlords was a bit tense. When the Mounties told him he'd need a permit to buy a handgun, he must have been as surprised as the American prospectors who were forced to turn in their sidearms at the Alaska-Yukon border during the Klondike Gold Rush. The Mounties ultimately issued Hoge a permit to buy a Colt .22 pistol for target practice.

While Hoge was searching for a route, the 35th Engineer Regiment was involved in a race against time: it had to reach and cross the frozen Peace River, fifty miles from Dawson Creek, before the ice melted. Otherwise, it would have to wait weeks until the ice was completely gone so that a ferry could operate. At stake was on-time completion of the highway. Across the Peace River was Fort St. John, but the 35th's destination was Fort Nelson, 240 miles further north, where it was to start construction. There was a rough provincial road from Dawson Creek to Fort St. John — interrupted by the river — and from there to Fort Nelson a trail pioneered by the Hudson's Bay Company. The trail was only passable during the winter when the underlying muskeg (jelly-like earth found in many places up north) was frozen solid.

The vanguard of the 35th arrived from Fort Ord in California in the first of four trains on March 10, 1942, and left the following day for Fort St. John. When the first troops reached the Peace River, the weather was unseasonably warm, threatening the stability of the ice. The troops spread sawdust from one bank to the other of the 1,800-foot-wide river and on top laid planks in order to provide insulation and spread the weight of the bulldozers and other heavy equipment that were to cross. The 35th reached Fort Nelson on April 5 with all its equipment and 900 tons of food and other supplies, enough to last four or five months.

The Peace River broke up at the end of the month, leaving the 35th isolated until floatplanes could again land on ice-free water. Six days later, after the chaplain had blessed the soldiers, they started work on the Fort St. John–Watson Lake portion of the highway, a distance of 326 miles. Working around the clock in shifts, the troops could clear three or four miles a day. This was a region of forest and muskeg traversed only by dogsled or horseback. The few people who lived there were trappers of fox and beaver, Indians and a handful of whites.

Hoge received his first report on highway construction from his executive officer, Maj. Alvin C. Welling, on March 27, and it wasn't very encouraging. "Tractor operators have been found along the road, crying violently, so great was the cold," said Welling, who held a Master's degree in civil engineering from the Massachusetts Institute of Technology. "Men transported in the back of dump trucks and cargo trucks could scarcely walk upon arrival at their destinations."[44]

Before he got his own planes to take photographs, Hoge employed the interim services of two Canadians from the Ontario Department of Highways and one of its planes. R.A.N. Johnston, a forester, and K.H. Siddall, an engineer, took photographs from an altitude of up to 10,000 feet on seventy-five-foot rolls. By June of 1942, Hoge had his own Army Air Forces planes for aerial photography. Film was flown nightly to the state of Washington for development and printing.[45] Officers of the Corps of Engineers then laid the prints on the floor of a former dance hall in Whitehorse for review and selection of routes for Army surveyors.

The survey teams, using Indian guides, traveled by dogsled when there was still snow on the ground, then by horseback, sometimes on a tractor and sled, and sometimes on foot. Anxious to start working, the troops sometimes couldn't wait for a surveyor to mark the route. "I'd tell my tree cutters to head off into the bush and shake the tallest tree," explained General Hoge. "Then I'd tell the bulldozer drivers to head for the trembling tree."[46] As a result, the final road was crooked, which convinced many northern residents that this was an attempt to make bombing or strafing of highway traffic more difficult for Japanese planes.

Each regiment was supposed to receive twenty D-8 Caterpillar bulldozers, twenty-four D-4 bulldozers and R-4 tractors, two half-yard power shovels, fifty to ninety dump trucks, twelve pickup trucks, six tractor-drawn graders, one portable sawmill, one truck crane, six twelve-cubic-yard carryalls, and two pile drivers, plus small tools and shovels

7— Heading North

The survey team from the 97th Regiment uses packhorses for transportation and to carry supplies and equipment (courtesy William E. Griggs).

and axes. However, most civilians who ventured up north had never seen D-8 bulldozers, then the largest in the world, so they sought adequate descriptions. The D-8s were likened to the elephant in India, the camel in the desert and the wild boar in the jungle (the latter for its noise).[47] Those who saw them in action could become lyrical in their descriptions. The British high commissioner to Canada, Malcolm MacDonald, wrote after visiting the highway, "Each of these monsters is driven and managed by one man. He rides it as some hero of old might have ridden a dragon. But as a matter of fact the bulldozer's appearance is deceptive. It certainly possesses Herculean strength. It is powerfully armed and looks as vicious as could be. Yet in truth it is docile. It is a slave completely subservient to its master's will. I never saw a creature more sensitive to a man's slightest whim."[48] The correspondent for London's *News-Chronicle* also gave flesh-and-blood qualities to the D-8: "A bulldozer would assault a tree at its foot and shake it as a dog shakes a rat."[49] One Indian chief in the Fort Nelson area told of his first meeting with a D-8: "I thought it was the old devil himself, kicking down trees and digging in the earth."[50]

Operating four or five abreast, the bulldozers cleared a path one hundred feet wide. A second wave of bulldozers pushed aside the uprooted trees and brush. Ten D-8s could

An enlisted man from the 93rd Regiment uses a jackhammer to chip away glacial ice along the Alcan Highway (courtesy City of Edmonton Archives, EA-10-2873).

clear up to three miles a day. Then a second team of surveyors delineated the road, placing stakes along the centerline and each side. Graders followed, smoothing out the road. Big dips and running water were overcome by the construction of log culverts. The troops felled and sawed trees by hand; power saws were rare and seldom used, as they weighed 150 pounds and needed two men to operate. The first trucks transiting a newly built section were those moving the camp forward. "I had a squad of ten to twelve men and I was responsible for them," said Sgt. John A. Bollin of the 93rd Regiment. "We'd take a section where there was nothing but trees and we'd go through and knock the trees down and get them to the side. Once we got all the trees off the road, a tractor and a road grader would come along and shape the road."[51] Civilian contractors from the Public Roads Administration followed behind, making improvements to the pioneer road.

Because speed was of the essence, delays were not tolerated. That often meant abandoning machines rather than repairing them. Norman Harlin, a civilian catskinner (as the drivers of the Caterpillar tractors were called), told of such an incident: "We had a Cat there with a track off, and the captain wanted to leave it, and I said, 'No!

We can pull it back down off the grade and we can fix that thing up.' And it finally ended up that it was holdin' up seven other bulldozers, and he says, 'Push 'er over the side.' And that's where the Cat is today, under the grade."[52]

Two words not heard before came into popular usage during the building of the highway: *muskeg* and *permafrost*. Muskeg — the name given by Algonquin and Cree Indians — is a swampy accumulation of leaves and other vegetable matter that has not decayed into soil because it is frozen for much of the year; permafrost is the permanently frozen subsoil found inches below the surface. Both had to be overcome if the highway was to be built.

Largely ice or water, muskeg can be fifty or sixty feet deep. When the Corps of Engineers arrived, the muskeg had been undisturbed for centuries. The surveyors soon recognized where the muskeg was because spruce and tamarack trees thrived in the soggy soil. If possible, the surveyors skirted the route around the muskeg, adding miles to the road. If the muskeg was only a foot or two deep, it would be scooped out and rocks and gravel packed down in its place. If the muskeg was deep, a bed of brush would be laid down and trees would be cut and trimmed to make logs, which were laid sidewise, and then more brush and logs were added until the road was solid enough for gravel to be spread. This was a *corduroy* road, similar to those built by the Romans. The Alcan Highway had more than two hundred miles of corduroy. Unfortunately, until the Corps of Engineers mastered the muskeg, many tractors and other vehicles were simply swallowed up. "They called it muskeg; we called it quicksand," said Fred Spencer, a demolitionist with the 93rd. "We lost dozens of vehicles in it. They'd sink until all you could see was the cab, then they'd call me to blow it up."[53] Said Otis E. Lee, a staff sergeant of the 95th in charge of a motor pool: "I lost two bulldozers, D-7s, D-8s, in muskeg. They were just sinking and I had nothing to yank them out of there. Gurgle, gurgle, gurgle."[54]

Because of permafrost, which covers 80 percent of Alaska and 50 percent of Canada above the 49th parallel, trees have shallow roots. That made it easy for the D-8s to knock down trees but difficult for those patching the road together. The solution was to keep the permafrost from thawing. The layer above the frozen earth, usually moss, would be scraped off and replaced by brush to protect the area from the sun since it was no longer in the shade, the foliage having been removed by the D-8s. Then the road would be built. Glacial ice was often found in the permafrost, impeding the grading of the roads.

As time wore on, the actions of the Japanese during the summer of 1942 would prompt the Army to convert the pioneer road into the Alaska Highway itself.

8

Japanese Attack Justifies the Alcan Highway

"It was supposed to be a secret mission."

Construction of the Alcan Highway was altered on June 3, 1942, when Japanese warplanes dropped through cloud cover and bombed the naval base at Dutch Harbor in the Aleutian Islands, which stretch out into the Pacific Ocean between North America and Asia. A fleet of two aircraft carriers (the *Junyo* and the *Ryujo*), five cruisers, twelve destroyers, six submarines and four transports loaded with soldiers waited offshore. The initial raid was unsuccessful, for half of the thirty-four Japanese bombers and fighter escorts that took off from the carriers never made it to Dutch Harbor, either getting shot down or lost in fog and crashing. Japanese intelligence was faulty: the nearest American airbase was not on Kodiak Island, 600 miles northeast, as the commanding admiral had been told; disguised as salmon canneries were hangars at Umnak, sixty miles from Dutch Harbor, and at Cold Bay, eighty miles away. The Aleutian Tigers' P-40 fighters from the two bases thwarted the initial Japanese attack.

The following day the Japanese reorganized and returned to Dutch Harbor, setting the base's oil tanks ablaze, damaging the hospital and a naval ship. Over the next several days, Japanese land forces went ashore and seized and occupied the Aleutian islands of Kiska and Attu. The ten-man naval weather detachment on Kiska eventually surrendered after burning its codes and confidential reports; the detachment's leader, Mate W. Charles House, was the last to give up (near starvation) fifty days later. There were no military forces based on Attu, the most westerly island, located 750 miles from air and naval bases on Japan's Kurile Islands. Two whites, including the Indian Department's schoolteacher, and forty-three Aleuts surrendered after exchanging rifle fire with the invaders. A third island, Agattu, located between Kiska and Attu, was uninhabited; the Japanese left a landing party there. More than one hundred Americans, between members of the military and civilians, were killed or wounded in the invasion.[1]

The bombing of Tokyo forty-five days earlier by sixteen B-25 bombers led by Lt. Col. James H. Doolittle from the aircraft carrier *Hornet* had set in motion Japanese plans to invade the Aleutian Islands. The Japanese thought the American planes might have flown from a base in the Aleutians, so the Imperial High Command decided to take action. It assigned the job to Adm. Isoroko Yamamoto. His plan was to seize Midway Island on the western end of the Hawaiian chain of islands and then move on to the Aleutians. He envisioned Midway and the Aleutians anchoring Japanese control of shipping in the North Pacific and maybe luring the U.S. Pacific Fleet into a final, decisive battle six months after Pearl Harbor. He attacked Midway on 5 May, but his plans went awry. He lost four aircraft carriers, 250 airplanes and the battle. But he decided to go ahead with the invasion of the Aleutians regardless.[2]

At the time of the Japanese bombing of Dutch Harbor, only one hundred miles of the Alcan Highway had been built. Questions about the value of the highway stopped almost immediately, including those raised by a Senate Foreign Relations subcommittee in Washington. The subcommittee's chairman, Senator Bennett Champ Clark of Missouri, said in a report that it "would be futile, a waste of vitally necessary time and an unwarrantable interference with the strategic efforts of the Army" if further investigation of the highway were undertaken.[3]

Writing in the *Saturday Evening Post*, Edgar Snow, one of the top journalists of the day, said, "The Japanese attack on Dutch Harbor and the landing of Japanese forces on the island of Attu have focused the attention of Americans on their northern possessions, and have brought home to them the strategic value of this barren land as our next best bridge to Asia.... Alaska and the Aleutians constitute the vital potential route across which we can throw a lifeline toward Asia. We should be developing that route without a single hour's unnecessary delay."[4]

Residents of Alaska were convinced that Japan was about to move inland from the Aleutians when fighters and bombers emblazoned with the rising sun were reported flying over the route of the Alcan Highway. They turned out to be Lend-Lease American planes painted with the Soviet red star heading to the Soviet Union on the Northwest Staging Route. The Japanese did shell Fort Stevens, Oregon, on June 20 and a lighthouse on Vancouver Island in British Columbia the following day. Later that summer Japanese planes released incendiary balloons that drifted inland over California, Oregon, Washington State and British Columbia, starting forest fires.

Because of the Japanese threat, General Hoge told the Public Roads Administration that it should abandon plans to use the Army's pioneer road to bring in equipment and supplies for the construction of a standard highway. Instead, the PRA and its private contractors were to follow behind the soldiers, gravel the surface and make improvements so that the pioneer, or access, road would become *the* highway. What was most important was finishing a highway as soon as possible. The criteria: a road that could be traversed by an Army truck. This was one of the general's last decisions up north.

When General Hoge was appointed, he was put in charge of the entire highway, from Dawson Creek to Fairbanks. Based at the midpoint (Whitehorse), Hoge found he didn't know what was happening elsewhere. Travel could only be done by airplane; conversations were limited to radio-telephone transmissions often affected by magnetic disturbances. "I couldn't cover it all," said Hoge. "It was impossible flying, and the weather would be so bad that for days you were stuck up there, three or four days."[5]

The Army's solution was two-fold: create two commands, the Northern Sector and the Southern Sector, and install 2,000 miles of telephone lines from Edmonton to Fairbanks so communication would be guaranteed. Hoge was given responsibility for the toughest section, from Watson Lake (just north of the Yukon–British Columbia border) to Big Delta, Alaska; James A. ("Patsy") O'Connor, then a colonel soon to be promoted to brigadier general, was given command of the Southern Sector based in Fort St. John. Then fifty-seven, O'Connor took up his new post in May of 1942. He had the services of the black 95th Regiment and the white 35th and 341st to build 800 miles. Hoge had two black regiments (the 93rd and 97th) and two white (the 18th and 340th) to build the other 800 miles.

Born and raised in Michigan, O'Connor was studying to be a lawyer when he obtained a congressional appointment to West Point. Like Hoge, he had served in the Philippines, where he was in charge of tunneling at the Corregidor fortress. He had experience working with black civilians in 1920–1922 when he fought Mississippi River floods while assigned to the district engineer's office at Vicksburg, Mississippi. At the time of his appointment, he was engineer officer of the Western Defense Command headquartered in San Francisco. A short, affable man, he was destined to see his military career advance in the Far North while Hoge's suffered a detour.

Nearly 20,000 civilian workers began to arrive up north in June and only started work in July, three months later than the troops. The arrangement between the Army and the federal road agency was never a happy one. Hoge was in charge of route selection and construction of the highway but PRA people on the scene took their orders from PRA commissioner Thomas MacDonald in Washington. The PRA judged its roads from the viewpoint of the motorist; the Corps of Engineers was guided by military needs. The Alcan Highway was the biggest construction project in which the PRA had ever been involved. The salaries paid to the 15,900 American workers — all white — by PRA contractors dwarfed the pay of the enlisted men in the Army as well as the lower hourly rates paid under Canadian law to the 3,700 Canadian workers.

One American reporter who checked on salaries paid by private contractors learned that carpenters were making $500 to $800 a month, welders and mechanics $800 to $900, plumbers $1,000 to $1,200, and cooks $600; even camp mess waiters and dishwashers received $250 to $300 a month with meals free. The Army's enlisted men made less than $100 a month for doing similar jobs on the highway.[6] Cpl. James Rebouche, a welder, found himself working alongside a civilian welder. "We have to get over this and everybody's got the right to have a good job if they can, I guess," he said philosophically.[7] Canadian workers unhappy about receiving lower salaries than their American counterparts staged a slowdown on the section of the highway between Fort Nelson and Watson Lake. Canada's Selective Service resolved the problem by freezing Canadian workers to their jobs on the highway.[8]

General Hoge received a visit in August from two of his bosses in Washington, Maj. Gen. Brehon B. Somervell, the chief of the Army's Service of Supply, and Maj.

Gen. Eugene Reybold, chief of engineers. Two months earlier Somervell's face had graced the cover of *Time* magazine because of his role in outfitting and arming the troops in Europe. The two visiting officers decided that Hoge had done a poor job and that troops working on the Northern Sector of the highway were ill prepared for winter, whereas General O'Connor had done a "first class construction job" in his Southern Sector.[9] Hoge was relieved of his command and replaced by O'Connor as head of a new organization with expanded responsibility: the Northwest Service Command, based in Whitehorse. O'Connor was put in charge of the Alcan Highway, the Canol pipeline, the White Pass and Yukon Railway and the telephone system being built between Edmonton and Fairbanks. Col. Robert Ingalls, who had accompanied Hoge on his February trip to Edmonton and Dawson Creek, replaced O'Connor as head of the Southern Sector in Fort St. John; Col. Earl Paules replaced Hoge as head of the Northern Sector in Whitehorse.

Hoge blamed his firing in part on the same issue of *Time* that had put Somervell on its cover. The magazine had sent one of its top reporters, Bill Rowland, to do a story on the Alcan Highway. Hotel space being at a premium, Rowland had stayed as a guest at Hoge's home. "*Time* published quite an article ... at the time, and I think Somervell, after a fashion, was jealous of that publicity," said Hoge later. "I didn't seek it and I know the War Department called me up. They wanted to stop this business. It was supposed to be a secret mission, but I had no ability to keep people out of that territory."[10]

Hoge moved out of the former Mountie barracks he used as headquarters in Whitehorse and O'Connor moved in. Whitehorse — the town got its name from the whitecaps, or white horses, of the nearby Miles Canyon Rapids — sprang up during the gold rush. Since most of the prospectors traveled down the Yukon River from Whitehorse, the town became a transit and supply center. It would have become a ghost town when the gold petered out had it not been for the new Yukon and White Pass Railway that linked Whitehorse to Skagway on the Alaska coast. Still, the town only had a population of about 500 when the Army arrived. Within two years the population had swollen to 20,000. For the old-timers, it seemed like the gold rush days had returned. There were only three hotels in town, and space was so scarce that two and three people were obliged to share a room; sometimes people slept in shifts in the same bed. One small restaurant boasted of having served 900 meals in one day.[11] The most popular place in Whitehorse was the government's liquor store, where block-long lineups were common to buy whiskey and rum at double or triple the price back home.

Up to fifteen trains per day were soon bringing in troops, government and civilian workers, building supplies and food over the 110-mile, narrow-gauge railway. "All of a sudden, after some rumors, but very little actual information, the trains started arriving," said local historian Helene Dobrowolsky. "There are hundreds and hundreds of U.S. Army soldiers pouring off there and marching on up to the escarpment to set up their tent camps. Well, they're here to build this road. All of a sudden, you're made to feel like a stranger in your own country. I think the locals certainly did feel invaded. When you get a lot of people like that in a small area there are inevitable social distresses, problems with alcohol."[12]

The railroad followed the trail of the Klondike prospectors over the White Pass, twenty miles outside of Skagway, a 2,900-foot climb that required the combined pushing and pulling of three or four locomotives. The White Pass was notorious for blizzards, avalanches and freezing temperatures that could hold a train captive for days (once as long as eleven days). Couplings joining the railroad cars had to be separated by blowtorches while exhaust steam from the locomotives froze stiff the overalls of the trainmen.

The railway only had twelve locomotives, some of them in service since operations began in 1900. So the Army decided to take over the railway and expand its rolling stock. The Canadian government agreed to lease the railway for the duration of the war. The Army kept the civilian crews, who knew the idiosyncrasies of the railroad, but brought in members of the 770th Railway Operating Battalion of the U.S. Military Railway Service to oversee operations. The troops assigned had worked for seventeen major railroads in the United States. Their commanding officer, Lt. Col. W.P. Wilson, had been superintendent of the Burlington lines in the Rocky Mountains and earlier had worked on narrow-gauge lines for fifteen years.

Teams were sent to old mining railways in Colorado, Arizona and Idaho, where narrow-gauge rolling stock was commandeered. Ten locomotives scheduled for use in Iran were instead shipped to Skagway. The troops christened the locomotives with a favorite girl's name, or a movie star's, just as pilots did with their airplanes.[13] When Colonel Wilson assured Col. K.B. Bush, General O'Connor's chief of staff, that there'd be no problem, given his experience with narrow-gauge railways, Bush replied, "Colonel, you've never seen a railroad like this one, wide gauge, narrow gauge or meter gauge."[14]

By the fall of 1942 there were 6,000 troops stationed in Whitehorse, so many that buildings abandoned since the gold rush days were pressed into service as barracks and storage sites. Safeguarding the supplies was inevitably lax. "At night everybody swiped stuff," said one old-timer. "It wasn't guarded. Take what you could carry." According to him, he did.[15]

Those stationed in Whitehorse, as well as thousands more located nearby, would often come into town on leave or for a night of fun. But Whitehorse, like all towns up north, was off-limits to black troops. Under Brig. Gen. Simon Bolivar Buckner's policy, all black troops due leave had to go back to the lower forty-eight to enjoy it. "We knew someone had given orders that we couldn't take our furloughs up north," said Sgt. Reginald Beverly of the 95th Regiment.[16] Sgt. Otis E. Lee, also of the 95th, said he'd have been better off not going home at all on furlough. "I had to get drunk to go back north," he said. "My brother put me on the train."[17]

Because there was sunlight for up to twenty-four hours during the summer, the soldiers worked around the clock on three eight-hour shifts. Often they worked a seven-day week, with their day off given to fighting the forest fires that were caused by their equipment and living conditions. Fires were started by everything from discarded cigarette butts, welding machines, and sawmills to soldiers trying to keep mosquitoes at bay with smoke (the mosquitoes usually won).

When the Army dispatched over 10,000 soldiers to build the Alcan Highway, it failed to issue them bug repellant or protective netting against the mosquito (sometimes jokingly called Alaska's state bird), although troops sent to Europe and Asia had received repellants and netting. Thomas Griggs, a former governor of Alaska and a member of the International Highway Commission that recommended construction of the highway, had warned the Army about the mosquitoes. "Please do not underestimate the mosquito plague," he wrote. "I have had horses killed by mosquitoes in the country into which you must go."[18]

The troops tried to shrug off the mosquitoes by making jokes about them, such as the two soldiers who pumped several hundred gallons of gasoline into one mosquito before realizing it wasn't a Douglas C-47, the military version of the ubiquitous DC-3. Or the soldier who was awakened in his tent by two mosquitoes discussing what to do with him. "Shall we eat him here, or shall we take him down to the river?" asked one mosquito. The other replied, "No, we'd better eat him here, or the big ones down there will take him away from us."

Even the author of an official Army report on the building of the Canol pipeline in Canada's Northwest Territories by Task Force 2600 (the name given the military workforce) found stories about mosquitoes to be humorous: "Canadian mosquitoes were a revelation, even to soldiers from swampy Southern states. The legend still persists among men who served with Task Force 2600 that at least half the planes serviced at airports during the early days were really mosquitoes in disguise. It was alleged by hard bitten soldiers that government planes were painted bright red, not to make them easier to find if forced down, but to distinguish them from mosquitoes."[19]

General Hoge blamed the War Department for lack of foresight. "Nobody knew or could realize in Washington how bad and terrible the mosquito problem was," he said. "When I tried to get head nets for the GIs the requisitions were ignored."[20] As the mosquito plague worsened, Hoge flew to Washington, barged into the office of the quartermaster-general and demanded 10,000 mosquito nets. "Why, there should be no problem about that," the quartermaster-general told him. "We have a million of them right here." "I know you've got them," retorted Hoge. "But I've got a million mosquitoes for every net you've got — and I can't get any nets."[21] A boxcar full of mosquito nets was soon on its way north.

A Canadian guide working for the Army was surprised at American reaction to the northern mosquitoes. "You'd think those Yanks would know about skeeters, but their home-grown kind down South were just little fellows," he said. "Up that way, we grew them big, with two engines and pontoons. Even I got to admit they were bad that year when we built the highway. They damn near killed them colored boys. Well, if

Black soldiers wear netting over campaign hats from World War I to ward off mosquitoes (courtesy William E. Griggs).

the truth were known, that year they damn near killed me too. Somebody said they must be part of the Jap invasion."[22] Virginia Smarch, an aboriginal at the settlement of Teslin, recalled seeing black soldiers working on the highway for the first time. "It was really warm in June and there must have been twenty [black soldiers] lying on the ground and the mosquitoes [were] just terrible," she said. "The colored people endured hard times while they were here."[23]

Pfc. Richard E. Trent, a member of the 95th Regiment from Pennsylvania, recalled the day he finally received mosquito repellant. He described it as "yellow gunk" that the mosquitoes seemed to enjoy.[24] "The mosquitoes like to have eat me up in the summertime," reported Clifton B. Monk, a sergeant with the 97th Regiment from Newton Grove, North Carolina.[25] "You had mosquitoes that dive-bombed you," said Hayward L. Oubre, also of the 97th. "They'd dive like the Japanese with the dive-bombing. They'd dive and hit you."[26] "[There were] one thousand per square yard," calculated William E. Griggs of the 97th. "We slept under netting and wore World War I hats which were covered with netting to protect our faces."[27] Col. Walter Dudrow of the 93rd Regiment said, "We wore mosquito nets all the time. You could reach up and smack the back of your neck and have fifty mosquitoes in your hand."[28] And just when the men thought the mosquitoes were satiated, large, blood-sucking bull flies, which usually attacked animals, came. The men of the 388th had a saying: "Mosquitoes at ease, bull flies take over."[29]

General Hoge used to wear his hat with netting to the mess hall for meals. "You had to eat with your head net on, and you would raise the head net and by the time you got food on the spoon up to your mouth it would be covered with mosquitoes," he explained. "You were eating mosquitoes half the time, and then you had to pull it right down again."[30] Some of the soldiers probably felt that the mosquitoes added a bit of flavor to the monotonous meals served to them.

Since the black regiments were sent to the most remote areas, they had to take enough food to last up to six months. Capt. Robert Platt Boyd, Jr., of "C" Company of the 93rd Regiment reported on his food allotment: "We were issued powdered eggs and milk, some powdered vegetables which tasted like a good grade of cardboard. The meat was all canned — Spam, Vienna sausage and meat stew. We did get coffee, sugar and flour and salt, but we had to bake our own bread."[31] Army humor prompted the men to dub the sausages "Yukon shrimp." Canadian war correspondent Peter Stursberg had occasion to sample the food when he was sent north to do a report on the Alcan Highway. "I had always understood that the American Army prided itself on the quality of the food which it gave its men," he said. "Whether this is true or not, the meals at the army camps along the road were, without exception, bad; in fact, they were the worst I had ever eaten."[32]

Members of the black regiments did what they could to improve the menu. The only village ever seen by the 97th in Alaska was a Native American settlement where a missionary lived with his family. Soldiers used to take chili con carne to the settlement and trade it for smoked salmon. "Finally, the Indians told us to bring something else to trade," said Sergeant Griggs of the 97th. "They were tired of chili con carne."[33] The 93rd tried to trade Army fare with Indians at Haines Junction, ninety miles west of Whitehorse. "My grandmother and other people didn't want to take the food because they thought their skin would turn black if they ate it," said Casey McLaughlin. "They believed the soldiers were black because of their diet."[34]

Captain Boyd of the 93rd once shot a moose that weighed over a thousand pounds and treated his men in "C" Company to fresh meat. "We had a good butcher among my mess personnel, so we had moose steaks for supper. Delicious!" he said. "The next morning I had moose brains and eggs for breakfast, and moose liver for lunch. We also had moose stew for several meals."[35] Boyd shot four moose and a caribou, plus rabbits, squirrels and ptarmigan, while working on the road.

Only the company commander was allowed to have a rifle and sidearm, kept under lock and key in his tent. But sometimes an enlisted man would gain access and go hunting for food. Pfc. Andrew Jackson of the 97th said he often shot moose and bear. "Bear steaks taste as good as T-bone steaks," he claimed.[36] "We did kill a bear, a huge

An enlisted man shows off the antlers from a moose shot for food (courtesy City of Edmonton Archives, EA-10-2848).

black bear, about nine, ten feet tall, and those chops were delicious," said Donald W. Noland, a Baltimore native and member of the 93rd Regiment.[37]

The Corps of Engineers, in a report, recognized there was a problem with Army food up north:

> Rations were particularly poor during the spring and summer. On the basis that fresh foods could not be shipped because of a shortage of shipping space, tons of canned "C" rations accompanied each unit, and while this food was undoubtedly nourishing, its sameness and lack of variety very soon palled on the appetites of all personnel. The troops on the field, working from ten to sixteen hours a day, were forced to eat Vienna sausage, chili con carne and corned beef hash, at practically every meal, until, after a reasonable time, they began to throw it away untouched.[38]

Sometimes supplies that were neither ordered nor needed arrived by boat in Skagway, such as forty-five tons of beer (alcoholic drinks being forbidden in the Army camps). The beer was received along with one hundred tons of coal and several hundred cords of slab wood for which the Army had no use. The boat docked in May of 1942 at a time when construction equipment was desperately needed. "The several bulldozers, or carryalls, or graders, which could have been brought in place of these shipments would have shortened the construction time by weeks," lamented the Corps of Engineers.[39]

Because the camps were moved every three or four days as road construction progressed, the soldiers lived in tents; these ranged from one-man to six-man dark green pyramid tents, most of them mounted on wooden frames. There were seldom any cots. The men slept in sleeping bags on the ground, usually on a bed of pine boughs. The officers had makeshift showers, but not the enlisted men. If there was a nearby creek or river, they had a freezing wash there. Otherwise, they'd heat water and swab in their helmets and use the water to shave. Some men grew beards.

As there was little to do except work, sleep and eat, the soldiers often explored the wooded areas around camp. Six members of the 95th did so and became lost. Four showed up the following day. An Indian tracker led a search party in the direction taken by the other two, one of whom staggered into a PRA camp a month later. The sixth was never found and presumed dead. After that the Army issued safety tips on how to avoid losing one's way and what to do if lost:

> Orient yourself before you start out by noticing all visible features of land and sky in relation to the course you intend to travel.
> Follow a compass course with penciled notes or strip map.
> Blaze your trail, including the far side of the trees so that you can see them coming back. Mark blaze with a pencil so you can identify it as yours. A trail can be marked by blazing trees, breaking off twigs or branches, sticking branches in the ground, piling up stones, trampling down underbrush, dropping bits of paper or cloth.
>
> Action if lost:
>
> Don't get panicky.
> Don't get lost from the place where you are, start marking your trail so that you can always backtrack to make a fresh start. Generally, the place where you first became lost is not far from the right path.
> Follow streams down. They get wider and generally lead to a house or a road.
> Don't follow old trails, they may lead anywhere.
>
> To attract attention, do any of the following:
>
> Shout.
> Blow a whistle.
> Fire a gun (if authorized to carry one).
> Make a smudge fire and send up smoke signals.
> To observe, get on high ground or climb a tree.
> Keep in mind that planes may be looking for you. Look for them. Get to a clearing or make one. Wave something white — use your underwear if need. Send up smoke signals.
>
> Porcupines can be killed for food.
> Don't separate your party under *any* circumstances.
> Make definite plans and execute them in an orderly fashion.

Private Trent of the 95th enjoyed the woods and even asked one of the Indian guides to teach him directional skills. When he tried them out, he got lost and climbed a tall tree to see if he could he get his bearings. He was found by a rescue team.[40] "Looking for stray Negroes who became hopelessly lost if they strayed far from road or camp soon became a major occupation for Indian guides and scouts," said Philip H. Godsell, a Hudson's Bay Company fur trader.[41]

Black Army historian Ulysses Lee was critical of what the troops faced up north, especially the black troops:

> For more than a year after their arrival, the wisdom of sending the Negro engineer units so far north was debated within the receiving command, within the War Department, and in other executive agencies of the government. Travelers, observers, and residents of the areas gave conflicting reports on both their efficiency and their desirability in northern areas. The morale of many United States troops in Alaska and Northwest Canada in the first year of the war was dangerously low, because of insufficient clothing, monotonous food, poor shelter, long tours of duty, and the visible contrast between troop conditions and those of contract laborers who, often employed on the same jobs, were better fed, more adequately clothed, and better paid. Few troops going to northern regions in 1942 had had special preparatory training, such as that given to mountain and desert troops; nor in many cases was appropriate clothing and equipment provided for them. Often units were sent directly from warmer camps in the continental United States without any previous cold weather experience; frequently the officers were as ignorant as their men of the proper use of the different items provided for cold weather use. For Negro troops, the problems of the Far North were greater than for the average American unit. Few Negroes in the service units sent there had had experience living in even the colder parts of the United States; they were completely unacquainted with northern wilderness conditions.[42]

The Native American and Canadian guides took back to their settlements diseases picked up from the soldiers; those soldiers who went to the settlements also contracted diseases. Said one report: "In less than one year, successive epidemics of measles, German measles, dysentery, jaundice, whooping cough, mumps, tonsillitis and meningitis swept through the [native] community."[43] The Corps of Engineers sent medics into settlements in Alaska and the Yukon to attend to the ailing. "We helped the people with medical services," said Sergeant Griggs of his regiment, assigned to Alaska.[44] Pearl Keenan, who lived near the aboriginal settlement of Teslin, said, "Measles, chickenpox, whooping cough — you name it, they brought it. But the soldiers were good people. They built our highway."[45]

Yellow jaundice, a liver infection, spread through the Army camps and killed a member of the 97th in Valdez, Alaska. "He must've been nineteen, never even got to turn a shovelful of dirt on the highway," said Lt. Walter Parsons. "The cemetery said they didn't have any place to bury colored people. I noticed that there was an acre they weren't using on the other side of a stream, so they let us put him over there by himself."[46] The jaundice outbreak was later traced to improperly sterilized vaccine needles.[47] Sgt. Otis E. Lee of the 95th said most of the men in his motor pool came down with jaundice. "I went in and spent time with the men hoping I'd get it so badly I'd be sent home," he admitted. "I never did get it."[48]

Given the back-breaking nature of the work, most of the black soldiers might well have looked for any excuse to remain in their tents.

9

The 93rd and 95th Start Off with Picks And Shovels

"Some of the white officers didn't want the black soldiers operating heavy equipment."

Operating the lead D-8 Caterpillar, the black soldier from the 93rd Regiment's "C" Company broke through the trees to a clearing where he found himself looking at McGregor's trading post and the Indian settlement of Teslin, population 300. A sergeant from the Royal Canadian Mounted Police barred any further advance. "I am the law in these parts and I don't want Negro soldiers mixing with my Indians," said the Mountie, echoing the racial policy of Brig. Gen. Simon Bolivar Buckner, the military commander in charge of the defense of Alaska.[1] General William Hoge had ordered the 93rd to build a service road from Carcross to the Teslin River, a distance of seventy miles over swampy, mountainous and often frozen terrain. That would allow the white 340th Regiment to transport its equipment by water to start its section of the road to Watson Lake, saving weeks in building time.

Capt. Robert Platt Boyd, whose "C" Company was given the lead role because of his engineering background, told the Mountie he was there under a treaty between the United States and Canada and had orders to put through the road to the river beyond the settlement. Boyd then used his radiotelephone to call Col. Frank M.S. Johnson, the commanding officer of the 93rd, and told him of the standoff. The colonel told the captain to maintain his present course but not to allow his men to enter the settlement. McGregor, the Scotsman who owned the store bearing his name, said the black soldiers were welcome at the trading post. The Mountie grudgingly let them enter the store, where they emptied many of the shelves. "Later on I am sure there was some comingling of my soldiers and the Indian belles," said Captain Boyd. "I never caught any miscreants, but the first sergeant said he ran into several visitors out at our campsite."[2]

One of the first things that Colonel Johnson did when the 93rd arrived in Carcross by train from Skagway on May 5, 1942, was to check in with the RCMP. "Information regarding the Game and Fishing laws of the Yukon Territory was given him and cooperation is acknowledged to the highest degree in every way," reported the Mounties.[3] Given General Buckner's policy and the rape in Skagway involving a soldier from the 93rd, Johnson must have told the Mounties that the troops were not to go into any settlements. The soldiers pitched their tents away from Carcross, an Indian village that owed its name to the famous writer Jack London: he had shortened it from the original Caribou Crossing.

Since the 93rd hadn't received its heavy equipment, the troops literally started work with picks and shovels. Pfc. Anthony Mouton remembered those early days working alongside former plantation workers. "They'd sing all day long when they were working," he said. "We had picks and shovels and were working on the road and they were singing these gospel hymns like they did back on the plantation."[4] After Colonel Johnson borrowed two D-8 bulldozers from the 18th Regiment, he ordered potential operators among the enlisted men to take driving lessons. "Some of the white officers didn't want the black soldiers operating heavy equipment," said John A. Bollin, a sergeant with "F" Company. "But some of the soldiers came out of Mississippi and Louisiana and had worked on farms and the levees and knew about tractors and graders."[5] Added Private Mouton, "Those guys from Mississippi and Louisiana and Alabama and Georgia, they put them on tractors and they knew how to drive them. I had never seen a black man driving a tractor in the little town of Lafayette, Louisiana. I thought that was so amazing. They were illiterate, but they were hard, hard workers. When I used to hear them talk at night about how bad it was back home, how their bosses used to treat them, and they'd tease each other. 'Your boss treated you worse than my boss.' This was an accepted way of life. I'd sit there with my mouth wide open, I was so young."[6]

"Few Negro soldiers have operated D-8 tractors or heavy trucks or shovels before they came in the Army," said a report written by Lt. Col. James L. Lewis of the 93rd. "This type of duty is especially attractive to the average enlisted man, since exercising control of an expensive machine capable of performing large quantities of work gives him a sense of personal achievement and importance that ordinary physical labor lacks."[7] But Lewis questioned the mechanical skills of the black soldiers. "Most Negro mechanics have an inherent liking for taking machines completely apart and can rarely accomplish this without scattering and losing many of the parts," he wrote. "This tendency must be sharply curtailed particularly in repairs performed in the field under adverse weather conditions."[8] However, a 93rd lieutenant, Leslie ("Bud") Schnurstein, had nothing but praise for the regiment's mechanics. "The guys would get out there and get on those tractors and would pull them apart and do all sorts of things — with gloves on. I don't know how they did it, but they fixed them," he said. "They were good."[9]

The 93rd went from Carcross to Tagish to Jake's Corner to Teslin and the river. The Public Roads Administration, which usually followed the engineer regiments, built the fifty-mile section from Jake's Corner to Whitehorse, effectively keeping black soldiers out of the Yukon's largest town. But a handful of members of the 93rd managed to spend several hours in Whitehorse when they were changing campsites. Although not a drinker, Sergeant Bollin stopped in a bar and struck up a conversation about boxer Sugar Ray Robinson with some white soldiers. "That was the only thing we had in common," Bollin said. "They knew Ray Robinson, I knew Ray Robinson."[10] Those were the only white soldiers Bollin saw during eight months in the Yukon and White-

9—The 93rd and 95th Start Off with Picks and Shovels

The 93rd Regiment operates its portable sawmill in the Yukon (courtesy U.S. Army Military History Institute).

horse was the only town he visited. "I saw only the road and trees and trees," he said. "That was it."[11]

The 93rd faced some of the Alcan Highway's worst building conditions, requiring more physical labor than usual. One stretch of road consisted of over three-quarters of a mile of muskeg. The 93rd had to fell by hand, trim, haul and lay out 8,000 trees to make a roadbed over the soggy ground. "After laying them on this long stretch, we put three feet of gravel on it, and it appeared to be fine," said Captain Boyd of "C" Company. "Yet within a few days it began to undulate whenever a heavy truck crossed."[12]

After reaching Teslin Lake on June 17, part of the 93rd doubled back and improved the road it had just built. Another part of the regiment boarded barges and traveled down Teslin Lake to Morley Bay, where it set up camp and started improving the road just completed by the white 340th Regiment.

Companies "A" and "B" of the 93rd spent October and November building barracks and rest stops for truckers, while Company "C" patrolled portions of the highway, looking for truckers in distress. Once the highway was open from Dawson Creek to Fairbanks, some members of the 93rd were assigned to relay teams to drive freight trucks to Whitehorse, where other drivers would take over. A truck brought the others immediately back to a camp on the highway.

Of the four black Corps of Engineer regiments that served in the Far North during World War II, only one — the 93rd — saw duty on the Alcan Highway, the Canol project and the Aleutian Islands. Detachments from Companies "B" and "C" were assigned to build part of the Canol road out of Johnson's Crossing in the Yukon Territory.[13] Afterward, General Buckner, who had originally opposed any black regiments being sent up north, asked that the 93rd Regiment be assigned to the Aleutian Islands to work on projects for a planned offensive against the Japanese holding Attu and Kiska.[14] The needs of war must have softened Buckner's opposition to black troops because he already had three black port battalions (the 372nd, the 383rd and the 483rd) unloading ships; in 1944 he also accepted a black infantry regiment, the 364th. However, Gen. James A. O'Connor, the head of the Northwest Service Command, rejected offers of the War Department to send up to four more black engineer general service regiments to relieve or supplement the four already up north.[15]

When Colonel Johnson left the 93rd, he had nothing but praise for the black troops. He said in his farewell letter, "The record of the Ninety Third Engineers speaks for itself—240 miles of Alcan Highway constructed from June 5, 1942, to October 1, 1942, and this road went through muskeg swamps, mountains and deep canyons. The Ninety Third Engineers' section of the road was, as stated by General Sturdevant, Assistant Chief of Engineers, 'The best section of road on the Alcan Highway.'"[16] Johnson additionally recommended the regiment be given a "Meritorious Unit Citation" for distinguished service in a foreign theater.[17] The Army awarded the 93rd "Battle Streamers"—silk ribbons to attach to its organizational flag—for its work on the highway.[18]

The day after Christmas 1942, the 93rd started moving by rail from the Yukon to Skagway, where they boarded the Army transport ship *David W. Branch* for the Chilkoot Barracks at Haines, Alaska. There they were outfitted with much-needed new gear, including rubberized jackets, pants and boots, because of the rain in the Aleutian Islands. The entire regiment left by ship on February 27 for Cold Bay in the upper Aleutian Islands. They were split into two battalions; the first remained at the Cold Bay Naval Base while the second battalion went to Fort Glen on Umnak Island. As occurred at Army posts in the southern United States, military authorities at Fort Glen assigned the 93rd to a remote area away from white troops and civilian employees.[19]

The First Battalion was kept busy at Cold Bay for the next seventeen months, during which time it constructed a 2,700-foot runway extension and resurfaced the rest, built twenty-nine miles of post roads, laid water and sewer lines, and assembled fuel storage tanks, mess halls and a segregated theater. They also built barracks for the Royal Canadian Air Force, whose pilots would take part in action against the Japanese. The Second Battalion on Umnak built hangars, docks, a water system and barracks. The 93rd unfortunately lost one of its men, Wilbur W. Loston, on the Fourth of July, a regular workday, when his truck overturned. So skilled had the 93rd's bulldozer operators become that nine of them were selected in July 1943 to work with a white engineer unit on Adak, effectively integrating the unit (at least for a few weeks).[20]

Fred Spencer was a company plumber for the 93rd on Umnak, where Soviet boats often docked to drop off lumber for building projects. "One day I had to carry some messages to a Russian ship," he said. He was surprised to be met at the foot of the gangplank by a woman, who escorted him to the captain's office. He soon realized that the crew was female. "They was just as nice to us. They had to give you something, had to give you a hug, had to give you something to eat. They fixed me a bowl of stuff I took back with me."[21]

The 93rd went from moving their tents every three or four days on the Alcan Highway to living in barracks that had indoor latrines and showers. "The change in living conditions this organization has undergone the past few months is amazing," said one officer in a report. "Four months ago we were living in poorly-heated tents in temperatures from thirty degrees to sixty degrees below zero. The present conditions of weatherproof, well-insulated buildings, and electricity seems to be the height of luxury. Ah, life in the balmy Aleutians."[22]

Stable living meant the soldiers were able to participate in sporting events. Sergeant Bollin became the ping-pong champion among black troops stationed in the Aleutians. The Red Cross put on boxing matches. The 93rd also organized a baseball team; when they ran out of black opponents, they started playing against white teams. The team's

When the 93rd Regiment ran out of black teams to play in the Aleutian Islands, it challenged white teams (courtesy Office of History Collection, U.S. Army Corps of Engineers).

star pitcher was Anthony Mouton, now five-foot-four. "I pitched a game against Pete Demetrovich, a fellow they said belonged to the Brooklyn Dodgers," Mouton said. "He was a pitcher they talked about all over Umnak. I beat him one-nothing."[23]

Most of the members of the 93rd hadn't seen a movie since leaving the training camp in the South. "Negro soldiers of this unit are permitted to attend post theaters and recreational programs and have a regular quota of the total number of seats which are reserved for this unit," said a report on the 93rd. "Segregation in the seating arrangement is considered desirable."[24] The troops wouldn't have agreed. "They had movies for white guys and we couldn't go to them. Just before we left the island, we went to this movie," said Joseph Haskin. "Then we were chastised for going there. We got punished."[25] Fred Spencer's only experience at a movie up north almost led to blood-letting. "When we left there was a bunch of white soldiers waiting outside and they picked on us," he said. "We fixed bayonets and were going to fight, but it didn't happen."[26] Spencer, then a sergeant, was demoted to Technician Fifth Grade, or T-5, the pay equivalent of a corporal.

Sometimes there'd be live entertainment, such as the "Wings Over Jordan" black gospel choir. The 93rd also saw comedian Red Skelton perform. After the black engineer regiments had left the Far North, heavyweight champion Joe Louis, a sergeant in the Army, made appearances in the Aleutians and along the Alcan Highway. If the performers were going to be there for more than one day, there was a separate show for blacks. If there was just one performance, there'd be a segregated area at the back for blacks. "We were used to it," said Spencer. "We'd been trained like that all our lives."[27]

The 93rd ultimately spent two years and three months up north, more than twice as long as any of the other three black regiments.

The 95th was the best trained of the three black regiments that helped build the Alcan Highway, probably the equal of any of the four white regiments. Yet it was the seventh and last regiment assigned to the project, selected on April 6 almost as an afterthought. Worse still, its heavy equipment was given to a less experienced white regiment. Activated as a battalion a year earlier, it was one of the first units to train at the Engineer Replacement Center at Fort Belvoir, Virginia, where many of its men learned to drive Caterpillar bulldozers; the 93rd, 97th and 388th had no such specialized training. Unlike many training camps, Fort Belvoir had a cadre of seasoned black instructors.[28] The 95th was also an active participant in the Carolina Maneuvers, a nearly eight-week exercise in the fall of 1941 that involved more than half a million troops, one-third of the peacetime Army at that time. Divided into a Blue Army and a Red Army, the troops had fought a mock battle. In addition, the 95th built a road under simulated war conditions at Virginia's Camp A.P. Hill, named after a Confederate general.

By the time it relocated to Fort Bragg, North Carolina, for another ten weeks of training, the 95th had added a second battalion and was reclassified as a regiment. "As one of the first units activated we got more than our share of the 'cream,'" said a report written for the regimental commander. "The physical condition of our men was well above average. The high intelligence of our unit is shown by the classification test scores and by the large number of our men who have successfully completed the course of study at the Officer Candidate Schools."[29] One of those enlisted men who completed the course attained the rank of lieutenant colonel, the highest of any black soldier assigned to the Far North during World War II.

The 95th arguably had more high school graduates and university students than the other three black regiments because fewer members came from the Deep South. As personnel clerk at the 95th's headquarters in Dawson Creek, Pvt. Henry Easter of Baltimore was aware of the educational background of the enlisted men. "There were quite a few guys who had gone to college," he said.[30] Chaplain Edward G. Carroll had an explanation: "Most of the fellows were conscripted from Baltimore and Washington. Some were teachers, some finished Morgan [State University, Baltimore]. Some finished Howard [University, Washington], some finished Minor Teachers College. Our clerk was one of the top students at Minor Teachers College."[31]

The 95th arrived in Dawson Creek, British Columbia, over a four-day period ending May 29 —1,250 troops plus tractors and graders and other heavy equipment needed for highway construction. The following day it left for Fort St. John, its members never venturing into town. When the then commander, Col. David L. Neuman, told Brig. Gen James A. O'Connor, head of the Southern Sector, that the 95th was ready to start work, he was given the bad news: the 95th would have to cede most of its heavy equipment to the white 341st Regiment, which had been activated only three months earlier at Fort Ord, California. It was made up of men and officers left over from the 35th Regiment, the first to arrive up north, and from two other service regiments. It had been sent north on such short notice that it was not accompanied by its allotment of twenty D-8 bulldozers and twenty-four D-4s. But now the 341st was given the lead role in constructing 265 miles of highway from Fort St. John to Fort Nelson in British Columbia. Some of the 95th's officers grumbled that since their men were experienced catskinners and the 341st's weren't, the white regiment didn't want to be shown up by black troops. So the 341st pressed for the 95th's equipment.

General Hoge, then in overall charge, made the decision to downgrade the 95th's role. In a letter written on April 17 to Brig. Gen. Clarence L. Sturdevant, No. 2 in the Corps of Engineers, he recommended that the black regiment receive fewer bulldozers and more trucks. "There is only one point that occurs to me concerning this seventh regiment and that is with regard to its equipment," he wrote about the 95th. "This regiment will have some pioneer work but most of its work will be maintenance and surfacing."[32] The 95th did not initiate construction of a single new mile on the Alcan Highway. Why would General Hoge favor an inexperienced white regiment over a veteran black regiment? He had shown little understanding of, or sympathy for, black troops, and probably believed the 95th should play a secondary role since it was last to arrive. The 341st had already worked up north for a month by the time the 95th arrived, so Hoge probably felt it was already familiar with problems such as building a road over muskeg.

What would be worse for troop morale — choosing a black regiment over a white one, or consigning the blacks to the rear, a position to which they were accustomed? The 95th was literally consigned to the rear, following the 341st and doing cleanup work and building culverts. "They thought we could cook and use picks and shovels, but they didn't think we had the intelligence to do engineering," said Chaplain Carroll.[33] "They gave you nothing to work with," declared Sgt. Otis E. Lee. "We had educated people."[34] "The men were bitter," said Pfc. James F. Jones. "But we had a job to do."[35]

The first stop for the 95th was Fort St. John, where some of the old-timers still told tales of the first black man to call the settlement home: Nigger Dan Williams. Born a slave on a plantation in Prince George County, Virginia, Williams escaped to Canada on the Underground Railroad, with a Bible given him by abolitionists tucked under his arm. After working on boats on the Great Lakes, he moved west and became known as the first person to grow wheat in the Peace River region. He arrived in Fort St. John in 1869 seeking gold. He built a shack on the north side of the Peace River across from the Hudson's Bay Company trading post, the only commercial structure in the settlement. When he returned four years later after discovering gold in the Omineca Peace region in the northeastern corner of British Columbia, he found the company had joined him as a neighbor and was encroaching on his land. He was arrested and tried for firing a shot at the Bay's factor, James McKinley. The testimony of a fellow miner named Banjo Mike saved Williams from a lengthy jail sentence. "Gentlemen, let me tell you this," the miner said. "I know, as many other miners know, that Dan Williams at a distance of one hundred yards can take the eye out of a jack-rabbit at every pop. Well, gentlemen, had Dan Williams had the slightest intention of harming Mr. McKinley, Mr. McKinley would not be here today to tell you this amusing little story."[36] Williams's marksmanship was dead on when he later shot and killed a Mountie, for which he was hanged in Calgary, Alberta, in 1884.

The 95th spent much of the month of June at Charlie Lake, seven miles northwest of Fort St. John, fending off the rain. "This [is] awful country, nothing but cold rain, mud and trees," reported one journalist who visited the 95th.[37] "We worked twelve and fourteen hours a day in the rain, and the flies and mosquitoes made life miserable for us, particularly in the open mess camps," said Master Sgt. George H. Burke of Washington, D.C. "We began to think we would never make the first four miles because we couldn't get our drainage work done. The mud became so bad that our trucks got stuck and then we had to walk. We didn't like it at all. We hardly had any free time and most of what we did we spent playing cards and pitching horseshoes."[38] (The horseshoes were a gift to the 95th from a nearby Canadian farmer.)

Before the 95th arrived, Charlie Lake was the site of one of the worst disasters to occur during the building of the highway on May 14, 1942: twelve members of the 341st Regiment drowned when the pontoon boat in which they were riding overturned during

9—The 93rd and 95th Start Off with Picks and Shovels

Members of a black regiment construct a culvert on the Alcan Highway (courtesy Archives Canada).

a sudden squall. A trapper who had been watching the boat through his binoculars twice rowed out a mile in his homemade fourteen-foot boat and rescued five soldiers.

Maybe losing its heavy equipment to the 341st made members of the 95th more determined than ever to show the generals that they had made a mistake in their assignment. "Units of the 341st Regiment were ahead of us and we worked to keep up with them," said Sergeant Burke. "They slashed the pioneer road and cleared it with bulldozers and we followed behind them, doing the grading, building the bridges and putting in the culverts, often eight and ten to a mile. Sometimes, after the road had been built, changes would be made and we would have to go over it again. We worked in companies, each with ten or fifteen miles of road to build, and we pushed the 341st so hard they skipped a section of the road altogether and left us to build it."[39] The 95th kept up the pressure by hand, shovel, axe and wheelbarrow. Sgts. John Ross of Beltsville, Maryland, and John Wilson of Portsmouth, Virginia, once built forty-four culverts in four days. "Everything had to be sawed by hand with two-man saws," said Pfc. Nate Dulin. "The 95th got more of the dirty work to do than any regiment."[40] Cpl. Jonathan Welch wrote in a letter home, "That old Southern principle of keeping Negroes as slaves is still being practiced."[41] The regiment's weekly Operation Report mentions a typical period: "one platoon fought forest fire at mile 90," "graveling and filling over corduroy," "opening ditches, repairing culverts," "cleared side hill of trees and brush," "hand labor employed most of week draining water from road."[42]

The 95th had two easily identified problems: food and the behavior of its commander. The fresh food that the regiment brought was soon consumed. "They lived on C-rations for about three months," said General Hoge. "They only had three things: vegetable hash, meat hash and chili con carne. Sometimes they had chili con carne for breakfast and sometimes they had it for dinner, but they always had three choices."[43] In addition, Colonel Neuman had injured a leg, which affected his mobility and ability to command; he took to drinking in his tent, which affected the regiment's morale. "He was a problem," said Private Dulin. "They told us he was sent home for his health."[44] Lt. Col. Heath Twichell, second in command of the 35th Regiment, replaced him.

Like most of the other officers up north, Twichell had never before commanded black troops. "The fact that [his new] troops were black I think gave him pause," said Twichell's son, also named Heath. "I mean, he had the same negative stereotypes in his head that all of his contemporaries and most Americans had at that point about black soldiers."[45] Unfamiliar with commanding black troops, Twichell decided to use some psychology. Needing to boost the morale of the 95th, he issued a challenge he thought the men could meet with the limited tools at their disposal: build a wooden bridge across the 220-foot-wide Sikanni (SEE-canny) Chief River at milepost 119, midway between Fort St. John and Fort Nelson. The bridge would replace a temporary pontoon bridge. General O'Connor and his staff at the Southern Sector headquarters must have been surprised by Twichell's proposal, but they went along with him. When engineers from headquarters first saw the river, they estimated construction would take two weeks, but O'Connor only gave the 95th five days to do the job. Many of the men from the 95th bet their monthly paychecks with white troops, who had come up from Dawson Creek, that they could build the bridge in just four days. Most satisfying for them was the fact that the 341st, which took their heavy equipment, had been scheduled to build the bridge.

All told, 166 men from "A" Company worked on the bridge, starting from both sides of the river in a friendly competition. The two key men in the actual construction were Lt. Lloyd B. Lee from Virginia, acting commander of "A" Company, and acting Staff Sgt. Gordon Brawley of Lewiston, North Carolina. Brawley, who had gained experience in bridge building at Fort Belvoir, was promoted to staff sergeant after completion of the bridge. "Sgt. Brawley, do you think we can do this in four days?" Lee asked him. "Yessir, Lieutenant Lee, yessir!" the sergeant replied. "We can get it done in four days, you and me." [46] The work was divided up among the platoons, with one cutting the trees, another trimming, debarking and dragging them by hooks to the river's edge, and another doing the actual construction. Brawley and Sgt. James A. Price of Baltimore

9—The 93rd and 95th Start Off with Picks and Shovels

Members of the 95th Regiment, who bet white soldiers their paychecks that they could build a bridge across the Sikanni Chief River in fewer than five days, carry logs for the construction (courtesy Office of History Collection, U.S. Army Corps of Engineers).

took one group of men across to the northern side on rafts built from empty oil drums and logs. First Sgt. Herbert Tucker of Washington, D.C., and Staff Sgt. Thomas Bond of Alexandria, Virginia, led the southern side. The biggest and strongest men were selected to put the logs into place, like Pfc. Richard Roundtree of Winston Salem, North Carolina. Once both teams were ready, a signal was given to start work. Given the fact that the glacial waters coursed by at ten miles an hour, the men tied ropes around their waists and to trees so they wouldn't be swept away. At one point Lieutenant Lee stripped to the waist and waded into the chest-high water to direct his men. Staff Sgt. Harvey Walker of Burgess Store, Virginia, and Allen Hickens of Chillicothe, Ohio, were in charge of selecting the tallest and straightest trees for cutting, hundreds of them, all felled with handsaws. "I was with the platoon that trimmed the trees and sawed them, made posts for the bridge," said Private Dulin. "It was a big thing to do."[47] Bridge carpenters included Pfcs. Don Wilmore of Philadelphia and Otis Waldrum of Wheeling, West Virginia.

When ice floes as big as grand pianos started accumulating at the pilings, Sergeant Price destroyed them with dynamite blasts without damaging the structure. "If that fellow was a civilian I'd hire him in two shakes," a Canadian contractor told General O'Connor. "He's the best demolition man I ever saw."[48] Some of the men worked twenty-four hours at a stretch. Company cooks brought hot coffee and biscuits to the men all day long. When the light started to dim near midnight, the headlights of the company's trucks would be turned on to illuminate the construction. Often the men would sing to keep awake and in good spirits.

At high noon on Friday, June 24, 1942, eighty-four hours after construction had started, Chaplain Carroll was given the honor of driving in the last nail. "I almost missed it," he later confessed.[49] Then Pvt. Walter Henry of Philadelphia drove a command car across the new Sikanni Chief River Bridge. The structure held. The 95th had beaten the time set by the Southern Sector headquarters by a day and a half.

Although alcohol was forbidden at all Army camps on the Alcan Highway, the 95th deserved a drink to celebrate their success in beating the deadline. So as soon as Private Henry had tested the bridge, Lieutenant Lee and Sergeant Brawley left by Jeep on a 324-mile round trip to Dawson Creek to find some beer or liquor. They returned early Sunday morning with a large keg of beer. "We stayed up all night waiting for them," said Private Dulin. "Once they started drinking guys were dancing with one another."[50]

Other companies of the

Members of the 95th have to work in fast-moving frigid water as they construct the Sikanni Chief bridge (courtesy National Archives).

95th working south of the bridge soon heard news of the completion. "The fellows in the 95th bet their paychecks that they could finish it in record time," said Reginald Beverly of "B" Company. "We didn't have to give our paychecks away."[51] Word also spread quickly throughout the Far North via Army drivers and leaders of packhorses, even reaching as far as the 97th Regiment working on the highway in Alaska. "We heard about that. Yes, we did," said Lee Young of the 97th. "We had great engineers. We had great bridge men. We took pride in the building of the Sikanni Chief River Bridge."[52]

At 10:30 A.M. on Sunday, July 26, Chaplain Carroll officiated at a dedication and religious service. Colonel Twichell was present, as were Maj. Ronald J. Munro, Capt. Sidney A. Martin and Capt. Carmelo Terlizzi and their lieutenants. The structure was named the Twichell-Munro Bridge. "We have built this bridge as a symbol to the democracy we love," the chaplain said.[53] Timothy Womack of Americus, Georgia, played "I'll Never Turn Back" on a hand-cranked organ and the chaplain played on his record player a recording of Marian Anderson singing "Ave Maria." Then everyone sang "The Star Spangled Banner," after which the soldiers started up their vehicles and crossed the bridge to continue their cleanup work behind the 341st. Sgt. Walter Simon of Brooklyn, editor of the mimeographed *Alcan Dispatch*, wrote in the camp paper, "We're a lucky outfit, lucky because we are good. If we weren't, we could never have been chosen to lose our reputation, our own personal pride by 'slipping up.' It's tough going, it will be tougher, but our will to see this 'baby' through will keep that road going."[54]

When General O'Connor heard of the 95th's feat, he said, "Some day the achievements of these colored soldiers — achievements accomplished far from their homes — will occupy a major place in the lore of the North Country."[55] Lt. Richard L. Neuberger, O'Connor's aide and a future senator from Oregon, called the work done by the 95th a "construction miracle": "It is one thing to build a road leisurely, with ample time, with sources of supply near at hand. To construct a road under pressure, miles from town or village or railway, is a totally different undertaking. That is the kind of job the Alcan Highway has been. The Negroes who bridged the Sikanni Chief and the Racing, who crossed the Alaskan Range, have lived in their chilly tents, eaten monotonous meals of canned meat, gone days without mail or news from the outside. It has been no picnic. At few places on the globe have troops undergone more sustained hardships."[56]

The building of the bridge so moved Hollywood writer Norman Rosten, future co-author of a book on Marilyn Monroe, that he included the feat in an epic narrative poem he wrote in 1945 about the Alcan Highway. In it he states that news of the feat reached Whitehorse four days later and soon afterward became known to members of the 97th regiment in Alaska.[57]

As will be seen, the achievement of the 97th, the only regiment deployed on the Alaska portion of the highway, would rival that of the 95th.

10

The 97th Completes the Highway

"The soil is ours, the toil has been yours."

General Simon Bolivar Buckner didn't welcome the 97th Regiment's 1,185 black enlisted men to Alaska, where he was in charge of the territory's defense: he initially opposed supplying the regiment from his stock of provisions, goods and material. When he did agree to do so, he did not want the black soldiers to pick the supplies up, which would mean going into settlements. The issue was bucked to the War Department. General Sturdevant, assistant chief of engineers, instructed General Hoge to arrange "for *white* handling detachments" to look after supplies for the 97th.[1]

There was two feet of snow on the ground when the 97th disembarked on April 3, 1942, in Valdez, a tiny fishing village at the end of the 350-mile-long Richardson Highway to Fairbanks, Alaska's only highway of consequence. "This regiment of blacks, most of whom came from the Florida area, had been constructing runways at Eglin Field, Florida," said Col. Donald H. Fischer, a battalion commander. "Most of the soldiers and a few officers had never seen snow. There was some trepidation when they learned their destination."[2] Said Sgt. Clifton B. Monk of Newton Grove, North Carolina: "It looked like Hell on Earth."[3] Regimental headquarters was set up in a clearing in Valdez, but the rest of the troops had to march thirteen miles until they found a suitable campsite alongside the Richardson Highway.

As it turned out, the 97th had the worst assignment of any of the seven regiments on the highway: the worst weather, the most mountainous terrain and the greatest isolation. The other six regiments operating in the Yukon could count on trails used by trappers over which supplies could be brought in; there were no such trails in the region where the 97th labored. Like the 93rd and the 95th, the 97th had a problem getting its equipment, including bulldozers. Before leaving Seattle, Col. Stephen C. Whipple, the 97th's commander, had rejected the fleet of used trucks assigned to it and requisitioned new ones. The new trucks never arrived; weeks late, the old ones showed up, still needing repairs. Several more weeks were spent unloading equipment and supplies. The troops were surprised to see coffins being unloaded, but a couple would eventually be used by the 97th before it finished its tour up north.[4]

An argument could be made that the 97th faced more racial obstacles than did the two black regiments operating in the Yukon Territory. Although the Army abolished segregated latrines worldwide in October 1942, they continued to be in use in Alaska

Segregated outhouses remained in operation in Alaska after the U.S. Army banned them worldwide (courtesy William E. Griggs).

while the 97th was there; there were separate entrances marked for white officers, white enlisted men and colored troops. Once segregated latrines became illegal, Sgt. William E. Griggs, photographer for the 97th Regiment, took a photograph of one of the outhouses and gave a print to Chaplain Carroll of the 95th, a fellow Baltimorean, for delivery to the War Department's inspector general.[5] An inspector subsequently visited the troops without their knowledge, but the segregated facilities remained while the 97th was stationed in Alaska.[6]

A restaurant in Valdez refused to serve enlisted members of a company commanded by Lt. Andrew Henry of Zanesville, Ohio. The colonel to whom he reported subsequently declared the restaurant off-limits for all military personnel and posted military policemen outside to make sure his order was obeyed. "We may have been criticized by some generals," the lieutenant said. "But when all was said and done ... we were a pretty top outfit."[7] The restaurants, bars and nightclubs in Fairbanks were more welcoming of the 97th, but some of the local residents were not. When a group of them complained to military authorities, Fairbanks was placed off-limits to black soldiers.[8] Said Sergeant Monk: "When you do a good job and then they treat you like the enemy, I'm telling you, we'd just come back after we'd done suffered in the cold."[9]

The largest town in Alaska's interior, Fairbanks had a population of 6,000 that would more than double during the war, not counting the Army Air Base at Ladd Field, where 7,000 troops—all of them white—would be stationed and 20,000 civilians employed. The air base had housing (some of it underground), canteens, movie theaters, clubs, swimming pools and bowling alleys, all spread over forty square miles.[10] The town itself had modern office buildings, hotels and apartment houses, restaurants and drugstores, but also a skid row down by the Chena River and anything-goes places like the Wagon Wheel.[11]

Although the northern end of the Alcan Highway was Fairbanks, there was already a serviceable road from the town to Big Delta, at the confluence of the Delta and Tanana (TA-nah-nah) rivers, ninety-nine miles south. Therefore, construction of the highway was to proceed from Big Delta southeast to the Canadian border. Since the first leg from Big Delta was near settlements, it was given to the Public Roads Administration. The 97th was assigned to start work at the village of Slana, 200 miles north of Valdez. This was not work on the Alcan Highway itself but on an access road—the Tok Cutoff, or shortcut—over which it would transport equipment and supplies to Tok, where the highway would pass. Major Charles Mitchem, battalion commander of the 97th, made the preliminary survey of the Slana-to-Tok route through the Wrangell Mountains. He and his party of enlisted men walked most of the way, although aided by packhorses. Aerial photos were not yet available to help him. But first the rest of the 97th had to get out of the port, where it was held captive by snow up to twelve feet deep in mountain passes on the Richardson Highway, built in 1898 to provide an all–American route to the Klondike during the gold rush.

By mid–May the 97th moved out of Valdez and started repairing the Richardson Highway for the Alaska Highway Commission—pick and shovel and wheelbarrow work—so that its heavy equipment could be moved. But that heavy equipment didn't reach Valdez until June and then had to be delivered to where the men were. "We were just learning," James C. Coleman, a captain from Bridgeport, West Virginia, said of "C" Company, which he commanded. "It was a learning experience for the first several months. We'd never touched that kind of equipment until we got to Alaska. We never had a bulldozer assigned for training. We had a little garden tractor."[12] One enlisted man who did have experience operating a bulldozer was Sgt. Lee Young from Engelhard, North Carolina. He was taught at Eglin Field in Florida by trainers from the Caterpillar plant at Champagne, Illinois. "Sometimes I had to train the new men," he said. "We had some guys off the plantation. These were smart guys. We were happy to be able to operate equipment because we were happy to get away from the farms. I was very proud when I was promoted to train the guys. I was one of the oldest operators there and I was only twenty-two. The other guys were eighteen to twenty. They were easy to train."[13]

"They learned real fast," said Sergeant Monk. "If anybody tells you a colored soldier ain't a smart man and can't learn anything, you just tell them they are a doggone liar. Those men took that machinery and built those roads. It was just amazing how they learned to operate and cooperate. It was out of this world."[14] "The men learned new skills," said Sergeant Griggs. "The men learned on the job and became experts operating bulldozers and other big equipment."[15] "For the most part, the men in my outfit couldn't read or write. They said they couldn't use heavy equipment," Sgt. Hayward L. Oubre recalled. "But these men became experts with that heavy equipment."[16] The men became so adept at operating the bulldozers that they'd borrow some from the PRA crews whenever they had the opportunity. "We didn't steal them," said Sergeant Young. "We just took and used them. I operated some of that equipment. They had a little more modern equipment. They'd park them and we'd just start them up and use them and leave them where we were working."[17]

When the 97th finally started work, it was the slowest of any of the seven regiments on the highway. The reasons were many: the snow delayed the start of their work; their heavy equipment arrived ten weeks after they did; the terrain was the most challenging of any regiment's. But the main obstacle was the Mentasta Pass between Slana and Tok, a narrow area cut through the Wrangell Mountains. "Our big problem was we started at Slana and we went up to a pass where there was no way of getting things in there," said Walter Mason, motor officer of "A" Company. "From June 7 to August 7 we only moved thirty miles."[18] Mason said he well remembered the date of June 7: "I was standing on the side of the D-8 Cat angle dozer when it made the first cut," he said.[19]

"All our work was in the mountains," said Sergeant Young. "We did more work in the mountains than any regiment. We followed the mountains around."[20] There were mudslides, washouts and flooding. Glacial ice had to be removed by pickaxe or dynamite. Some of the men learned to operate bulldozers on muddy mountain passes; the bulldozers would lose their tracks, which sometimes had to be threaded back on the sprockets while the equipment was dangling over a precipice. "The son-of-a-gun got to know how to drop that blade to keep from tumbling down the mountain," said Sergeant Monk, who was learning on the job. "The Army don't tell you how to do it. They just tell you you've got to do it."[21]

As with the 95th, there was a problem with the regimental commander. Colonel Whipple was described as "a fussy, plodding nitpicker who lacked rapport with his troops."[22] After a visit to the 97th by General Hoge and General Sturdevant, Whipple was replaced by his executive officer, Lt. Col. Lionel E. Robinson, a man with building experience in civilian life. "Robinson reorganized the regiment," said Captain Coleman. "We were really struggling at cross-purposes. Robinson called all the officers together one night and said he was reorganizing the regiment. Each company was given a specific role."[23] Company "A" was given three D-8 tractors and made lead company. Company "B" chopped trees and brush for corduroy road material. Company "C" did dirt removal. Company "D" built bridges. "This reorganization made all the difference," said Coleman. "Now every officer had a definite assignment and responsibility. Construction moved steadily ahead and on schedule."[24]

One civilian engineer who assessed the 97th after spending time with it in the mountains was Harold Richardson, western editor of the *Engineering News-Record* magazine. "This regiment, the Negro 97th, had some pretty hard going from the first," he reported. "It started right out in the Wrangell Mountains, and in the first ten days, they made only one mile total progress. During the next ten days it made three miles, which was still mighty discouraging as the schedule called for at least two miles a day. However, as the troops became more experienced and hardened, progress became better, though the country didn't."[25]

To save time, Colonel Robinson decided to make the access road to Tok just one-way, not two-way as originally planned. Even graders were used to pull trailers and sleds filled with supplies, tents and light equipment on one-way trips. Half-filled fuel drums that could float were pushed into the Little Tok River and retrieved downstream. This way, the 97th was able to make up some of the lost time. "Our men's effectiveness was very good considering that during the summer they worked seven days a week and nearly twenty-four hours a day," said Lt. Col. Howard A. Garber, former commanding officer of "F" Company. "Their soldierly behavior was all that was required in view of the work schedule. We did not hold any formations nor drills and it wasn't necessary to call the roll as the men had no place to go AWOL."[26]

The 97th reached the Tanana River on August 16, but was unable to cross to Tok

The 97th saves construction time by contracting a civilian sternwheeler to transport its heavy equipment across the Tanana River (courtesy William E. Griggs).

10—The 97th Completes the Highway

because its pontoon boats and bridging equipment had been mistakenly sent to Whitehorse for delivery to the 18th Regiment. The 97th could have waited for the PRA, which had orders to build a 365-foot timber bridge across the river, but this would have occasioned a delay, time Colonel Robinson couldn't afford. Major Mitchem and Capt. Andrew McMeekin provided a solution. They flagged down a small sternwheel riverboat and negotiated a price with the captain, who agreed to transport the 97th's bulldozers, graders, trucks and other equipment across the swift-flowing river. "This move saved the 97th Engineers at least two weeks in construction of the highway," said Lieutenant Mason. "At this point, the regiment was still one hundred miles from the Alaska-Canadian border."[27] It had taken the regiment two months to build the seventy-eight miles of road from Slana to Tok, where its section of the Alcan Highway began.

When the 97th finally started building its assigned section of the Alcan Highway east from Tok in Alaska, the regiment was one hundred wooded and swampy miles from the Canadian border. One hundred miles on the other side of the border was the 18th Regiment working westward. This was one of two gaps on the highway. The other was between the 340th and the 35th, which would meet on September 24, 1942, on a tributary of the Liard River, thereafter known as Contact Creek. That meant the highway was then open from Dawson Creek in British Columbia to Whitehorse in the Yukon Territory, a distance of 1,030 miles. Anticipating the linkup, Cpl. Otto H. Gronke of Chicago and Pfc. Robert Bowe of Minneapolis were deployed to test the highway by driving from Dawson Creek to Whitehorse in a Dodge 4 × 4 half-ton weapons carrier; they left September 22, averaged fifteen miles an hour and made the trip in seventy-one hours (over five days) of driving time. The road was so rough that a fender was shaken off the first day out. Three days after their arrival, regular supply runs to Whitehorse began. The final link to Fairbanks would be completed when the 97th and the white 18th Regiment met. Secretary of War Henry L. Stimson announced that the highway would be opened by December 1.

Given the fact that winter starts early up north, there was fear that snow and freezing weather might prevent the 97th and 18th from fulfilling Stimson's prediction. Construction conditions were destined to become more difficult. Once ice started to form in the rivers, trucks could not easily ford them; ice would lock wheels and crack the axles.

Completion of the Alcan Highway was not intended to be a race between the two regiments to see which got to the border first because there had never been plans for the 97th to operate in Canada. However, radio contact was maintained between the regimental headquarters, so the 97th and the 18th each had a pretty good idea where the other was.

Col. Earl G. Paules, who oversaw both regiments as commander of the Northern Sector, decided to save precious time. He ordered the 97th and 18th to build the final seventy-miles more or less as a simple, one-lane winter trail that could be upgraded the following spring by the Public Roads Administration. The temperatures were already dropping; frozen ground was not suitable for normal road building.

The 97th made faster headway than the 18th, crossing into Canadian territory and putting up a cocky sign reading "Los Angeles City Limits" at the border.[28] They knew they were in Canada when they saw a pole with Indian carvings to mark the border.[29] The 18th was expected to best the 97th because of the speed with which it had built the first 150 miles of road westward from Whitehorse. It was by far the fastest of all seven regiments at that point. However, during the final stretch the 18th encountered one hundred miles of permafrost that required the time-consuming placement of layers of insulating foliage topped off by logs laid side by side in corduroy fashion.[30]

Near Beaver Creek at dusk on October 25, 1942, Cpl. Refines Sims, Jr., from Philadelphia was operating one of the 97th's D-8 bulldozers some twenty miles past the Alaska-Yukon border, moving so fast that branches snapping back were bloodying his face. When he saw spruce trees starting to topple in his direction, he immediately slammed on the brakes and put the D-8 in reverse. Past the fallen trees emerged another bulldozer, this one operated by Pfc. Alfred Jalufka of Kennedy, Texas, a member of the 18th Regiment. "I never saw anything so exciting and so filled with history," said Harold Richardson of the *Engineering News-Record*, who witnessed the virtual nose-to-nose meeting of the two bulldozers.[31] Accompanying Richardson were two lieutenants from the 97th, Ralph W. Hunt and G.H. Jones, who had thought the two regiments might meet that afternoon. With his motor idling, Jalufka had heard a noise and thought he was about to meet a herd of moose or a bear or two. "He raised the blade of the Cat half way and crouching down prepared for the attack," said a colleague. "Raising his head slightly he saw another Cat with its blade at half-mast coming towards him."[32] Sims and Jalufka sat silently on their bulldozers for nearly a minute, just looking at each other.[33]

A Canadian who arrived on the scene shortly after the meeting imagined the conversation that might have taken place between the two soldiers:

> SIMS: "Wonder how much further northward those fellows are now. Are we going to have to build The Road all the way to Whitehorse ourselves?"
> *A loud noise!*
> SIMS: "Could it really be?"
> JALUFKA: "Hi there, Ninety-seven!"
> SIMS: "Well, blow me down. You the Eighteenth?"
> JALUFKA: "Shake, pardner."
> SIMS: "I guess we made it."
> JALUFKA: "I guess we did."
> SIMS: "What took you so long?"
> JALUFKA: "What took you so long?"

Richardson of the *Engineering News-Record* had a camera, but the foliage was so heavy where the two bulldozers met that there wasn't enough light for a photo, especially as northern days were becoming shorter. The two men moved their Caterpillars down

A black corporal and a white private meet on their bulldozers October 25, 1942, linking up the Alcan Highway (courtesy Office of History Collection, U.S. Army Corps of Engineers).

to a nearby creek where the light was better. "So the picture was taken a quarter of a mile from where it happened," explained Walter Parsons, then a lieutenant with the 97th.[35] Ignoring a "golden spike" moment like those when the linking of railway tracks was celebrated, Sims and Jalufka then turned around their machines and started widening the trail. The 97th had just completed the construction of 230 miles of highway through mountains and muskeg.

The Alcan Highway had been linked — and the 97th had beaten the 18th. Richardson's photo was published in hundreds of American newspapers, one of the first public recognitions of the contributions of black soldiers to the war effort, albeit in northern Canada. Had the War Department stage-managed the linkup, it could not have come up with a better scenario at a time of racial disturbances in the United States: a black man and a white man shaking hands after jointly completing an important wartime mission.

However, the United States was not the first to announce the completion of the

Alcan Highway: Japan was. A broadcast from Tokyo congratulated the Army, saying the highway would help the Japanese military in its coming invasion of the Western Hemisphere.[36] Just how the Japanese managed to scoop the American news media was a mystery.

Four days after the linkup, Secretary Stimson announced that the highway was completed and traffic flowing:

> Trucks started to roll the entire 1,671-mile length of the Alcan Highway this week, carrying munitions and material to troops in Alaska.... Thousands of trucks will run all winter carrying soldiers and supplies to Alaskan posts, Plans are under way to haul strategic raw materials southward on the return trips.[37]

(Stimson erred in his figure for the length of the highway. It was then 1,650 miles, but would become shorter as the Public Roads Administration straightened the highway by reducing some curves.)

Eight months and twelve days after President Roosevelt had approved the project, the highway was completed, although much upgrading and permanent bridge building were still to be done. "We were anxious to meet the boys of the 18th," said the 97th's Sgt. Lee Young, who heard the news as it spread from company to company. "It was getting cold. We had to finish before we got snowed in."[38]

An official dedication ceremony was held on November 20, 1942. The actual site of the meeting between Sims and Jalufka was too remote for the ceremony, so Brig. Gen. James A. O'Connor's staff sought a location closer to Whitehorse. They chose the most elevated section of the highway at mile 1,061 built by the 18th Regiment—located 162 miles west of Whitehorse, it commanded a view of Kluane (CLUE-ah-nay) Lake and the Ruby and Nisling mountains guarding it; to the west were the St. Elias Mountains, whose peaks rose 12,000 feet. The site was named Soldiers Summit. The ceremony was originally to have been held November 15, but the capricious northern weather caused a postponement: a chinook—a dry, warm wind from the ocean that can lift temperatures by as much as seventy degrees in several hours—drove the thermometer up to fifty-five degrees; the resulting thaw swelled rivers and knocked out bridges, a preview of damage that would occur over the coming winter. The highway was effectively closed while repairs were made.

Barracks were hastily assembled near Slim's River bridge at the south end of Kluane Lake, a ten-mile drive from Soldiers Summit, for the 200 invited guests and one hundred troops participating in the ceremony. General O'Connor wanted an authentic lunch, so his staff obtained the necessary ingredients. Maj. Dick Luckow sent out a hunting party that came back with fresh moose, mountain sheep and bear meat. Stateside fare was given local names, such as Dawson Creek Crackers and Fairbanks Cheese. Hothouse tomatoes and lettuce were served in Slim's River Salad. There were also Pickhandle beans, Karskawalsh potatoes, Burwash prunes, Takkini corn, Spinach à la Kloo, Horse Camp pudding and Coffee à la Yukon. One of the cooks was Cpl. James Johnson, a native of Norfolk, Virginia, and a member of the 95th Regiment. He had been a cook at a hospital in Clifton Forge, Virginia, when he was drafted.

A black private from Baltimore named Philip Bush had been assigned to ensure the wood stoves in the barracks were giving off sufficient heat. On his rounds, he saw General O'Connor in his sleeping bag, and shook him awake. "General, suh," he said, handing O'Connor one of the programs prepared for the ceremony. "Will you put yuh name on my program for me?" Now awake, the general asked, "What did you say, young man?" When the private repeated his request, O'Connor said, "Sure I will," and looked for his glasses and a pen. E.L. ("Bob") Bartlett, Alaska's secretary of state, marveled afterward, "That's the sort of thing we're fighting for."[39]

By 9:30 A.M. on November 20, the benevolent chinook wind had blown itself out and given way to a more typical northern winter day: thirty below zero. Probably the most admired participants were the eight members of the RCMP honor guard who eschewed their normal buffalo winter coats and appeared in their scarlet dress tunics. Since there were no Canadian troops present, the Mounties stood by the fluttering Union Jack — Canada did not yet have its own flag — while the American troops, wearing parkas with the hoods up, flanked the Stars and Stripes. Some of the local civilians wore reindeer-skin parkas. Bonfires were lit so participants could warm up, creating a smoky pall over Soldiers Summit.

As befitting the interracial nature of the construction and of the final linkup, two black and two white enlisted men held the thirty-foot red, white and blue ribbon that represented the Alaska-Yukon border. "Four outstanding soldiers of the American Army have been selected to hold the ribbon which will be cut by representatives of the Canadian and Alaskan governments," said the master of ceremonies, Col. K.B. Bush, chief of staff of the Northwest Service Command, whose bare hands turned blue as he read from his notes. "These enlisted men are representatives also. They represent the thousands of soldiers whose loyalty, toil and effort have made this road a reality. Fittingly, these men will be introduced by the commanding officers of their respective sectors." Col. E.G. Paules introduced the men from the Whitehorse sector, and Col. Robert D. Ingalls did likewise for the Fort St. John sector. Corporal Sims and Private Jalufka were to have a lead role, holding the ribbon. But Sims became ill and was furloughed home. Another member of the 97th Regiment, Sgt. Alfred Sharp of Montgomery, Alabama, replaced him.[40] The other black enlisted man was Pfc. John T. Reilly of the 95th, a native of Detroit. "These enlisted men," said Paules and Ingalls in a joint statement, "are worthy representatives of the thousands of American soldiers who have done such a magnificent job in building this road."

There were also black and white bands, those of the 95th and 18th Regiments. The black band was led by Sgt. Benjamin S. Smith of Washington, a graduate of Howard University and the Washington College of Music. He was conductor of the Washington Philharmonic Band when he was drafted. Cpl. James J. Butler, a native of Philadelphia and member of the 95th, composed the regimental march that was played at the opening.

Sgt. Alfred Sharp of Montgomery, Alabama (left), and Pfc. Alfred Jalufka flank Col. E.G. Paules at the opening ceremony of the Alaska Highway (courtesy U.S. Army Military History Institute).

Despite his musical talents — he played various instruments, including the euphonium — he was a pick-and-shovel man on the highway. He said his job then was "supplying the company with wood" for the stoves in the tents and kitchen.[41] The bands kept their instruments heated in a nearby tent so they could make a last-minute dash to the ceremony; they applied alcohol instead of valve oil to keep their instruments from freezing up.

The guests of honor included Alaska's Secretary Bartlett, standing in for Governor Ernest Gruening; Ian Mackenzie, Canada's health minister; Dr. Charles Camsell, commissioner of the Northwest Territories; and Maj. Gen. H.N. Ganong, commander of Canada's 8th Division. Brig. Gen. William M. Hoge, the man who began the actual construction of the highway, was not in attendance.[42] Mackenzie read the remarks of Prime Minister Mackenzie King, who said, "This is one more symbol of the peace and friendship that have endured for so many years between our two lands. The soil is ours, the toil has been yours. We have built the skyway — you the highway — to this great Alaska base. This road is built for war, but it will remain for peace, bringing, in happier days, tens of thousands of your people across the magnificent terrain of this great north to the edge of the Arctic shores."[43]

When the broadcasting equipment used by the Canadian Broadcasting Corporation to tape the ceremony started to pick up a strange clicking sound, crewmembers sought the source of the noise. They found the mike used by the Canadian minister was open and that the cold caused his false teeth to chatter.[44]

The main American message was that from Secretary of War Stimson: "Connection of the Alcan Highway, far in advance of schedule, was made possible by the determination and devotion of individuals who have had part in its construction. The wilderness barrier has been conquered by men to provide a vital military link between interior North America and the Territory of Alaska. I congratulate them all — the United States Army Corps of Engineers who conceived and planned the highway, as well as the civilian contractors and crews who, with the military, pushed across this formidable terrain."

Said General O'Connor: "The Alcan Highway, as we call it, is truly a joint effort of our two nations. The name we have given it symbolizes that. It combines the first syllables of Alaska and Canada. No designation could be more appropriate." Appropriate or not, Congress would change the name of the highway within a year.

After these remarks, Bartlett and Mackenzie cut the ribbon with a pair of scissors whose blades were plated with genuine Alaska gold. One blade was later sent to President Roosevelt while General O'Connor personally delivered the other to Prime Minister King. Irwin T. May, chaplain of the 18th Regiment, pronounced the benediction and Father Charles Hamel, pastor of Whitehorse's Catholic Church, read the invocation.

Capt. Edward G. Carroll, chaplain of the 95th, managed to get a piece of the ribbon as a souvenir. Carroll, a graduate of Columbia University and the Yale School of Divinity, said, "By and large the colored troops coming under my surveillance have adapted themselves to these new surroundings, new work and new climate. A man who used to be a dining car waiter is now one of our best bulldozer operators; a soldier who wrote fiction for pulp magazines is an excellent cook." Then he singled out Reilly, one of the two black soldiers who participated in the ceremony: "Cpl. Reilly, one of our finest soldiers, is known all over Detroit for his splendid tone voice. His singing thrills his comrades on many occasions."[45] Reilly had studied music at Howard University in Washington. "I've sung concerts in Detroit, Cleveland, Chicago and other places," Reilly said. "When I wasn't singing, I was selling insurance."[46]

Corporal Gronke and Private Bowe then got into their Dodge 4 × 4 and headed for Fairbanks, 600 miles away, leading a convoy of freight trucks to complete their inaugural drive on the Alcan Highway. They left to the strains of "The Maple Leaf Forever" and "The Washington Post March" played by the band of the 18th Regiment. For their pioneering effort, Gronke was named General O'Connor's driver while Bowe was assigned to an indoor job as a mail clerk. At the formal luncheon, the guests feasted on moose and bear steaks and slices of mountain goat, and toasted the Alcan Highway with coffee and water.

J. Frank Willis, a top broadcaster for the Canadian Broadcasting Corporation who was covering the event, said with a bit of hyperbole, "Surely this road will rank for all time among the greatest engineering feats the world has ever seen. From Dawson Creek to Fairbanks in Alaska, a distance of 1,650 miles, American Army Engineers have punched through this highway at the blitzkrieg speed of eight miles a day."[47] An American Army transport flew Willis's tape to Edmonton for a Sunday afternoon hookup with the Mutual Broadcasting System and the British Broadcasting Corporation, as well as for transmission within Canada.

Once the highway was completed, the 97th helped maintain it and operated terminals for trucks in what was dubbed the "Fairbanks Freight"—the fleet of Army supply trucks. One company at Cathedral Rapids was given the task of chopping glaciers off the highway by hand or building bypass roads around them.[48]

Historian Walter R. Borneman would say of the regiment's achievements, "By carving the most miles in the final stretch, the 97th had done as much on the ground to silence generations of prejudice as the famed Tuskegee airmen were about to do in the air."[49]

Upon his retirement in 1974, General Hoge was not as glowing in his assessment of the 97th. He termed the regiment "practically useless" during an Army debriefing interview.[50] When Hoge's comments became known, Lt. Col. Lyman L. Woodman, the Corps of Engineers wartime public information officer in Alaska, investigated them and found them to be unsubstantiated. One of those who responded to Woodman's inquiry was Col. Donald H. Fischer, a former commander of the 97th, who said, "I must strongly disagree with the person who was so uncomplimentary of the black troops. He probably did not realize that these men were, for the most part, uneducated, afraid, in an environment so new and strange and wondering if they were going to survive. I found them to respond very well to leadership and to be cheerful, willing, hard workers, and [they] developed into damn good soldiers."[51]

While the 97th enjoyed its moment of fame with the completion of the highway, the black 388th Regiment was at work in the neighboring Northwest Territories on the Canol project to supply fuel to the Army trucks and planes operating in the Yukon and Alaska.

11

The 388th Does the Heavy Lifting

"Dusky hepcats entertained their redskin hosts."

As the black 388th Regiment left Camp Claiborne, Louisiana, in early June of 1942 on three trains bound for northern Canada and work on the Canol pipeline, the Japanese were bombing Dutch Harbor and invading the Aleutian Islands. If the Alcan Highway had its genesis in the Klondike Gold Rush, the pipeline was a spur-of-the-moment project — and a very secret one — inspired by Japan. The War Department feared — correctly — that Japan was planning an invasion that could prevent oil from reaching Alaska by sea. So the Roosevelt administration approved plans for construction of a 595-mile-long pipeline from the producing oilfield at Norman Wells in Canada's Northwest Territories to a refinery to be built in Whitehorse in the Yukon. Since the War Department wanted oil to be flowing by December 31, common sense called for construction to start at both ends of the pipeline. But Japan's seizure of Kiska, Attu and Agattu theoretically placed Whitehorse within range of Japanese bombers, so most of the work was done from more remote Norman Wells. The opening date for the pipeline was pushed back a year. To compensate, construction was ordered on what became known as Canol 2, a pipeline from Skagway to Whitehorse for the storage of oil from the lower forty-eight states brought in by petroleum tankers.

Although the decision to build the Alcan Highway was prompted by the Japanese attack on Pearl Harbor, American and Canadian commissions had spent decades studying the possibility of a land route from the lower forty-eight. No such study preceded the decision to build the Canol pipeline. The pipeline proposal was approved based on a one-page memo written following a one-day conference by an engineer who had never been up north and whose specialty was railroading. James H. Graham, a dollar-a-year man, must have been surprised when his old friend, Maj. Gen. Brehon B. Somervell, in charge of logistics for the entire Army, accepted his pipeline proposal without question. Those in attendance — three generals from the War Department and representatives of Standard Oil of New Jersey, now known as ExxonMobil, and its Canadian subsidiary, Imperial Oil — agreed that the project was feasible but would be difficult to carry out. No one asked the opinion of the Navy because Somervell felt this matter was none of its business.[1]

Afterward, there were some second thoughts by Standard Oil of California, contracted by the Army to operate the pipeline and refinery, and Imperial Oil, which operated the producing Norman Wells field. Secretary of the interior Harold Ickes, who was President Roosevelt's wartime oil czar, also had reservations. Roosevelt sought to reassure Ickes. "The recent attack on Dutch Harbor discloses the possibility of great military need for this additional source of supply," the president told him. "We are daily taking greater chances and, in view of the military needs of Alaska, the project has my full approval."[2] The goal was a daily production of 3,000 barrels.

The Army Corps of Engineers had not anticipated the challenges that would balloon the costs of the Canol project to $134 million, almost $100 million more than James Graham had estimated. That figure grew to $300 million if military costs were factored in.[3] More miles of road were built for the Canol pipeline project than for the Alcan Highway and more airfields than on the Northwest Staging Route.[4] Some 52,900 people worked on the project, including 2,500 soldiers; because of the brutal weather and working conditions, 28,000 civilians quit before completing their nine-month contracts.[5]

The officer in charge of the Canol project was a controversial colonel named Theodore Wyman, Jr., cleared of charges of "private and public misconduct" while serving as the Army's district engineer in Hawaii at the time of Pearl Harbor.[6] Wyman arrived in Edmonton on May 18 and set up his headquarters in the Alberta city. Neither he nor his staff had any operational experience in the Far North. He left almost immediately for Waterways, a northern Alberta town so small that it didn't even have a hotel. He booked a room in Fort McMurray, five miles away, at its only hotel, the New Franklin, and hired the only available car in town, a taxi, and its driver. He then found a vacant field for pitching tents that he named Camp Prairie, and also contracted riverboats from the Hudson's Bay Company and the Northern Transportation Company Limited. One Army officer opposed to Wyman was General William Hoge, who accused him of getting equipment diverted from the Alcan Highway to the Canol project. "He was a ruthless man who tried to commandeer everything," Hoge remarked. "It irked me to think of all this equipment diverted onto Canol, a badly conceived project which I thought served no purpose."[7]

At Wyman's request, Grant McConachie, general manager of Canadian Pacific Airlines, obtained a plane for use in locating a route for the pipeline. McConachie flew the plane, a twin-engine Barkley-Grow with pontoons, to Norman Wells before turning it over to another pilot. No one had ever before flown from Norman Wells to Whitehorse over the Mackenzie Mountains. The one flight in mid–June was sufficient for the Army to determine the general path of the pipeline, as compared to the decades spent studying possible routes for what became the Alcan Highway. The difficult part came later in the year when Army ground parties, helped by Indian guides, sought a feasible trail through the mountains. "The first two crews used horses, but they had to turn back when they got stuck," explained General James O'Connor, head of the Northwest Service Command, which was responsible for the Canol project as well as the Alcan Highway. "Two other crews went into the mountains with tractors, pulling their supplies on sleighs. They too got stuck. The other three crews used dogteams. Two of them couldn't make it, but the third got through and found a route."[8] The parties often ran short of food and had to exist on the game they shot. Native Canadian George Blondin, from Fort Norman, was eighteen when he signed on as a guide for the Army. "Most elders in the area didn't know there was a war until the Americans came in 1942," he said. "I was more than happy to help them."[9]

Most of the work on the Canol project was done by the Army during that first summer, bringing in the pipe and supplies that the private contractors would need. Bechtel, the main private contractor, had been upfront in its description of life on the project. Its recruiting announcement read as follows:

This Is No Picnic

Working and living conditions on this job are as difficult as those encountered on any construction job ever done in the united states or foreign territory. Men hired for this job will be required to work and live under the most extreme conditions imaginable. Temperatures will range from 90 degrees above zero to 70 degrees below zero. Men will have to fight swamps, rivers, ice and cold. Mosquitoes, flies and gnats will not only be annoying but will cause bodily harm. If you are not prepared to work under these and similar conditions

Do Not Apply

Those were also the conditions faced by troops of the 388th Regiment who didn't have the option of quitting their jobs if it got too cold. After disembarking on June 7 at the end of the railroad in Waterways, the members of the 388th were trucked to Camp Prairie, the segregated base outside of town. "We slept on the ground in pup tents the first night," said First Sgt. Wansley Hill. "There was still ice on the ground. It was cold!"[10] An Army report confirmed the living conditions at Camp Prairie: "Here's what the soldiers discovered: Rain. Cold. Mud. No place to sleep but the ground, with last winter's frost still in it. No tent stoves. No sleeping bags or cots. No Arctic socks or shoepacs."[11] (Shoepacs were laced leather boots with rubberized lower tops and soles.)

The challenge was how to supply a remote oil field seventy-five miles south of the Arctic Circle with the material to install a pipeline. That was the job given to the 388th, whose black enlisted members made up half of the American soldiers serving in the Northwest Territories and northern Alberta. If the three black regiments on the Alcan Highway did pick-and-shovel work, the 388th did mainly stevedore work on the Canol project, repeatedly unloading and loading pipe, as there was no uninterrupted waterway from the end of the railroad to the oil field. As noted in an Army report, "When they found that their orders called for moving 30,000 tons of freight, mostly pipe, over 1,171 miles of rivers and lakes in three months, they almost tossed in the sponge then and there."[12] That 30,000 estimate proved too low as 55,000 tons were eventually destined for Norman Wells and its oil field. Ironically, Waterways and its twin town, Fort McMurray, were then sitting on one of the world's greatest oil reserves, the Athabasca Tar Sands, which would be developed half a century later.

Two wood-burning, sternwheel steamboats of pre–Great War vintage operated

The 388th spends much of its time cutting and stacking cordwood to fuel the sternwheelers contracted by the American Army for the Canol project (courtesy Archives Canada).

between Waterways and Fort Fitzgerald, making the 287-mile run on the Clearwater, Athabasca and Slave rivers, crossing Lake Athabasca en route. The white troops from the 89th and 90th Heavy Pontoon Battalions fashioned pontoon rafts, loaded them with supplies and tried the voyage themselves. The first two rafts capsized in rough waters on Lake Athabasca, but the third attempt was successful. The waves would be much stronger on Great Slave Lake on the second leg to Norman Wells. But first, all cargo had to be unloaded at Fort Fitzgerald and trucked to Fort Smith over a sixteen-mile portage around a series of rapids, one of them aptly named Rapids of the Drowned. The next set of boats, also including sternwheelers, operated from Fort Smith, making an eight-hour crossing of Great Slave Lake and then entering the Mackenzie River. The Great Slave is the fifth largest lake in the Western Hemisphere, a 12,000-square-mile inland sea, and one of the most treacherous in the world, subject to Arctic winds that produce ocean-sized waves that can play havoc with shipping; more than one bulldozer destined for the Canol project ended up on the lake's floor.

The approach to the Mackenzie River is dangerous because of submerged rocks. The river, which empties into the Arctic Ocean, is surpassed in length in North America

Members of the 388th wait on a barge at dockside in Waterways for the trip downriver to Fort Smith (courtesy Archives Canada).

only by the Mississippi. The entire river system was ice-free for only four to four and a half months of the year. One of the jobs assigned to the 388th was cutting by hand and stacking firewood for the two ancient sternwheelers that pushed barges between Waterways and Fort Fitzgerald, as well as the others that operated out of Fort Smith. On one occasion, the troops had cut and stacked 2,000 cords of wood only to have them consumed by a forest fire. After that, a fireguard was posted at each stack of firewood.

The 388th had to unload thirty to seventy-five boxcars of freight every day, sometimes working twenty hours a day, seven days a week. One company once worked sixty-nine straight days without a break, loading and unloading pipe, cutting and stacking firewood, and fighting fires (often started innocently by the troops to ward off mosquitoes). Because of a shortage of tracks, boxcars had to be immediately emptied. Nor were there warehouses, so everything had to be piled on makeshift platforms and transferred to barges as quickly as possible. One of the assignments given the 388th was laying a railway siding for boxcars waiting to be unloaded at Waterways.

The first troops to leave Waterways were eighty men from "A" and "B" Companies who loaded two barges with pipe and climbed on top as the steamboat *Athabasca* headed downriver on June 11 to Fort Fitzgerald and the portage to Fort Smith, where the headquarters for the 388th was to be established. The company commanders met with Dr. J.A. Urquhart, the top federal government official in the Northwest Territories, and Inspector A.G. Berch of the Royal Canadian Mounted Police. "The Americans found the Canadian officials most cooperative," the Army reported.[13] The next day tents were pitched on vacant land outside of town commandeered by the Army as a campsite for the black troops.

There was almost an international incident when the first truck carrying soldiers approached the camp area. The owner of the land, who opposed turning it over to the Army, had appealed to the RCMP for support. He and a Mountie were blocking the entrance when the truck, driven by a black corporal, pulled up. A resident relayed the conversation: "Mah Loo'tenant he done say I'se to use this hyar road. Outta mah way, Mountie — outta mah way fo' I'se a-comin'through!" The Mountie and the owner stood aside and the truck passed by.[14]

Father William A. Leising, a farm boy from upstate New York who became an Oblate missionary priest in the Far North, remembered the arrival of the 388th in Fort Smith. "Children ran to the school windows — the teacher's head above their little ones — straining to see 'all those tanned men' marching in squads to the river to unload pipe," he said. "One thousand two hundred and eighteen colored troops from the 388th Regiment had set up their tents that night on the bend of the street known as 'Axhandle Alley,' deep in the poplar wood south of town."[15] That day the Hudson's Bay trading post closed its doors at 1 P.M., as the black troops had purchased practically all of its merchandise. Two other stores did likewise. "Those Americans have come into the North and that is the end of our peaceful days," said the Catholic archbishop.[16]

While the white-gloved matrons married to public servants sent from Ottawa were not happy to see the black soldiers, the local residents enjoyed them, according to one longtime northern resident. "Here at Fort Smith happy Negroes joined with redmen, half-breeds and trappers in tripping the light fantastic to the tune of squeaking fiddles, swinging their aboriginal partners," he wrote.[17] The caller chanted as the black soldiers were introduced to square dancing, northern style:

> S'lute your ladies, all together!
> Ladies opposite, the same
> Hit the lumber with your leathers,
> Balance all and swing yer dame
> Bunch the moose cows in the middle
> Circle stags and do-se-do
> Pay attention to the fiddle,
> Swing her 'round and off you go!

"In return, colored troops — the kuskitayweasuk, or black meats, as the Indians called them — reciprocated and dusky hepcats entertained their redskin hosts with an open-air concert by their fifteen-piece Negro band," the old-timer added.[18]

One hundred and sixty black soldiers were bound for Norman Wells aboard the Hudson's Bay steamboat *Distributor* when it encountered a storm on Great Slave Lake, forcing the ship's captain to seek shelter at Hay River. The storm lasted three days, during which time Capt. Robert Jackson, the company commander, ordered his men to go ashore for calisthenics. He was unaware that an Indian, hidden in scanty spruce brush, was watching. Since these were the first soldiers the native had ever seen, he concluded that they were performing a war dance as they were singing, jumping, toe touching and doing other never-before-seen maneuvers. He reported this to his tribe's chief, who then asked Captain Jackson if his men could repeat their war dance at the Indian settlement. The captain was amused and accepted the invitation. The Indian members reciprocated and performed a ceremonial dance for their black guests.[19]

Not all the natives, however, were initially as welcoming of the black troops. Sgt. Franklin J. Brehon claimed white officers often warned local people about the troops. "They laid down their talk about us," he said of the officers in the province of Alberta and the Northwest Territories. "When we got up there and started unloading our equipment and things, they stayed in their houses. Keep out. Keep out. When they came out of their houses two weeks later, they'd stand off at a distance and look at us."[20]

Most of the 388th's energy was spent on the pipe, 550 miles of it that had to be handled by hand at least six times before reaching its destination. That meant that the soldiers were posted all along the route from Waterways to Norman Wells. Each pipe was twenty-two feet long and weighed 230 pounds. Britain's high commissioner to Canada, Malcolm MacDonald, gave a rather undiplomatic account of pipe rolling by the 388th during a visit he made to the Canol project: "We went to watch Negroes packing lengths of pipeline on scows moored against the riverbank. It was a strange sight. A couple of buck Negroes at the top of the bank started each bit of pipe on its downhill journey by giving it hearty kicks. Other men posted at intervals down the slope helped it on its way with more kicks. You might have thought you were watching a scene somewhere on the banks of the Mississippi in the Deep South instead of beside the Slave River north of parallel 60."[21]

One way of dealing with the pipe was through humor, so the members of the 388th came up with chants such as this:

> Crackers in the morning, crackers at night,
> here comes the *Athabasca* with mo' damn pipe.

Another favorite was:

> The night is light,
> the mosquitoes sho, do bite
> look up da river
> and see mo' damn pipe.[22]

The troops staged competitions between squads to see which one could unload or load the most pipe in a given period of time.[23]

The main job of the 388th was loading and unloading 550 miles of pipe by hand (courtesy Archives Canada).

An Army report stated, "It was a strange northland setting as the Negro soldiers, first of their race whom most of the natives had seen, labored through the long hours of daylight against a background of dark, cold, and dangerous waters on one side and the stunted spruce jack pine, and aspen poplars on the other."[24]

As he was supervising stevedore work at the dockside in Waterways on June 28, Lt. Willis G. Gardener, commander of "C" Company of the 388th, slipped on a wet plank and fell into the Clearwater River. Seeing the officer floundering, two of his men, Sgt. Robert Hayes and Technician Fifth Grade Hubert Massie, realized that he couldn't swim and was in danger of drowning. Although neither man was a proficient swimmer, both jumped into the river fully clothed, including their heavy boots. Struggling against the current, they eventually managed to pull Gardener to the riverbank. For that, Hayes, twenty-seven, from Columbia, South Carolina, and Massie, twenty-three, from Waynesboro, Virginia, were awarded the Soldier's Medal for "for heroism at Waterways, Alberta, Canada," at a ceremony held at the 388th's headquarters in Fort Smith. No other soldier working on the Canol project or the Alcan Highway would be so honored.[25]

During the war, no American soldiers were posted further north than the members of the 388th Regiment. Company "D" was based seventy miles below the Arctic Circle; some men were at Norman Wells but most at a camp on the other side of the Mackenzie River. Norman Wells was just a small company town run by the Imperial Oil Company.

It shipped by river barge its then limited supply of oil from the field south of town to nearby mines, including one at Port Radium on Great Bear Lake; uranium from that mine was used in the atomic bombs dropped on Hiroshima and Nagasaki to end the war in the Pacific in 1945. The Canol project required the laying of pipe under the Mackenzie River to a pumping station at a camp named Camp Canol. Company "D" was assigned to help build the camp, four miles west across the river from Norman Wells.

Colonel Wyman, in charge of the Canol project, had flown to Norman Wells and was waiting for the *Distributor* carrying 166 black troops when it docked on July 13, 1942. Sixteen members of Company "D" remained in Norman Wells to build a dock, unload pipe and other cargo, and cut firewood for the steamboat. The remainder crossed the Mackenzie River, some to work at a sawmill cutting lumber for Camp Canol and others to do construction work. They produced 45,000 feet of lumber used to build a headquarters building and three barracks. The site chosen for the camp had to be moved twice, for structures at the first two sites started to sink in the muskeg and mud.

The *Edmonton Bulletin* notes the heroism of Sgt. Robert Hayes and Pvt. Hubert Massie, who saved a white officer from drowning (courtesy U.S. Army Military History Institute).

Eventually 1,700 civilians, including fifty women (most of them secretaries), were based at Camp Canol, making it the largest settlement in the Northwest Territories, without counting members of the 388th. The camp even boasted a renowned restaurateur, Victor Leval, maitre d' of the Congress Hotel in Chicago and a former president of the International Caterers Association.[26] He served up to 90,000 meals a month to those at Camp Canol, but none to the 600 black troops of the 388th who were eventually stationed there; they had their own segregated mess.[27] They built log cabins for themselves, chinking the structures with moss, and lived in them during the winter of 1942-1943. Their colleagues at the sawmill weren't so fortunate; during the winter, they slept fully clothed in canvas pyramid tents.[28]

Besides Waterways, Fort Smith, Fort Fitzgerald, Norman Wells and Camp Canol, members of the 388th were sent on temporary or permanent assignments to Sawmill Snye and Embarras Portage in Alberta, and, in the Northwest Territories, Fort Resolution, Wrigley Harbor, Mills Lake, Hay River, Resdelta, Yellowknife Sawmill on Great Slave Lake and Bear Island off Norman Wells. They did construction, felled trees for lumber and firewood and did stevedoring when riverboats docked. Bear Island was the site of an emergency appendectomy performed by a medical corpsman, Lt. Sidney

Smith, on Pfc. Willie Nix of the 388th. The successful operation took place in a log cabin and the operating table was a cot placed on boards and propped up between a gas barrel and a box.[29]

Since the water highway from Waterways to Norman Wells operated only four or four and a half months of the year, unlike the Alcan Highway, the Army sought to move the maximum amount of freight during the short season. The 89th and 90th Battalions built pontoon rafts to supplement the old riverboats being used by the Army, but these proved inefficient. Then the Army brought in diesel boats, complete with captains and pilots, from the Mississippi and Missouri rivers. But most of the craft were not built for the shallow Mackenzie River, where the draft was just seven feet. The flat-bottomed sternwheelers drew only two feet.

Colonel Wyman ordered the building of fourteen airfields so that civilian workers could be flown in as well as supplies and equipment to supplement the riverboats: Fort McMurray, Norman Wells, Fort Smith, Fort Simpson, Mills Lake, Fort Fitzgerald, Embarras Portage, Hay River, Fort Providence, Fort Good Hope, Arctic Red River, Fort McPherson, Aklavik and Old Crow. Places such as Aklavik were so far north of the Norman Wells oil field that some Canadians wondered if the United States was planning to extract the region's mineral wealth after the war. Ten of the airfields were built by October 1942, spaced about one hundred miles apart.

Wyman, in fact, had ordered the airfields built without seeking Canadian permission or even informing Ottawa, let alone the War Department in Washington.[30] When Canada's External Affairs Department learned of the airfields, it summoned American minister J. Pierrepont Moffat. External Affairs' Hugh Keenleyside, Canadian representative on the Permanent Joint Board on Defense, told Moffat, "It was very important that we should be informed first, as soon as the United States authorities began to discuss any new projects in the field."[31] Partly because of Canadian opposition to Wyman, he was replaced in 1943 as head of Canol operations by Col. Ludson D. Worsham, soon to be promoted to brigadier general.

This was not the first time that American aviation policy was implemented up North without Canadian knowledge. Canada's director of civilian aviation ordered grounded in Edmonton a Northwest Airlines DC-3 carrying fourteen civilians on Alcan Highway business. The plane had arrived unannounced in Winnipeg, Manitoba, and then continued on to Edmonton. The issue was defused in the House of Commons by Canada's American-born minister of munitions and supply, C.D. Howe. "I found that everybody there has assumed that someone had asked Canada for permission for this plane, and it was explained that the Army wished to engage this airline to do certain transport work," he said. "The necessary permission was given that very day."[32]

Members of the 388th were assigned to airfield construction in Waterways, Fort Smith and Embarras Portage in northern Alberta, but increased cargo flights didn't solve the problem of supplying Norman Wells when the Mackenzie River froze in October. A detail from Company "B" experienced the freeze firsthand. It was marooned for three weeks on an island in the Great Slave River near Fort Smith. The men had gone there to cut wood for the steamboats. When their rations started to grow scarce, they discovered that ice in the river was too heavy for boats to pick them up but not thick enough to allow them to walk out. The temperature dipped to twenty below zero before the ice thickened and they could leave.

Back in Washington, General Somervell, the Army's chief logician, realized that all the freight in Waterways wouldn't reach Norman Wells by the freeze up, so he ordered the 388th and the two white battalions to remain up north through the winter while Colonel Wyman found a solution to the transportation problem. Less than two-thirds of the freight destined for the Canol project had left Waterways. The remainder would be warehoused for the next eight or nine months unless an alternative delivery system was put into place.

Three years earlier, a tractor had dragged sleds loaded with supplies from the end of the rail at Grimshaw, Alberta, across the frozen Great Slave Lake to the goldmine center of Yellowknife, a distance of some 500 miles. Colonel Wyman decided that Caterpillar bulldozers and trucks could perform a similar operation if a thousand-mile-long winter trail was built to Camp Canol. That could only be done once the muskeg had frozen solid, enabling a trail to be cleared on top. As long as the ground remained frozen, no surfacing such as gravel was required. The 388th was called upon again, this time to help build a winter trail from Grimshaw to Fort Simpson, a distance of 414 miles. After the war, Grimshaw became Mile Zero on the Mackenzie Highway to Fort Simpson on the Mackenzie River.

The pipe and other material stored at Waterways were put on the Northern Alberta Railway and shipped south to Edmonton and then back north to the railhead of Peace River, twelve miles from Grimshaw. The camp at Camp Prairie outside of Waterways moved to Peace River and opened on October 2, 1942, as Camp Pioneer. The segregated camp housed 400 soldiers, "C" Company from the 388th and a company from the white 90th Battalion. While "C" was getting settled, "B" Company from Fort Smith was constructing a sector of the winter trail to Hay River, 193 miles of muskeg and swamp.

Since no members of "C" Company had ever driven a Caterpillar tractor before, two civilian catskinners were hired to teach them. "They showed us the procedure to operate a bulldozer. 'You're on your own,'" recalled Sgt. Franklin J. Brehon. "That was it."[33] Maintenance of the heavy equipment was assigned to civilian mechanics, but they all quit within two weeks because of the cold. On October 23, Lieutenant Gardener, the officer saved from drowning by two of his enlisted men, left camp with an integrated work crew consisting of twenty-five black soldiers and nine white soldiers from the 90th Battalion. An old wagon trail led out of Peace River, so the initial clearing was relatively easy. Immediately behind the bulldozers came civilian workers driving the freight trucks and tractors that towed between six and ten sleds each. Some Cats pulled cabooses and messes as the men ate and slept on the trail. By Thanksgiving, the tem-

Three unidentified members of the 95th Regiment warm their hands over a fire (courtesy Office of History Collection, U.S. Army Corps of Engineers).

perature had dropped to forty below and the civilian drivers started to quit because of the cold, even though they had heaters in their trucks, while the Army trucks driven by soldiers lacked heaters. One day Sergeant Brehon was sent to pick up containers of water. "By the time I got back, my hands were frozen [on the steering wheel]," he said. "The guys had to pry them off."[34] The last civilian driver quit in December.

On January 17, 1943, a tractor train with five soldiers left Fort Simpson carrying fuel and supplies to the road builders. It was twenty miles from its destination when the diesel fuel in its tank congealed at sixty degrees below zero and the Caterpillar shut down. The men decided to continue on foot; one froze a foot and another suffered hallucinations. That winter, the lowest recorded temperature on the trail was seventy-two below zero.

A battalion from the 95th Regiment was deployed from Dawson Creek in October to help on the Canol project. It teamed up with the white 35th Engineers to build a winter trail from Fort Nelson on the Alcan Highway to Fort Simpson on the Mackenzie River, a distance of 280 miles. That would enable Canol supplies brought into Skagway to be trucked on the Alcan Highway and then on to Norman Wells. The following month a company from the 93rd was assigned to work on a road from Johnson's Crossing to the access road alongside the pipeline. "It took us three weeks to build twenty-six miles, and the 'dozer then broke through the ice over an unexpected and unseen stream," said Capt. Robert Platt Boyd, Jr., commander of "C" Company. "The more we tried to get free, the worse it became stuck."[35] As that was the company's only bulldozer, the 93rd's contribution to the Canol project came to an early end.

Fifty-two members of Company "C" of the 388th who had been working on the Embarras Portage airfield were on the last riverboat from Fort Fitzgerald to Waterways on October 13, 1942, after which the river route was declared closed. Two riverboats, the sternwheeler *Mackenzie River* and the diesel-powered *Dease River*, were unable to leave Camp Canol and were ice-bound over the winter. The Army feared the spring breakup might damage the boats, so it was prepared to use trench mortars and aerial bombs if necessary to control the ice. They were not needed.

Its work done, the rest of Company "C" of the 388th was ordered to leave Peace River and take the winter trail to regimental headquarters in Fort Smith for the balance of the winter. Company "B" had built barracks in Fort Smith, while there were only tents in Peace River.

Pfc. Howard G. Conley of the 388th thought that the War Department should be apprised of work conditions on the Canol project, so he wrote a letter to Truman K. Gibson, who had replaced Judge William H. Hastie as civilian aide to Secretary of War Henry L. Stimson. "We worked in almost unbearable weather conditions. Men were freezing their hands, feet, etc., and when they would report on sick call, they would be told by our Medical Officers that nothing was wrong with them," he wrote. "If they were not marked 'Quarters' on the sick book, when they returned to their companies, they were punished by having to do a tour of extra duty. When duty called in the morning, and men would build fires to keep warm awaiting the remainder of the group, and when the Commanding Officer would come by and see such, he would kick the fires out, and speak mean words to the group. Conditions of that nature existed throughout our stay there, and we were helpless to do anything about it. If such can be investigated, and corrected, we would be quite grateful and much relieved."[36]

Conley would have received a sympathetic hearing from Philip L. Fradkin, winner of the coveted Pulitzer Prize while a reporter for the *Los Angeles Times*, who later investigated living and working conditions on the Canol project. "Seventy-seven years after the end of the Civil War, the project was to show that blacks — in this case a Negro engineer battalion — had progressed little beyond the state of slavery," Franklin wrote. "They arrived in Waterways — having taken the train direct from Camp Claiborne, Louisiana — lacking mosquito netting and repellent, proper clothing, proper outdoor training, and the knowledge of where they were and why. The troops of the 388th were to live and eat separately from whites, get the most menial jobs, be last in line for winter housing, be stationed farthest north, and generally suffer the most."[37]

Despite all the activity surrounding the Canol project, its very existence was kept secret for more than a year after the 388th Regiment and the two white battalions had been deployed to Canada's Northwest. Canadian journalist Richard Finnie, who'd later be hired by the American Army as a consultant, had anticipated the pipeline in a January 11, 1942, article in the *New York Herald Tribune* titled, "Sub-Arctic Canada's Oil Field May Supply Alaskan War Bases." That reference, however, must have been forgotten amid all the war news. Stenographers, secretaries and others at Canol headquarters in Edmonton knew about the project, of course, but were sworn to secrecy. Edmonton residents saw trucks on the street with CANOL stenciled on the sides. One writer said small boys spent long summer days spying on Canol's comings and goings at the airport and the Northern Alberta Railway yards and that Canol gossip was common at Edmonton beer parlors.[38]

When the Army announced the appointment of General O'Connor as head of the newly formed Northwest Service Command, it made no mention of the Canol project, although it was under his command. When black enlisted men Hayes and Massie saved their company commander from drowning, the awarding of the Soldier's Medal was delayed for a year for fear of revealing the Canol project. Trips to the Northwest Territories were off-limits to those who were not traveling on official business. Nor were there newspapers, as in neighboring Yukon, that could have reported on the project. The *Vancouver Sun* partially lifted the veil of secrecy in early May 1942, saying an oil pipeline would run across the top of the world. Commenting on the newspaper report, the Alaska Defense Command felt constrained about what it could say. "The undertaking has been a closely guarded secret," it reported. "Censorship still forbids disclosure of many details."[39] When Undersecretary of War Robert P. Patterson was asked a year later about the Canol project, he confirmed it. "It has been very successful," he told a press conference on June 20, 1943.[40]

Did the members of the 388th Regiment know the purpose of the project? "We knew what the project was all about," said Sgt. Wansley Hill of "B" Company assigned to regimental headquarters in Fort Smith. "The men were handling pipe, but we couldn't mention the project to anybody." Not even in letters back home. "We were told what we shouldn't mention in letters," Hill said. "Our letters were censored by the company commander in the company office before they were sent out."[41] If anything was deemed to be in violation of security, the commander would call in the enlisted man who wrote the letter, explain the situation, and ink out the words.

Most members of the 388th Regiment spent the winter of 1942-1943 in Fort Smith and Camp Canol. Those at smaller posts transferred to Fort Smith, especially as their rations began running out. Until the Army obtained winter clothing for the men, frostbite was a problem. Since there was little daylight during the short winter days, the men had difficulty watching each other for signs of frostbite: white spots on black faces meant frostbite. By February, those who had been working on the winter trail were back in camp. There was no regular work to be done. "It was just a matter of surviving

The military band of the 388th Regiment performs at Fort Smith in the Northwest Territories in 1942. Note the mosquito netting on the pianist's hat (courtesy Glenbow Archives, NA-1527-1).

the cold until spring," said Sergeant Hill. "The men cut wood for the stoves and tried to keep warm. We had to keep the trucks running so they wouldn't freeze up. That's what we did until the ice went out."[42]

Someone in the Army with a diabolical sense of humor (or no common sense) decided to send ice skates and skis to the 388th, whose members were mainly from the South and had never before seen snow, let alone practiced winter sports. A patch of snow was tamped down and flooded with water to form an ice rink. Raised in Jackson, Mississippi, Hill had never seen ice-skating in his life, but he gave it a try. "There was no enjoyment," he said. "It was just too cold."[43] There was no one to show the fundamentals of skiing to the men, so the skis mainly went unused. But movies, which started arriving in the middle of winter, were popular with the men. A band was formed among those wintering at Fort Smith, but if anyone felt like dancing, he had to do so with a fellow soldier.

During the winter, the men of "B" Company kept showing up late for roll call, much to the annoyance of the company commander. The men claimed they couldn't hear the bugle sounding reveille. Sergeant Hill decided to investigate. "I got up one morning before the bugler, a man named Bridges," he said. "When I heard the bugle, it was sticking out of a corner of the tent."[44] Bridges was sounding reveille while still warm in his sleeping bag, but his supine position didn't allow him enough wind to make the call heard clearly throughout the camp. The company commander imposed a punishment of KP (Army shorthand for Kitchen Patrol, as washing dishes and peeling potatoes was euphemistically called).

Construction of the pipeline itself had been suspended pending the results of the drilling of new wells in the Norman Wells field. Although oil had been discovered in 1920, the wells were then capped for a dozen years until successful regional mining projects provided a market for Imperial Oil's production. Nearly sixty producing wells were brought in under the Canol project, so many that the field was considered comparable to the average major field in the United States, although not up to East Texas levels.[45]

The fact that the Army was paying for the drilling and giving title to the oil to Imperial Oil and parent Standard Oil of New Jersey rankled some of the American troops. "Not many of us GIs were happy about building the Canol Pipeline Road," said one soldier from the white 35th Engineers who had been transferred from the Alcan Highway to the Canol project. "One reason was that we were building it for some big oil company, at enormous personal risk to ourselves because of the weather." He said another reason was the fact the civilian workers made more money in one or two days than the soldiers did in a month.[46]

At least one officer and seven enlisted men were killed on the Canol project, including three members of the 388th. Pfcs. Clarence Tucker and William E. Logan were burned to death in an explosion at the camp in Fort Smith. "These were some of the men I knew who gave their lives to establish a chain of airports and set up an inland defense backing up our west coast against attack," said American missionary William A. Leising.[47]

The 388th's section of the winter trail ended at Fort Simpson. Civilian contractors built the Camp Canol–Fort Simpson portion. On February 24, 1943, a bulldozer from the north met one from the south at Blackwater Lake, 150 miles south of Camp Canol. When the blades of the two Caterpillars accidentally touched, fisticuffs nearly resulted. "Why don't you look where you're going?" one civilian driver shouted. "Why don't you learn how to run a Cat?" the other yelled.[48] This hardly resembled the show of camaraderie when Sims and Jalufka of the 97th and 18th Regiments met at Beaver Creek in the Yukon to complete the linkup of the Alcan Highway. Convoys continued north from Peace River to Camp Canol until late April, when the winter trail started to turn to spring mud. Those that couldn't reach Camp Canol stopped at Fort Simpson, where the cargo was put on barges when river traffic resumed in the spring on the Mackenzie River. All the backlogged freight eventually reached Camp Canol in time.

The bulk of the civilian workers arrived in 1943: welders, carpenters, cooks, ironworkers, catskinners, crane operators, truck drivers, mechanics, office workers. They came from all over the United States—California, Oregon, Minnesota, Wisconsin, Kansas, Missouri and even New York City. The access road they built was much like the pioneer road that became the Alcan Highway: it was a rough all-weather road navigable by trucks carrying pipe, equipment and supplies. The access road was 595 miles long, but another 488 miles were built to connect the string of airstrips for cargo aircraft. Civilian employees worked on the road through the winter of 1942–1943 from both ends, setting up camps along the way. The workers adopted techniques learned on the Alcan Highway for road building over muskeg and permafrost. The winter trail was 1,000 miles long; 1,600 miles of pipeline were laid in the Northwest Territories, the Yukon and Alaska in 1942–1944.

Pipeline construction followed as soon as a stretch of road was finished. Normally pipelines are buried three or four feet below the surface. But because the ground up north is permanently frozen, pipes were supported on wooden blocks, laid on the ground and welded together. This was feasible as the crude oil had a paraffin base that allowed it to flow at temperatures down to seventy degrees below zero.

All told, the project consisted of four linked pipelines: Canol 1 from Norman Wells to Whitehorse, a distance of 595 miles; Canol 2 from Skagway to Whitehorse, a distance of 110 miles; Canol 3 from Carcross to Watson Lake, a distance of 297 miles; and Canol 4 from Whitehorse to Fairbanks, a distance of 600 miles. Canol 5, from Fairbanks to the rail connection with Anchorage at Nenana, was rejected by General Somervell, the Army's top logistics officer. Canol 6 was the name given to the winter trail on which the 388th Regiment worked.

Since a refinery built from scratch would have taken too much time, the Army looked for a used one that could be disassembled and shipped to Whitehorse. A partial refinery was found in Corpus Christi, Texas. It was dismantled and transported by rail and water to Skagway and then to Whitehorse on the White Pass and Yukon Railway at a cost of $24 million. Boilers for the refinery were found in an old power plant in Hamilton, Ontario. Turbines and generators came from an idle mill in Pinedale, California, and missing parts came from hundreds of suppliers in the United States. Although the refinery was built within the town, the Army cordoned off the area so that the facility was never seen close-up by local residents. It would become known as the most traveled refinery in the world.

As the Canol project stretched from Norman Wells to Fairbanks, the White Pass and Yukon Railway and the Alcan Highway were used for the shipment of supplies, supplementing the Waterways system. Additional dock and storage facilities had to be built at Prince Rupert (the end of rail in northwestern British Columbia) and in Skagway to handle the Canol freight.[49]

As had happened on the Alcan Highway, telephone communication was nonexistent along the route of the pipeline and in the settlements that supported the project. So a telephone line was built from Norman Wells to Whitehorse by American civilian teams under the direction of the Army Signal Corps. Holes for the poles had to be excavated by hand, sometimes with the help of dynamite, six feet in diameter and three feet deep. Horses were used to pull the poles into place and erect them. Miller Construction Company of Indianapolis, Indiana, which had worked on the Alcan Highway telephone system, also participated in building the Canol system.

12

An Unexpectedly Severe Winter

"Those deaths were deaths in battle, and I'd like those men honored."

The winter of 1942-1943 was called the coldest ever in the Far North, with the temperature dropping to seventy-two below zero and never rising above twenty below during one three-week period. Even antifreeze froze. At least four members of the 95th Regiment and two from the 97th froze to death when their trucks broke down and they tried to walk to camp. Military authorities tried to improve driver safety by threatening anyone who drove a truck into a ditch with five days of KP. Soon warm kitchens were filled with Army truck drivers.[1]

The troops weren't supposed to spend the winter up north. The original plan for Alcan Highway construction and Canol pipeline work was to transfer the Army units back to posts in the lower forty-eight until spring, leaving behind skeleton crews to guard equipment. "My instructions were to build a highway and pioneer road, as fast as we could, and that when winter came we would be brought back to the United States until spring came when we would go back to work again," said Brig. Gen. William M. Hoge. "But they reneged on that, and those men — many of them — those regiments stayed on all through the winter up there."[2]

The troops were, in fact, being penalized for having done a good job: finishing the highway ahead of schedule. Once the highway was open, the War Department decided to have troops from the engineer regiments maintain it during the winter so that truck convoys could continue without interruption from Dawson Creek to Fairbanks. The commanders of the four black regiments were apprehensive about spending the winter up north, as they had been led to believe that their enlisted men, most of them from the Deep South, wouldn't be able to stand the cold. "Our colored boys are allergic to cold weather, and it's going to be a problem to keep them well and happy I fear," one officer stated.[3]

The Army was aware of the disappointment of the men when they learned they'd be remaining up north. "There was no rejoicing among the troops at the prospect of spending a winter in the sub–Arctic regions," said one Army report. "At that time the men still were living in tents and even in August the temperature was falling steadily, with heavy rains adding to the discomfort at Camp Canol by creating areas of mud, deep and sticky."[4]

The first sergeant of "A" Company of the 388th had used the prospect of a southern winter as an incentive to get his men to improve their laundry habits. "You all who don't have your clothes washed is going to be automatically left here when we all moves out," he told his men.⁵ But soon he learned they were all staying. "We were told we'd be sent back to the States by September," said Sgt. Franklin J. Brehon of the 388th. "We finished the pipeline and orders came from Washington to stay. We were told we were going to build a road."⁶

An unnamed black soldier battles the winter of 1942-1943, when the temperature reaches seventy-two degrees below zero (courtesy Alaska State Library, Fred B. Dodge Photograph Collection, ASL-P42-100).

When the 95th Regiment reached Fort Nelson, British Columbia, in October, winter was approaching, and the men thought they were going home, as they had completed the roadwork originally assigned. "We were [then] ordered to improve the road to Watson Lake," said Master Sgt. George H. Burke. "There was already snow on the ground, the weather was bitterly cold and we were still living in tents. All of us were disappointed because we had hoped that when we had completed our section of the road we would be transferred back to the United States. We got busy, set up our own sawmill to cut lumber for a camp and started work on the new section."⁷

"Our regimental commander had told our troops that as soon as they met the regiment to the south we were just going to go down the road and go back home," said Lt. Walter Parsons of the 97th Regiment. "Now that wasn't a clever thing to say."⁸ One member of his regiment was so disconsolate about having to spend the winter up north that he decided to shoot off a toe so he could be invalided home. He missed and shot off his foot. He was dishonorably discharged.⁹

The 97th's problems began shortly after the October 25 meeting with the 18th Regiment at Beaver Creek, thus completing the road. The regiment had continued southwest, improving the section of the road to the nearby White River at milepost 1169 built by the 18th. "The colonel [Lionel E. Robinson] had been promised portable barracks for winter quarters when he arrived at the White River," said Warren Duesenberg, who with his brother, Milton, ran an Indianapolis, Indiana, contracting company that followed the 97th and made improvements to the road. "When we got there, there were no barracks. They were still in tents; the temperature was falling to forty below zero; food would freeze in their mess kits before they could eat."¹⁰ Duesenberg brought portable barracks for his workers.

Boulton B. Miller, a colonel assigned to the Northwest Service Command in

Whitehorse, said some units of the 97th Regiment were "cut off and frozen in" during the winter of 1942-1943. "Most of them were from Louisiana and found the severe cold of lower than fifty degrees below zero a major problem," he said.[11] Doing road maintenance, one company of the 97th Regiment found itself so far from its supply base in Whitehorse to the east that it was running out of food, fuel and proper winter clothing. "We went up there and didn't have but little pup tents, in forty below zero," said Clifton B. Monk. "I had one blanket, my buddy had one blanket, and an Army jacket."[12] By April of 1943 much of the regiment was transferred to Big Delta, one hundred miles southeast of Fairbanks. "The bugle would blow us out in the morning, but we'd be up to our hips in snow, so they stopped," said Sgt. Hayward Oubre of the 97th. "We had to survive. We had to find wood because we'd all freeze to death."[13]

The Northwest Service Command made a surprise visit to the 97th on a day when the temperature was sixty-eight below zero. It found the clothing of the troops to be in "abominable condition," as were their "wretched" living quarters. "The pathetically ill-equipped 97th is doing little but hibernating at present," it said.[14]

The ordeal of the 97th during the winter of 1942-1943 even merited a poem:

> It's a hooded troop of frozen men
> And for them you can hand out cheers,
> It's that fighting gang of Uncle Sam 97th Engineers.[15]

The poem was written by Frank C. Lee, who served in the 9th Battalion, 6th Infantry, in World War I. The cadence is similar to that found in the poems of Robert Service, the poet laureate of the Klondike Gold Rush.

Despite efforts at maintenance, the highway was closed for many weeks during the winter because of a northern phenomenon: water from underground warm springs flowed into culverts and ditches and onto the road, eventually freezing, making driving too difficult and dangerous. Rivers would freeze from the bottom up, pushing up mounds of ice that knocked out twenty-four of the 130 bridges on the highway.

The white 340th Regiment was losing a battle against ice that threatened to destroy a wooden bridge on the Upper Liard River in the Yukon. Members of the 95th Regiment were assigned to replace the white engineers. "This meant sending naked men into the water at well-below-zero temperatures," reported a stringer for *Time* magazine. "The longest the poor devils could stand it was fifteen to twenty minutes — when they would become paralyzed and numb and another relay would replace them. Some were so stiff and cold they had to be fished out."[16] The black soldiers were wrapped in blankets and taken back to camp to warm up.

Members of the 388th in the Northwest Territories were mainly divided between Fort Smith and Camp Canol, living in barracks or log cabins they had built themselves in anticipation of winter. It was so cold in Fort Smith that Sgt. George Young was able to preserve a side of fresh moose meat under his bunk. "It was like a refrigerator inside," he said.[17] Young had bought the moose meat from natives; he'd cut off a chunk and cook it for himself and his roommates whenever they wanted a change from mess-hall fare.

Tent life was challenging during the winter. When the troops moved, they had difficulty just setting up their tents: it was impossible to drive wooden stakes into the frozen ground. Steel spikes would be hammered in and water poured around them. They'd freeze in so hard there was no possibility of the tent coming down.[18] "We had heaters in the tents," said Sgt. Reginald Beverly of the 95th. "Around thirty or forty below zero the frost would form about an inch inside the tent. That was like insulation so we were warm."[19] Pfc. Nathaniel Dulin of the 95th felt so comfortable in his sleeping bag one morning that he refused to leave his tent. "It was way below zero," he said. "We were supposed to remove ice from the road. I stayed in my tent."[20] It took a visit from the company commander and a first sergeant to get him to the work detail. They must have sympathized with him, for he received no punishment. "When the cold weather came, I had my men make stoves out of oil drums and I had men cutting wood and keeping fire around the clock in the tents," said Sgt. Otis E. Lee of the 95th. "Nobody ever took off their clothes, took a bath. We slept in our clothes for weeks on end."[21] If clothes got too stiff to wear, they were boiled in a fuel can on the tent stove. "We didn't do a lot of changing in the winter time," explained Sgt. Lee Young of the 97th. "We didn't get lousy. I don't think the lice could live up there."[22] If there was a large enough tent available, the men would erect one-man tents inside. "That kept the frost off our little tents," said Young.[23]

The Army supplied kerosene heaters to many of the units. "This seemed like a great arrangement until we discovered that no kerosene would be issued because, like everything else in the Army in 1942, it was in short supply," said one company commander with the 93rd Regiment.[24] He converted the heater to burn wood; others used gasoline instead, a more dangerous solution given its flammability. Eugene Long of the 95th told of a soldier named Woodson being burned by an exploding stove as he slept in his sleeping bag, which was really two sleeping bags in one. The men got into the first one and then wiggled into the second one. "I got stuck in it one time," Long said. "I decided every time I got in that sleeping bag I'd have a knife with me."[25] Long, who visited Woodson in the hospital, said he believed the soldier died of his burns. Some men found a use for sleeping bags other than sleeping: they cut armholes in them and wore them as coats.

The men literally risked life and limb during the winter. "At one point, we couldn't stay outside more than an hour because your feet would start to freeze and you wouldn't feel it," said Sgt. Anthony Mouton. "We had to go in and put our bare feet in a bucket of snow, which we didn't feel. When we started feeling cold, we knew we had circulation back in our feet."[26] "The harsh, inhumane weather of Alaska, compounded by the inadequate and improper clothing, multiplied by the racism displayed toward blacks by the white officers in command, made it an almost intolerable situation," stated Paul W. Francis of the 93rd Regiment, which spent the latter part of the winter in the Aleutians.

"These same conditions resulted in my toes freezing and other medical problems brought on by their freezing. We were treated like convict labor."[27]

Francis was right in his complaint about clothing, at least as far as boots and gloves were concerned. Some gloves issued to the men had an opening for trigger fingers that had to be sewn up. And the Army-issue boots for winter were all-leather. "The boots they gave us were very nice, but they couldn't stand the cold. They'd freeze," said Sgt. Jesse Balthazar of the 97th. "The boys found it better just to wear plain galoshes and wear two or three pair of socks. That's what just about everybody would wear."[28] Some men used their boots — inside their tents — as a weather gauge. "You can tell how cold the temperature is by the number of eyelets that can be laced before the fingers can no longer hold the shoelaces," said one man. "After you warm your hands under your armpits, you can continue the lacing of the boots."[29] "Several layers of light clothing is infinitely warmer than a single layer of equal weight," the Army counseled.[30] It also warned the men that they risked freezing to death when their inner clothing became saturated with moisture from perspiration, drawing heat from their body.

The Northwest Service Command in Whitehorse conceded in a report stamped SECRET that there was a problem: "The issue of arctic clothing under present T.B.A. [Table of Basic Allowances] is inadequate to provide sufficient clothing for troops."[31] Solution: more outer clothing. Before the winter was over, each man was issued a knee-length fur-lined water-repellent parka with wolverine fur around the face, an arctic blanket-lined jacket, a fur cap with ear flaps, kersey-lined duck pants, a pair of water-repellent pants, a pair of fur gloves joined together by a strong cord that went behind the collar to keep from losing them, knee-length lace-up boots, and a pair of shoepacs with rubber feet and leather tops, plus woolen underwear and turtleneck sweaters. Many of the men, especially on the Canol project in the Northwest Territories, traded their Army-issue clothing for native winter garb: caribou-skin coats, gloves and moccasins.

How did the black soldiers fare in the cold? "During the most severe weather encountered, it is believed that Negro troops, properly led, have accomplished more physical labor than other troops in the same area engaged in similar work," according to Lt. Col. James L. Lewis of the 93rd Regiment, who wrote a report on the subject.[32] One of his company commanders, Capt. Robert Platt Boyd, wrote, "On one occasion when the temperature fell to seventy-two degrees below zero for one three-week period, they got along as well as anyone else. We employed the buddy system in Company 'C.' No one was allowed outside alone in sub freezing weather."[33]

Col. Walter F. von Zelinski, chief medical officer in Whitehorse, agreed that the black soldiers successfully withstood the cold. "We have learned a significant thing," he said. "The Negro can stand the heat better than the white man, and he stands the cold just as well. We may have a few more frozen ears and faces among the Negroes because they're more likely to expose themselves unnecessarily. But the Negro piles on all the clothes he's issued and goes right ahead with his work."[34]

Many black soldiers, such as this member of the 388th Regiment, traded their military-issue clothing for Indian garb (courtesy Archives Canada).

A Canadian trapper who lived at Charlie Lake in British Columbia, Pen Powell, described how some members of the 95th Regiment piled on clothes during the winter. "No Eskimo could touch 'em for clothes," he said. "There was no end to what they could pile on, and, of course, I guess the cantina or wherever they was gettin' those damn things, there was no end, they'd just give 'em everythin.' Christ, their feet'd be that long, great big fat boots, one end tied to the other. And they wouldn't get out of 'em for two or three weeks at a time 'til a Chinook would come, you know, and warm it up a little bit."[35]

Talking to a reporter, Staff Sgt. Augustus Chandler of the 97th said, "Tell the

Unidentified members of the 95th Regiment demonstrate the parkas issued for the winter (courtesy Office of History Collection, U.S. Army Corps of Engineers).

readers that we can take it. When we first arrived in Alaska, it was said that we were used to warm weather and that we could not stand too cold a climate, but after more than a year there, oftimes with not enough clothes or food, we have worked and are still living."36

One white officer had his own take on black troops and cold weather. "Most Negro soldiers fear they will have some more or less permanent effects from living in extreme cold and wet cold climates," he said in a report. "There is a common belief that each individual 'stores up cold in his chest' that only warm sunshine can eliminate and that the lasting effects of which are never overcome completely. Rheumatism, tuberculosis and arthritis are the diseases most feared and many believe that an individual cannot help losing his mind if he stays in such a climate very long."37

Capt. Richard L. Neuberger of the Northwest Service Command likened the hardships on the Alcan Highway during the winter of 1942-1943 to those of the Klondike days. "During the last great influx into the Yukon, that of the Klondike Gold Rush in 1898, men had died along the trail every day during December, January and February," he said. "The trek to Whitehorse and Dawson City was studded with pain. The present Yukon migration rivals that of '98."38

The winter was hard not only on the troops but also on their equipment, from bulldozers and trucks down to the common axe and hammer. Since steel loses its elasticity in extreme cold, the treads on the bulldozers would split, often obliging the work crews to abandon them rather than trying to repair them. Axes and hammers left outside had to be warmed before use; otherwise, the frozen handles would break with the first blow. But the main problem was with the trucks. If the temperature wasn't too low, some company commanders kept a bulldozer operating twenty-four hours a day to tow trucks in order to get them started. During the night, some commanders would have an enlisted man start a truck and drive it around for fifteen minutes in first gear and then take it back to its parking spot; he'd then repeat the operation for other trucks. When the weather was really cold, such as thirty or forty degrees below zero, all vehicles would be run around the clock. "I remember that it was so cold that the antifreeze we had to put in the trucks would freeze, so we had to run the truck twenty-four hours a day," said Sergeant Mouton of the 93rd.[39]

When a vehicle was fueled in cold weather, gasoline would be strained through a chamois cloth to remove as much water as possible and reduce the possibility of stoppages. Often the fuel line would freeze up when the vehicle was moving. The driver would then remove the fuel line with a wrench, thaw it out with a blowtorch and reinstall it. Sometimes this would have to be repeated every thirty minutes. "The drivers would use airplane gas as fuel in the trucks because it wouldn't freeze up like regular gas," said Sergeant Balthazar of the 97th.[40] After serving with the 97th, driver Clemmie L. Herron, Technician Fourth Grade, was transferred to the 770th Engineer Dump Truck Company, a newly activated black unit at Camp Butner, North Carolina. A taciturn man, after being asked if he was happy to be back, he finally replied, "Too cold up there. Yes, too damn cold!"[41]

Until the drivers learned how to deal with a stalled truck, their ignorance could be fatal. "I had some men coming back from a furlough in the States. They were driving a Studebaker truck that wasn't made for the north, should've been sent to Florida," said Sergeant Lee of the 95th. "The fuel line iced up and they probably didn't have the tools to get that ball of ice out of there. They tried to walk to the nearest camp to get help. They died along the way, three of them."[42] After that, Lee, who was in charge of the motor pool, placed an oil drum cut in half in every truck so that a driver could pour in gasoline and make a fire if he became stranded. Another member of the 95th died near Coal River on the Alcan Highway in British Columbia, near the Yukon border, when he stopped to rest after abandoning his frozen truck.

A lieutenant and an enlisted man from "E" Company of the 97th had left in a Studebaker truck in February of 1943 to pick up gas and diesel fuel. On the way back, the truck froze and the pair started walking back, the officer literally pulling along the enlisted man. Realizing both ran the risk of dying, the lieutenant left the black soldier and walked another ten miles to camp. A search party found the enlisted man on the third day, frozen in a sitting position. "After that, we built sheds every ten miles along our stretch of highway with a stove and food so that no one would be further than five miles from camp," said Sgt. William E. Griggs of the 97th.[43] A second member of the 97th died on the Slana cut-off in Alaska when his truck broke down. "Brush and cleared-away timber slashings enabled him to build a fire alongside the road," said Captain Neuberger of the Northwest Service Command. "Had he stuck by the fire, eventually he would have been rescued but he decided to walk the fourteen miles to camp. He froze to death on the way. The temperature was sixty-six degrees below zero that afternoon."[44]

Yukon native Harold Chambers, whose father was an Army guide, was twelve years old when he saw the body of a black soldier in a truck beside the road: "He was a Negro and he froze to death. He ran out of gas and that was it."[45] Local resident Oscar Albanati was driving a truck from Fort Nelson to Dawson Creek when he came upon a stopped Army convoy. He walked up to the lead truck and saw a black soldier leaning under the hood. "I gave him a tap on the shoulder and he fell over," said Albanati. "He was dead, frozen stiff."[46]

Local Canadian residents, and even some white troops, felt sorry for the black troops during the winter — not the calendar season of December 21 to March 20, but the northern winter that can cover nine months of freezing temperatures. Charlie Taylor's family ran a trading post where the Army often bought supplies. His father once sold all of his candles so that the black troops could have light in their tents during the winter, when darkness in December can last for most of the day. Taylor said the black troops, members of the 93rd Regiment, were so far removed from their Southern hometowns that they could have been on the moon. "They just shivered the whole winter," he said.[47] Mel Clarke farmed with his father near Dawson Creek during the war. "When we heard they wanted to build a highway up there, it sounded to us like going to Mars. And when we saw those boys from down South who were supposed to build it, well, we felt sorry for them."[48] Jim Sutton, a white American soldier, noted that the black troops were forced to live in tents, but not the white troops: "They were up here when we got here. We were put in barracks, wooden barracks, and we had stoves and everything."[49] Said Charles Russell, a self-described cowboy from California and catskinner with the 35th Regiment: "These black fellows, they had ... I don't understand it. They couldn't vote. But they drafted them. And then stick them in here, something like this."[50]

The winter experience was similar in all the black regiments. "Living in seventy-two-degree-below zero weather, we had frozen fingers, frozen ears," said Sgt. Nehemiah Atkinson of the 97th. "The tissue on your face would be burned off."[51] "Just about everybody got a little burn," noted Sgt. Lee Young of the 97th. "I had frostbite on my ears and nose and frosted feet. You couldn't eat with a fork, just sticking it in your mouth, your lip would stick to it."[52] He said the men had to warm their forks on their clothing before using them. "One man owned a brass whistle," said Sgt. Frank J. Brehon of the 388th. "When he blew it one day it froze to his lips. The skin tore away when it was removed."⁵³ "When they sent us back to the States, my feet were so frostbitten that I could scrape about half an inch of dead skin off them," recalled Sgt. George Young of the 388th. "It was terribly cold up there."⁵⁴ Said Paul W. Francis of the 93rd Regiment: "You'd see kids, eighteen or nineteen, crying like babies because they were so cold. You almost wanted to put them out of their misery."⁵⁵ Wesley Davis, a member of the 95th from Winter Haven, Florida, said, "I tell you, the first thing that comes to your mind is the cold. The cold and the living conditions really got your attention right away."⁵⁶ "Some of our men are reported to have lost their ears and other members of their bodies in the bitter cold," the *Chicago Defender* newspaper reported.⁵⁷ According to Pfc. Alexander Powell of Quincy, Florida, "With all that cold, it would come back to thirty or thirty-five below, it would actually feel warm to you."⁵⁸

How cold was it during the winter? Shaving cream froze inside the tent. A scotch and soda would freeze before it could be mixed. "I've seen the time when it was so cold they'd tell you not to open your mouth to breathe," said Staff Sgt. Clifton B. Monk of the 97th. "Breathe through your nose or your lungs would freeze up and you'd be dead. I've woke up in the morning and had ice in my nose where the fire in the diesel oil drums had gone out in the night."⁵⁹ Said Joseph Haskin of the 93rd: "It was so cold that if you spit, it would be a little ball of ice before it hit the ground."⁶⁰ "If you had a five-gallon container of water inside the tent, the next morning it would be ice," said Jesse Balthazar of the 97th. "And it was an experience going to the outhouse in the winter."⁶¹ The Army physician assigned to the Northwest Service Command in Whitehorse, Capt. Walter Tatum, did not take lightly the problem of winter treks to the outhouse. "In deep snow men are inclined not to use the latrines, particularly if they are out of doors," he said in a memo to commanders on the Alcan Highway. "It will be necessary for all commanders to take appropriate measures to see the ground is not polluted. Extra precautions now will pay dividends in the spring."⁶²

The black soldiers tried to use humor to help them through the winter. Seeing snow for the first time and hearing of Japanese raids, an enlisted man from Georgia said to the company lieutenant, "If them thar Japs come over here a-bombin' they jest couldn't miss us pore darkies — we all'd show up jest like flies in a milk bottle."⁶³ During a blizzard, one soldier commented, "Boy, we're certainly going to show up well against this background."⁶⁴ Catholic Bishop Jean Louis Coudert met a member of the 93rd guarding a bridge at Carcross in the Yukon and commented on how bundled up the soldier was. "You look like you're well dressed," the bishop said. "Are you cold?"

"Man, I sure *am* cold!"

"Well, what do you think of the Yukon?"

"Yukon? *Yukon* have it!"⁶⁵

Canadian war correspondent Peter Stursberg was walking through the camp of the 95th Regiment near Fort Nelson looking for someplace to get warm when he heard singing coming from a tent:

> Oh Lawd, I'se happy 'cause I'se warm
> Oh Lawd, I'se happy and warm

"The Negroes had not lost their native wit or cheerfulness despite the fact that they were in such a different climate," he said.[66]

There was little good cheer in the camps of the black soldiers on Christmas Day 1942. Since "A" Company of the 97th was literally isolated at Beaver Creek, the regiment's commander, Colonel Robinson, had frozen Christmas turkeys dropped by plane for the men. Unfortunately, the birds took two days to thaw in the cook shack mounted on a sled.[67] Capt. Albert L. Smith of Pittsburgh, chaplain of the 97th, remembered the temperature being seventy-two below that Christmas Day.[68] "I didn't even think about Christmas," said Sgt. John A. Bollin of "F" Company of the 93rd. "There was no turkey. I believe there was some Spam."[69] Anthony Mouton of "A" Company of the 93rd had beef hash that Christmas. "It was so lonely," he said. "I spent most of the day in my tent with John Lockott from Philadelphia. We had a record player and one record that was cracked, a record by Paul Whiteman and Helen Forrest, 'Serenade in Blue.' We played that all day long, just to hear something from home."[70] The lyrics tell of longing for a loved one left behind.

The headquarters company of the 97th Regiment spent Christmas and New Year's at an abandoned gold mining camp at Livengood, fifty miles north of Fairbanks. "There were old cabins there, but they were comfortable," said Sgt. Hayward Oubre. There were a couple of indigenous families living there among the old mining dredges. Oubre and other NCOs chipped in and asked an Army driver to buy them a shortwave radio the next time he made a trip to Fairbanks. "We heard Bing Crosby singing for the first time 'I'm Dreaming of a White Christmas,'" Oubre said.[71] They'd hear it many times that Christmas. The temperature dipped to seventy below zero, but the heavens cooperated. "The Northern Lights were like a Broadway show," Oubre added.[72]

Other companies of the 97th were spread around the Alaska Highway. Company "C" spent Christmas in wooden shacks built by civilian contractors at Cathedral Rapids, 150 miles east of Fairbanks. It moved to Livengood early in the spring of 1943.

Fred Spencer and some other members of the 93rd shared Christmas dinner with Canadian troops in Whitehorse after white American soldiers refused to eat at the same time and in the same mess hall as black soldiers. "We were to have Christmas dinner at a big mess hall that could seat 2,000 or 3,000 at once," Spencer said. "The black soldiers wasn't allowed to go into the mess hall with white soldiers. The white soldiers got together and decided the black soldiers could eat alone first on Christmas Day. But the Canadian Army didn't go along with this. So the Canadians ate with us. The white American soldiers were standing around outside waiting for us to finish. It was a cruel thing."[73] The men from the 93rd were in Whitehorse awaiting transfer to the Chilkoot Barracks in Alaska.

The severe winter produced an unusual court-martial when ten members of Company "F" of the 97th Regiment refused to board an open truck in thirty-degree-below-

During a New Year's Eve celebration, bunkmates of the 97th's Headquarters staff ring in 1943 by holding photographs of their wives or girlfriends. At the far right is Sgt. Hayward Oubre of New Orleans (courtesy William E. Griggs).

zero weather for a 138-mile trip. All the men were found guilty of mutiny at a military trial in Whitehorse and sentenced to prison, with the first sergeant, James M. Heard, from Elberton, Georgia, receiving the longest sentence: twenty years, one for each year that he had lived. According to testimony, Heard had told his men they'd be "damn fools" to ride in a truck that lacked a canvas cover and had ice and snow on its bed. He said he had heard that the Northwest Service Command issued orders that no one should ride in the back of a truck at thirty below. Less than a year later, all the men were back in uniform after their convictions were overturned.

This incident occurred on March 29, 1943, at Big Gerstle, Alaska, where the men had been on loan to another company to work on the bridge there. They were being taken to Fairbanks to rejoin their company. Sergeant Heard had gone to the orderly room to speak to the commanding officer, Lt. Dewitt C. Howell, promoted to captain by the time the three-day court-martial began on June 5. "The gist of the conversation was that it was too cold to make the trip and he rather questioned my authority," testified Howell. "I told the first sergeant to line up the men. When I went out to the trucks, the men were standing there in a group in front of them.... I pointed out that [mutiny] was a very serious crime and punishable by death."[74] Howell gave the men ten seconds to board the truck. When they refused, they were arrested, taken to Whitehorse and put in the stockade pending trial.

Capt. Walter Parsons, former commander of "F" Company, had been transferred to the Canol project to work on construction of the oil refinery in Whitehorse, since he had spent a decade in the oil business in his native Texas. When he heard that ten men whom he once commanded were now in the stockade, he visited them. They asked him to join their defense team, even though he had no legal experience. None of the officers hearing the case — most were attached to the Northwest Service Command or the Canol project — had worked on the highway or commanded black troops.

"They are of a different race," Parsons told the court. "That is no fault of theirs, but I bring it up because I want you to remember that, when it comes time to vote on the guilt or innocence of these men, they are of a different race that has not had the advantages you have had. Their advantages have been disadvantages. Many of them are from the South. You, who are from the South, know the schooling these men get." He said the accused were used to working at forty and fifty below zero. "But try riding in a truck when it is thirty degrees below zero," he said. "You'll find it's quite different." He concluded, "These men are guilty of nothing more serious than minor disobedience."[75] The military jury thought otherwise. Besides Heard, those sentenced were as follows: Pvt. Sims Bridges, age twenty-two, sentenced to eighteen years; Pvt. Lee I. Ratliff, nineteen, sentenced to twelve years; Pvts. Willie L. Howell and Robert M. Rucker, both twenty-four, sentenced to five years. The others were sentenced to three years: Pvts. Willie B. Calhoun, nineteen; James V. Hollingsworth, twenty; Josh Weaver, twenty-two; Warren H. Lindy, twenty-one; and Pfc. Eugene Fulks, twenty-four. An eleventh soldier was in the latrine when the others refused to board the truck. He, too, ended up in the stockade but was released before the court-martial.

Six weeks later, the Army's judge advocate eliminated the sentences of five of the men and reduced those of the others. "Considering all the facts in the case, including extenuating circumstances, the age of each of the accused, and no previous convictions, it is believed that the interests of justice and discipline will be best served by reducing the sentences," the judge advocate said.[76] The following year, Maj. Gen. C.H. Danielson of the War Department announced that all the men had been cleared of any misconduct.[77] "Their actions were found to constitute common sense, not mutiny."[78] Sergeant Heard returned to duty on May 12, 1944.

(Shortly after work started on the Alcan Highway near the tail end of the winter of 1941-1942, Brig. Gen. Clarence L. Sturdevant, assistant chief of the Corps of Engineers, had written a memorandum about the dangers of transporting troops in the back of trucks during freezing weather: "Men transported in trucks could scarcely walk upon arrival at destination. Once dragged inside a tent and piled near a fire, they fell quickly asleep. Some of the officers and non-commissioned, who were determined to keep going, soon learned to keep away from fires." Sturdevant was saying that under these circumstances sleep could become permanent.[79])

No official record of deaths — either military or civilian — on the Alcan Highway and the Canol pipeline was kept. It is estimated that fewer than one hundred people were drowned, frozen to death or killed in accidents. A stretch of highway in the Yukon known as Suicide Hill, a thirty-two-degree grade with a right angle at the bottom, was the scene of many fatalities. George Ford, who as a University of Alberta engineering student worked on the highway in 1942, said he was camped at the foot of the hill when a transport truck tipped over, killing thirty-two soldiers. "We had to pick up the bodies," he said.[80] When the operations ended on both projects, the Army disinterred the bodies of thirty-four Americans buried during the war in the Whitehorse cemetery and took them back to the United States for reburial.[81]

Lt. Col. Lionel E. Robinson, commander of the 97th Regiment, felt that soldiers who fought a losing battle against nature should be recognized as if they died in combat. "Those deaths were deaths in battle, and I'd like those men honored," the colonel said.[82]

13

Surviving Isolation

"We couldn't enjoy ourselves much in the wilderness."

When the Army decided in 1942 to appease Brig. Gen. Simon Bolivar Buckner by keeping the black troops out of northern settlements, it made a bad situation even worse for members of the 93rd, 95th, 97th and 388th regiments. All troops on the Alcan Highway and Canol projects had to battle the same tough terrain and weather. But the white troops could go into town to relax and meet people who looked like themselves. The black troops were barred from settlements, and even if they did manage to get into town, there were virtually no other black people up north. When the only black resident of Dawson City died in 1942, the local newspaper judged the death worthy of a story.[1] The white troops had service clubs such as the Red Cross that didn't admit blacks; the black troops didn't get their only Red Cross center until they were about to leave the Far North. Places like Whitehorse, Dawson Creek and Fairbanks had brothels patronized mainly by white soldiers and contract workers because black soldiers were kept out of these towns.

"It was a lonely time," said Staff Sgt. Clifton B. Monk of his assignment up north with the 97th Regiment. "We couldn't enjoy ourselves much in the wilderness."[2] "They didn't want black men coming in contact with any people. We were ostracized," said Hayward L. Oubre, like Monk a sergeant with the 97th.[3] According to another individual, "The officers' wives were flown in to be with them. But we didn't have that."[4] "When we arrived, we were taken from the train station to a cow pasture," said Pfc. Nathaniel Dulin of the 95th. "When 'A' Company left, we were taken directly to the train station. In between, we saw no towns or settlements. We had to stay on base. We weren't allowed to go to town."[5] Pvt. Henry Easter joined the 95th in Dawson Creek for its final three months in Canada. "I understood before I got to Dawson Creek that you weren't supposed to go into town," said Easter, a personnel clerk. "I never went in to Dawson Creek."[6] Said Joseph Haskin of the 93rd: "It was modern-day slavery for the Negro troops. They kept you where they wanted you. We wasn't allowed to go into villages."[7] Staff Sgt. Linton Freeman, a native of Georgia and member of the 95th, said, "There was not a thing up there. No towns. Nothing but trees. Even in the summer it was an awful, dusty affair. Almost unbearable. It brought out all that was in you, just to survive."[8] Willie Richardson, a member of the 93rd from Quincy, Florida, said the isolation bothered him. "I'd never been out of civilization so long," he said. "I was used

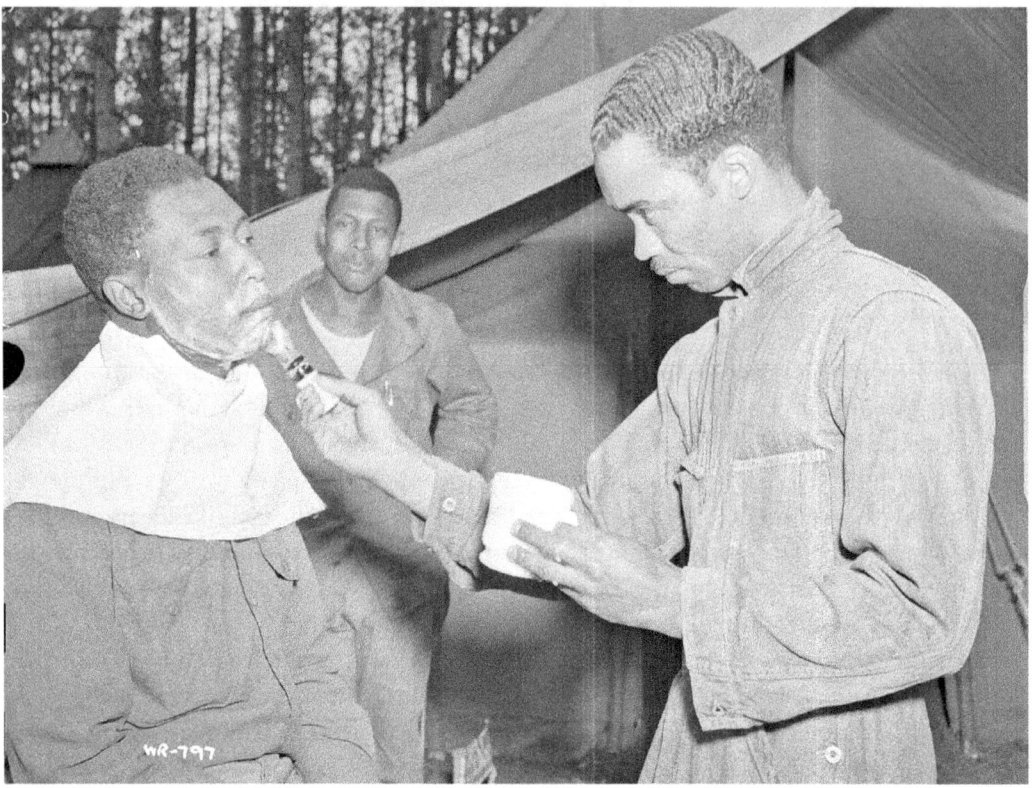

This unidentified soldier is getting all spruced up but there are no girls up north he's allowed to meet (courtesy Office of History Collection, U.S. Army Corps of Engineers).

to being with the girls."[9] According to Paul W. Francis, also of the 93rd, "One of the first things we heard: 'Don't go to town and don't say a word to the ladies.'"[10] Joseph Haskin added, "We were like [being] kept on a reservation. We couldn't go out and explore in the neighborhood or nothing."[11]

Canadian Allen W. Sowden recalled an incident in Fort St. John when three members of the 95th Regiment stationed at Charlie Lake walked the seven miles into town, where a monthly dance was being held. They were dancing with local girls when American military police armed with .45 caliber sidearms came looking for them. "The black soldiers ran out the back door," said Sowden, a teenager at the time. His mother ran a boarding house just 200 feet from the dance hall, and one of the soldiers sought refuge there. "He was really scared and said if he was caught they would shoot him," Sowden said. "My mother gave him a room overnight and didn't charge him. Up north, black or white didn't make any difference to us. They were just people. We couldn't figure out why the white American soldiers treated the blacks so differently."[12] The soldier left early the next morning to walk back to camp. Sowden said a second soldier also made it back but the third was arrested.

The lack of female companionship led some black soldiers to experiment with same-sex affairs. "The isolation became a serious problem," said photographer William E. Griggs of the 97th Regiment. "One of the serious problems was men acting like women."[13] Griggs took a photo of eighteen smiling young enlisted men that, years later, he anachronistically titled "Gay Boys Club." He said he assumed they were all heterosexuals frustrated by the remoteness of their camp.

Some of the commanders anticipated the impending isolation and joked about it with the troops. "Our commander told us, 'Men, don't worry, every tree you'll see, you'll see a woman behind it,'" said Albert E. France, a native of Cooksville, Maryland, who was a sergeant with Company "A" of the 93rd Regiment.[14] Staff Sgt. Otis E. Lee of the 95th was told the same tale, as were John A. Bollin of the 93rd and William Griggs of the 97th. "When we left the U.S., we were told there'd be lots of women up north," said Lee. "We'd find one behind every tree. They had stories in the Army about how nice it was going to be."[15]

The isolation of the black troops drew the sympathy of some of their commanders. Lt. Col. James L. Lewis of the 93rd said he understood that the problems that black soldiers up north had were unlike those of white soldiers. "Negroes are gregarious as a rule and like mixed gatherings, music, and opportunities to mingle with other people," he said. "On the highway and in the Aleutians there were no people outside of the regiment with whom they could associate freely. Natives of Alaska and Canada treated them with feelings of apprehension and distrust. The complete isolation of soldiers of this unit has made their problems in this respect far more serious than the average white soldier."[16] He added, "The average Negro soldier has felt keenly the absence of women, particularly those of his own race, throughout his overseas duty. Most conversations touch on the subject of sex before they are terminated."[17] Another colonel said, "I'm sorry for the first town they hit when they get away from here."[18]

Such a town was Dawson Creek on February 2, 1943, a Tuesday night. A black soldier from the 95th Regiment newly arrived from a wilderness camp assaulted a nurse while she was walking down the street. Maj. Samuel R. Dighton of the Corps of Military Police was sympathetic in the report he filed with Brig. Gen. James A. O'Connor, commander of the Northwest Service Command in Whitehorse. "Should I say here that these men had been in the bush for nine months and hadn't seen women in that time? White troops were able to see women," he wrote.[19] A military court sentenced the soldier to fifteen years in prison.[20] A member of the 388th was arrested in Fort McMurray, Alberta, and charged with assault of a white woman with intent to commit a felony, a case said to have outraged local authorities. He was quickly court-martialed and sentenced to twenty years at hard labor in Fort Leavenworth, Kansas.[21]

A fire in Dawson Creek ended the isolation for the 95th Regiment. On February 13, 1943, a driver for the Oman and Smith Construction Company parked his truck loaded with sixty cases of dynamite and twenty cases of percussion caps in the town's

Bentley livery stable while he ate dinner before heading north to Fort St. John. His cargo was destined for construction crews erecting the Army's Edmonton-to-Fairbanks telephone line. Since it was Saturday night, the streets of the town were packed. The driver, Glen Barnhardt, was finishing his meal when a fire broke out in the stable, which still had hay in the second-floor loft. Once apprised of the existence of the dynamite, local firemen tried to warn away onlookers, but to no avail. Passengers from a packed train that arrived during the fire augmented the crowd. "American military police brandishing automatics were trying to press back the solid crowd," said Dorthea Calverley, a Canadian government employee who witnessed the fire.[22]

The dynamite exploded at 6:37 P.M.—the clock on the Canadian Bank of Commerce building marked the time for several years—sending a fireball into the night sky. Six people were killed, including an American soldier who was struck by a flying keg of nails, and 164 injured. The blast rattled windows six miles away in the town of Pouce Coupé, from which water was hauled to fight the fire as Dawson Creek had none of its own. Due to the scarcity of water, firefighters didn't try to extinguish the fire but instead watered down nearby buildings to prevent it from spreading. The U.S. Army provided firefighting equipment and troops to help contain the fire. None of the soldiers were black, as members of the 95th Regiment, then stationed outside of Dawson Creek, were forbidden from entering the town.

The fire destroyed one of the town's six square blocks, leveling all businesses, hotels and restaurants except the Dawson Co-op Union store. Not a single café was left untouched. Three American doctors were flown in from Edmonton to help attend to the injured. The Army flew nine of the most badly burned to Edmonton. Many of the injured had been blown away by the blast from rooftops where they had gone to witness the fire. Many other people were left homeless by the destruction of the Dawson Hotel, the town's largest.[23] A Canadian living in London said he heard Lord Ha-Ha, the Briton found guilty of treason after the war for his role as a Nazi propagandist, mention the fire on the day it occurred: "Attention. Fifteen minutes ago Dawson Creek at the beginning of the Alcan Highway was blown up and the whole place is now on fire."[24]

As tired firefighters, both civilian and military, needed to rest, the Army relented and sent members of the 95th into town. Issued rifles, they initially guarded damaged buildings. Later they also cleaned up debris, boarded up missing doors and windows, and directed traffic.[25] Then they helped the Army rebuild Dawson Creek by putting in a water system from Pouce Coupé to the town. For some time, more black soldiers than white were seen on the town's streets. Good will was needed on the part of the Army as anti–American feelings ran high. The town council resigned in a dispute over how much compensation should be demanded from the United States.[26] The Miller Construction Company of Indianapolis was charged with "criminal negligence" but a judge threw out the case on the grounds that the company was unaware that a subcontractor—Oman and Smith—had stored the dynamite in the livery stable it leased.

Among the black soldiers active in the aftermath of the fire was Pfc. Charles

English, of Braeholm, West Virginia, photographer for the 95th Regiment, who recorded the damage with his camera. Local residents complimented English, who was drafted out of West Virginia State College, on the businesslike and gentlemanly way he did his work. He received a commendation from Col. Albert L. Lane, commander of the 95th: "Your work reflects great credit on yourself, your organization and the United States Army."27

Before the 95th moved *en masse* to Dawson Creek after completing work on the Alcan Highway, military inspectors had visited company camps and interviewed the enlisted men. Their report said:

Pfc. Charles P. English of the 95th Regiment, commended for his photographs of the aftermath of the Dawson Creek fire (courtesy Office of History Collection, U.S. Army Corps of Engineers).

> In general, the conditions in these military camps as regards cleanliness, sanitation, comfort and appearance of personnel were found to be below standard even considering the severe cold and other difficulties.
>
> Several of the mess halls were filthy, dark, poorly ventilated, and without tables where the men could sit down and eat. Practically no table equipment was observed, the men eating from individual mess kits.
>
> The cooks and bakers were not cleanly dressed. The entire set up in most of these mess halls was very uninviting. The food was not well prepared.
>
> The enlisted personnel are dirty in their persons and apparel. Most of them need haircuts and shaves. There is a marked shortage of washing, laundry and cleaning facilities.
>
> It was reported that sleeping bags are becoming very dirty and are losing their insulating qualities with continued use. Replacements and facilities for cleaning are required.
>
> Several officers stated that the above conditions are the result of a shortage of men and low morale.
>
> The latrines in most cases are not satisfactory....
>
> Discipline of the troops was reported to be satisfactory. Everything considered, their morale is as good as could be expected. The presence of civilian workers, with high wages and better living conditions to complete the work our armed forces have initiated under severe conditions, is, however, disturbing.

The report was dated February 15, 1943, and signed by Major Dighton of the Corps of Military Police. It was addressed to General O'Connor of the Northwest Service Command.[28]

The 95th was such a grubby lot when it arrived at its camp outside of Dawson Creek that its members overwhelmed the town's newly opened dry cleaner. "We were told these black troops had been in the bush nearly a year and needed spruced-up uniforms to go back home," said Dave Ho-Lem, one of the owners. "We told them we'd do it for the 300 going out only if it was shirts and trousers. However, when they came in they dumped tunics and parkas and every other kind of clothing on top of us. We worked forty-eight hours straight getting that job finished. In the end we were so tired we had to shout and sing and yell at each other to keep awake."[29]

The regiment's commander, Colonel Lane, gave an upbeat report on his troops to O'Connor: "The commendable performance of the 95th Engineer General Service Regiment while stationed at Dawson Creek Railhead and Depot should not pass unrecognized. For a period of four months this Regiment provided the bulk of the labor necessary to the establishment and operation of this Post and its numerous utility installations. Their effort reflected a continual efficient performance of duty and spirit of mutual cooperation that set a high standard by which other units could pattern their own activities. They exhibited an admirable ability to adapt and to create. Good morale was abundantly in evidence."[30]

Praise for the 95th even came from a Canadian civilian, William W. Barclay, who was employed by Curran & Briggs Ltd., a private contractor on the Alcan Highway. He wrote:

> Your regiment came into this bleak, somber and silent land and accomplished a task that has won the admiration and praise of free men everywhere. If it is permissible and only because they were more closely associated with us I would specifically mention Company "F" of Captain Richard Berne, his fellow officers, non-coms and men we cannot speak too highly. Under the most adverse conditions they kept their morale high, by their most exemplary conduct they have strengthened the tie that binds our two peoples in friendship. We will long remember them.
>
> In conclusion, sir, I would like you to know that I and my fellow countrymen are proud of the 95th Regiment as a whole and proud of that nation from whence they came.[31]

The 95th had worked alongside the private contractor at Mile 35 at Muskwa, British Columbia.

Among the projects undertaken by the regiment in Dawson Creek was the construction of the first Red Cross center to serve black troops in the Far North. It was a one-story, wooden hut, known as the Recreation House for Negro Soldiers, built at the 95th's camp. The men made the furniture, including a dressing table in the sleeping quarters for the director. They had been told the director was a young black woman, so they composed a letter of welcome and left it on the dressing table. It read in part, "We feel as if this war is really worth fighting for now that you have come to us and we know we will win this war."[32]

13 — Surviving Isolation

The Red Cross's Hazel Dixon Payne, of New Rochelle, New York, held a Master's degree in health and physical education. She flew into Dawson Creek on a day in early March 1943 when the temperature, as she recalled, was seventy below zero. She noted in an interview that the men had spent nearly a year up north without seeing a black woman. "The expression on their faces exhibited tension, anxiety and a grand appreciation for a Negro woman," she said.[33] Payne had brought pinup pictures of black women; she asked friends to send more when she realized how successful they were. "The folks back home should have seen them stand for hours at a time, staring at the pictures," she said.[34] The most popular pinups were those of black singer Lena Horne. Once, entertaining at Fort Riley, Kansas, she walked off the stage when she noticed German prisoners of war seated up front and black soldiers confined to the rear.

The Red Cross center had two ping-pong tables and two pool tables and showed four movies during a typical week. Almost shrine-like was the stage, over which the members of the 95th had carved the Corps of Engineers' crest, painted bright red and white. The stage was used for the first time on April 10, 1943, when the 95th put on a show called "Dozing Along," a play on the Caterpillar bulldozers used on the highway. Among the songs in the show were "Bugler Call Rag," "Blues in the Night," "Darktown Strutters Ball," and "I'm a Prisoner of Love." Cpl. James J. Butler, who had composed a regimental march for the opening ceremony of the highway, wrote the music for a song titled "Alcan Blues." Clifford Taylor tap danced to "Sweet Sue." There was also a dream number that included "I'm the lad who built Alcan." The highlight was a South Seas number for which the men made costumes of crepe paper, blonde wigs from rope and brassieres from strips of cotton; the men danced in their GI shorts and Army boots.[35]

Most members of the 95th Regiment were fortunate to be in Dawson Creek, because they had not only a Red Cross center but also barracks they had built for themselves. Not all of the black troops were as lucky during their first full winter in the Far North.

Ulysses Lee, the black Army historian, wrote of the problems faced by the troops up north. "The isolation of troops in Alaska and Northwest Canada, increased in the cases of Negro units by the refusal of many towns to admit them even to their streets and shops, contributed to low morale," he said.[36]

There was visual evidence that some of the black troops did get involved with aboriginal women in the Yukon and the Northwest Territories. There are native Canadians with curly hair and Negro features around Teslin, southeast of Whitehorse, where the 93rd worked.[37] Given the fact that the 388th was involved in river transportation, its members had more access to settlements along the waterways in northern Alberta and the Northwest Territories. "When I arrived in 1955, there were children eleven and twelve who had Negro features and curly hair," said a nurse practitioner from the Grey Nuns order who was based in Fort Smith. "Indians never had curly hair. These children were accepted. There was never any fuss in the north about color or religion."[38] Diamond Jenness, chief of the anthropological division of the National Museum of Canada, was obviously confused in a story he often told: "In 1943 colored employees of a firm that had contracted to build an oil pipeline in the region openly offered a prize of $500 to the first Indian woman who should give birth to a baby with black kinky hair."[39] (There were no blacks employed by private contractors on the highway and pipeline projects in Alaska, the Yukon and the Northwest Territories.) One native woman in regular contact with black soldiers was Rose Norwegian, who moved across the Mackenzie River from Fort Norman, where she was born, to Camp Canol. There she'd wash and mend the clothes of the black soldiers. "They were good to work for," she said. "They had their own cooks so they brought breakfast to me in my tent. When I was doing my work during the day, I could hear them singing in the woods."[40]

Several black soldiers returned north after the war and married native women. One of them was Jack Saunders, a member of the 93rd Regiment from Alabama who settled at Burwash Landing in the Yukon, where he and his wife raised seven children in a log cabin.[41]

What did the native Canadians think of the black soldiers? "They had been schooled with some ideas about what we would do and what we would look like, but they soon found out that we were just like any other human being," said Sgt. Hayward

A member of the 97th Regiment tries out a dogteam and sled brought to a campsite by a native Canadian fur trapper (courtesy William E. Griggs).

L. Oubre of the 97th.[42] "White soldiers would go into settlements before us and tell a whole lot of lies, that we were dangerous, so people would be afraid," said Fred Spencer of the 93rd. "Once the people knew us, we were a number one friend. We got along well with the Indians, the few we saw."[43] There was no word in the native languages for a black man. One chief in the Yukon gave some thought to the matter and found an answer: "Black white men."[44] When an Indian group saw black troops of the 388th disembarking at a port on the Mackenzie River, one member welcomed the soldiers by saying, "Hullo, midnight." A soldier took one look at the man and replied, "Holy Moses! Yo's just about a quarter to twelve yo'self."[45] Richard Frank, an Indian elder, recalled a black soldier arriving in Minto in the Yukon on a floatplane. One of the elders told a young native to go and pick up the soldier's gear. "I'll never forget that," the surprised soldier said of the courtesy shown him.[46]

The regiment farthest from civilization was the 97th in Alaska. "Tempers could flare because of isolation," said Sergeant Griggs. "One soldier shot another in the stomach and killed him."[47] Lt. Walter Mason of "A" Company claimed fellow soldiers had harassed the man. "He was so upset he sat down in the tent and said, 'I'm going to shoot the next man comes through the door,'" Mason said. "It was just a man feeling so depressed and harassed that he just said he was going to do that. And the next man that came through happened to be his best buddy, but he still did it."[48] The soldier was shot in the stomach but survived the initial assault. However, he died two days later when his stitches popped after he got out of hospital bed unattended. The shooting took place at Mineral Lake when the 97th was building the access road from Slana to Tok.

Jesse Balthazar, a sergeant with the 97th, had once taken a correspondence art course. When an officer from Teaneck, New Jersey, learned this, he had Balthazar paint a sign pointing to Teaneck. "I guess it was a morale booster as soon they were all making suggestions about their hometowns and states."[49] Such signs noting the distance of hometowns became popular with all troops.

Because of their isolation, most of the black troops working on the Alcan Highway rarely saw white troops. When they occasionally met in town, the result was not always pleasant. One resident described what happened in Dawson Creek when members of the 95th were working in town after the explosion that destroyed one block of buildings. "Soldiers fighting each other and white soldiers kicking black soldiers off the sidewalks, wooden sidewalks almost pounded into the mud," he said. "The Negro fellows were the work battalions and I thought they were slaves. Everybody kicked them around, and it was the first time I'd seen more than two black fellows together at once."[50] Orval Couch, a Yukon native who worked as a highway truck repair foreman, told of what could happen when whites met blacks on the town's narrow sidewalks. "I'd see groups of [white] GIs walking up the street there in Dawson Creek and they'd meet three or four Negroes and the Negroes would have to get off the sidewalks and walk on the street."[51] Canadian war correspondent Peter Stursberg related an incident he witnessed in Whitehorse. "American Military Police beat up a Negro soldier on the street," he said. "Some of the Canadians were ready to take the MPs apart, but they were stopped by the Mounties."[52]

When the movie made from songwriter Irving Berlin's "This Is the Army" musical had its Canadian premiere in Whitehorse in 1943, there were no blacks in attendance — just white officers, troops and dignitaries in the 500-seat theater, financed and built by one of the private contractors on the highway. Did the officers present know that Berlin had recruited several hundred members of the Army, black and white, for the show? Not only that, Berlin also insisted that the cast work and live together. His company, which did road shows in the United States and for troops in Europe, was then the only *integrated* company of black and white American soldiers. "He knew his gesture would at the least be progressive, and probably controversial," wrote a biographer. "But he believed the armed forces was the great leveler in American society."[53] Among the numbers performed by the black cast during the show and in the movie was an adaptation of "Puttin' on the Ritz," an ode to well-dressed, upscale blacks in Harlem that Berlin had written years earlier. Sgt. Joe Louis, the reigning heavyweight champion, appeared in the movie, as did Lt. Ronald Reagan, a future president.

The few instances when black and white troops got together usually involved the purchase of liquor, banned in Army camps. Army Air Forces pilots flying planes destined for the Soviet Union soon realized they could make money on the side by bootlegging. "The guys in the air force, when they'd go to the States, they'd bring a lot of liquor back," said Sergeant Haskin of the 93rd. "They'd drive down the portion of the highway that was built and sell us liquor."[54] Once the highway was open, Canadian truckers would bring in supplies for private contractors. Sergeant Lee of the 95th saw an opportunity when truckers bogged down and needed help. "I had some MP badges I'd put on my men," Lee explained. "They'd go down and help them out, pull them out. I'd say, 'You've got too much load on. You'll have to take some of this stuff off. Oh, that vodka, you'll have to take some of that off.' We'd take the vodka and eggs and the ham. We had better food than other units."[55] Some of the men driving the supply trucks were also in the bootlegging business. "There were supply trucks running up supplying the regiments, and there was alcohol hauled up the road," said Walter Mason, a lieutenant with the 97th. "Some of them were civilian drivers. Some liquor seeped into the camps from time to time. At times it caused us problems. The men never got completely out of hand."[56] Sergeant Oubre of the 97th said some of his men would get raisins and yeast and make liquor. "The officers didn't mind so much," he said. "They wanted it too."[57] Sergeant Griggs, the 97th's photographer, would use the tanks in the darkroom for a still. "People would come in and say there was a strange smell. I'd say, 'That's hypo.'"[58] Many company commanders removed vanilla extract from the camps because of its popularity. "I do remember when the first sergeant threw the head cook head first into a fire barrel to sober him up after he had become drunk from drinking all the vanilla extract in camp," said Capt. DeWitt C. Howell of the 97th Regiment, the officer who leveled mutiny charges against the troops who refused to ride in the back of a truck at thirty below.⁵⁹ Ralph McManus, a University of Alberta civil engineering student who worked in Dawson Creek during the war, recalled a man in town who'd buy rum and water it down and sell it to the black troops stationed nearby. "That's the only thing I heard of whites and blacks being together," he said.⁶⁰

Gambling was a popular pastime among the black troops, especially those in remote areas. It was also a source of income for the more skilled players. One of those was Sergeant Lee of the 95th, although as a noncommissioned officer he wasn't supposed to gamble with men of a lower rank. "I managed to make enough money in a poker game to send to my wife to buy a home," he said.⁶¹ Another big winner was Joseph Haskin of the 93rd. "I did pretty good gambling," he said. "I was considered a rich guy because I'd send home over $10,000 to my mother. There was nowhere to go to spend money."⁶² Shooting craps, Pvt. Joe Coliva of the 388th once won $9,000 from civilian workers on the Canol pipeline.⁶³

Sergeant Oubre was one of those who didn't gamble. "The fellows used to gamble outside of my tent," he said. "You want to hear some cuss words, you just listen to frustrated black soldiers in World War II. But I couldn't sleep, so I complained. The guys were told they could gamble if they didn't disturb the other men. Next day I heard mumbling outside my tent. They were cursing, the lowest kind of cursing, but in whispers."⁶⁴ Another non-gambler was Private Dulin, who set up his own private PX (post exchange) in Company "A" of the 95th. His customers tended to be players spending their winnings. He'd come across a mail-order catalogue from the Johnson Smith Company in Detroit and started placing orders. "I started ordering name-brand chewing gum and other things, candies, cigarettes, cigars," he said. "I sold them and made me some money. I had an order coming in every month. As soon as I got some money I'd get a money order and send it to my parents. I made pretty good up in the woods. I doubled the price that I paid. I was the PX man."⁶⁵

The enlisted men had money for gambling because they were paid in cash once a month; officers were paid by check. The Canadian Bank of Commerce, which had branches in Dawson Creek and Whitehorse, was authorized by the U.S. Treasury to handle payroll funds, as was the Royal Bank of Canada in Alberta and the Northwest Territories. An officer would make the pickup. "My jeep driver was a large black sergeant," said Lt. Samuel B. Land of the 95th Regiment. "When I told him we had over $100,000 in my bag and that it was possible we might be robbed, he said, 'Don't worry, Lieutenant, they will have to get by me first.' We both were armed with .45 caliber pistols, but as it turned out, did not need them. This sergeant, Murphy, was an extra good man."⁶⁶ Privates' pay was twenty-one dollars, while a private first class received thirty-two dollars, a corporal forty-two dollars, a sergeant fifty-six dollars, a staff sergeant seventy-six dollars, a technical sergeant $110 and a first sergeant $150.

One officer on the Canol pipeline worried about the morale of the men when they lacked entertainment. "So far, the soldiers, both white and black, on the Canol project, have no means for entertainment," he reported to his superiors. "I saw no games of any kind and no movies or other stage entertainment. I do not believe that soldiers working as hard as these men are compelled to work, sometimes as many as fourteen to sixteen hours a day, can maintain a high state of morale without some sort of recreation. Negroes generally laugh, joke or sing while working. I witnessed none of these while I was there."[67]

Army historian Ulysses Lee tried to disabuse white officers of the belief that the black soldiers could usually be found singing as they worked. "Guard against the popular conception that all Negroes can and like to sing and dance," he wrote in "Leadership and the Negro Soldier," a manual he prepared for the Army. "This is far from the truth. The American Negro, like other rural peoples, has developed a folk culture in this country that is unique and something to be proud of. To many Negroes, however, these cultural contributions of the group are no more a part of their own personal experiences than the square dance, hillbilly songs, and corn husking bees are a part of the experience of many white youths."[68] He could have been thinking of reports coming from white officers like one that appeared in the *Edmonton Journal*: "Light-hearted lads, heavy logs on their shoulder ... shuffling out of the brush to a red-hot vocalization of the 'Chattanooga Choo-Choo.'"[69]

As a way to combat loneliness, many of the men kept pets. It was a rare camp that didn't have bear cubs, moose calves, foxes, squirrels and even birds, such as great owls. Men at the headquarters of the 97th had a husky named Tok and bear cubs named Dynamite and TNT, orphaned when their mother was shot after attacking a soldier. Col. Albert L. Lane, commander of the 95th Regiment, told a story about one of his men who was swimming in a stream when he met a black bear. Since he was unarmed — and undressed — he punched the bear in the nose. The surprised animal beat a hasty retreat.[70]

Probably the best antidote for isolation was a letter from home. "The men have a deep and abiding attachment for their homes," said Chaplain Carroll of the 95th. "When mail comes in, the soldiers leave the most luscious repast on earth to get it. Some read the letters right away. Others carefully husband them, opening one a day to make them last as long as possible."[71] But the mail service was erratic. Before the Alcan Highway was passable, any airplane flying in would carry mail, landing with pontoons or skis. Once there was highway traffic, mail trucks drove in from Edmonton. Company commanders censored all outgoing mail. Men were told to write on only one side of a page so that offending material — any mention of the highway or the pipeline — could be cut out with scissors. Some commanders inked out the material. An entire letter judged inappropriate was forwarded to the War Department.

Opposite, top: A Husky dog watches as a member of the 97th Regiment feeds a pet bear cub (courtesy William E. Griggs). *Bottom:* Capt. Edward G. Carroll, chaplain of the 95th Regiment, leads a Sunday service (courtesy Office of History Collection, U.S. Army Corps of Engineers).

13 — Surviving Isolation

Once a private bringing mail to "C" Company of the 93rd from headquarters showed up with a sidearm, a .45 caliber Remington automatic pistol. Capt. Robert Platt Boyd, Jr., the company commander, told the private he did not allow anyone to carry a loaded weapon in the camp. The private reluctantly started to draw the weapon from his holster. "The next thing I knew it went off," said Boyd. "There was an unearthly scream from behind the canvas curtain where the cooks slept." The captain found one of the cooks thumping about the floor, still zipped in his sleeping bag. The doctor who was summoned broke out in laughter after examining the cook. "He said a surgeon couldn't have done a better job of circumcising the soldier," Boyd said. "The bullet had just skimmed the underside of the end of his penis. The doctor explained the incident by saying the soldier was probably sleeping on his back and dreaming of his girlfriend, and must have had an erection, and the round grazed him."[72]

Fortunately, the isolation of the troops was soon to come to an end.

14

The Highway Is Praised, the Pipeline Criticized

"This country am nothin' but miles and miles of nothin' but miles an' miles."

The military importance of the Alcan Highway and the Canol pipeline lessened in 1943 after American forces, aided by Canada, drove the Japanese out of the Aleutian Islands. When Gen. Simon Bolivar Buckner had assumed command of the Army in Alaska eighteen months before the attack on Pearl Harbor, the American military presence up north mainly consisted of a 400-man unit guarding the Chilkoot Trail, which led to the gold fields of the Klondike. As one writer facetiously put it, the troops in Alaska might have played a strategic role if the Royal Canadian Mounted Police attempted to invade.[1] By January of 1943, the brigadier general had at his disposal 94,000 troops. When the American Army went on the offensive in the Aleutian Islands, the Allies were also on the offensive in the European theater. American forces controlled most of Sicily; Mussolini had been deposed and the new Italian government was considering terms of surrender; American Liberator bombers were attacking oil fields in Rumania, the source of 90 percent of the German Air Force's fuel; the Soviet Army had stopped the Germans in the rich coalfields of the Ukraine's Donets Basin; and the British Army was advancing in North Africa.[2]

On May 11, 15,000 American troops invaded Attu, an island thirty-five miles long and fifteen miles wide. Company "A" of the black 383rd Port Battalion went ashore with the task force and unloaded landing barges. After seventeen days of fighting, between 700 and 1,000 surviving Japanese made a suicide attack on American forces. The following day, the Japanese announced the loss of Attu. Casualties totaled 549 American dead and 1,148 wounded, making the fight for Attu the second most costly Pacific theater battle, proportionately, after Iwo Jima.[3]

When a joint force of nearly 34,000 American and Canadian troops invaded Kiska on 15 August, they met no resistance. However, friendly fire, booby traps and mines killed twenty-one American soldiers, and the Navy lost seventy men when the destroyer *Amner Road* struck a mine. The Canadians suffered four dead. Kiska was declared secure on August 24, 1943.

The ouster of the Japanese from the Aleutians immediately changed the justification for construction of the highway and pipeline, especially since the pipeline still had not provided any fuel for the trucks on the highway and the airplanes bound for the Soviet Union. Given the success of its island-hopping strategy in the Pacific, the War Department scrapped plans for using Alaska as a major base for an attack on Japan.

Due to the changed conditions, Maj. Gen. Eugene Reybold, the head of the Corps of Engineers, together with officials of the Federal Works Agency (which oversaw the Public Roads Administration) discussed the possibility of lowering the standards for the Alcan Highway. As a result, the PRA was told to eliminate all unnecessary refinements to the highway. The route of the pioneer road was to be followed unless deviations would involve less work. The width of the finished highway was to be reduced from thirty-six to twenty-six feet and all surfacing done with available local materials.[4] All work was to be finished by October 31, 1943, a year after the pioneer road had been completed. Army engineers had built approximately 1,400 miles of road and the PRA 250 miles. The PRA closed its Whitehorse office on December 3, 1943, and turned over what little work remained — mainly permanent bridges — to the Northwest Service Command.

The command's lead officer, General O'Connor, was already putting the Japanese threat behind him that summer and thinking of the highway's role in getting Lend-Lease aircraft to the Soviet Union. "The importance of this route will depend upon the progress of the battle between the Russians and the Germans," he said. "If the Russians win, the need for the route will be small. If the Germans should have success, the need for the route will be correspondingly great."[5]

The first planes bound for the Soviet Union via the Northwest Staging Route left Ladd Field outside of Fairbanks on September 29, 1942 — twelve A-20 Havoc attack planes. American pilots had flown them from Great Falls, Montana, to Fairbanks, using the Alcan Highway as a guide. If the pilots found themselves short of fuel or had mechanical problems on the 2,500-mile route from Great Falls, they landed at one of fifteen intermediate airstrips. When any plane crashed in the northern wilderness, there was a novel rescue procedure: dog drops. If the crash was in an inaccessible area where a rescue plane couldn't land, a medical team parachuted in. If needed, the team ordered dogs and a toboggan dropped to evacuate the victim to a lake or another location where a rescue plane could land.[6]

Before the Northwest Staging Route became operational, there were two main ways to get Lend-Lease planes to the Soviet Union. One was by sea, usually to Murmansk or Archangel in the Arctic Sea; the other was by air, flying them to Belém in northern Brazil, across the Atlantic Ocean to Ascension Island, then to Ghana, Egypt, Iran and Iraq, where Soviet pilots took over. The Northwest Staging Route was considered the safest of the three routes.

The four black regiments left the Alcan Highway and the Canol project by the end of the summer of 1943. The 93rd was the first to depart. Company "F" left for the Aleutian Islands in October 1942, before the opening of the highway, and other companies followed over the next two months. Its work completed in Dawson Creek, the

95th left in May for Camp Claiborne, Louisiana. The 97th moved from Big Delta, Alaska, to Livengood to help build a proposed 512-mile highway from Fairbanks to Nome on the coast of the Bering Sea, a project favored by Maj. Gen. Brehon B. Somervell. Once the Japanese were driven from the Aleutians, however, Somervell cancelled construction. The 97th had built only two miles of road. The regiment left from Valdez for Camp Sutton in North Carolina. As soon as the Mackenzie River was navigable in 1943, members of the 388th were again assigned to the transportation of freight bound for Camp Canol and the provision of wood for the sternwheelers. As the private contractors received their equipment and supplies, the role of the 388th was phased out; the last members left the Far North for Camp Sutton by the end of September. The access road from Camp Canol to Whitehorse was completed on New Year's Eve of 1943, after which it became the main supply route for the Canol pipeline.

Before the departure of the regiments — black and white, as well as smaller units — the War Department honored them for their "meritorious conduct" in the construction of the Alcan Highway. The citation said:

> Commencing with the spring thaw and continuing on through the summer floods, the troops overcame the difficulties imposed by mountainous terrain, deep muskeg, torrential streams, heavy forests, and an ever lengthening supply line. By virtue of remarkable engineering ability, ingenious improvisations and unsurpassed devotion to duty, the units assigned to the highway construction completed their mission in one short working season and thereby opened a supply road to Alaska that is of inestimable strategic value to the war effort of their country.[7]

While the troops were departing, the highway they helped build was undergoing a name change. The Territorial Chamber of Commerce told Anthony J. Dimond, Alaska's delegate in Congress, that "Alcan Highway" lacked dignity as a name. He agreed: "It sounds too much like 'Ashcan.'"[8] Dimond suggested to the House of Representatives that it be named either the Alaska-Canadian Highway or the Canadian-Alaska Highway. After much debate, it became the Alaska Highway, even though five-sixths of the road was in Canada. The House of Representatives on March 24, 1943, approved a joint resolution. The Northwest Service Command on June 10, 1943, officially announced the new name as the Alaska Military Highway, but the *Military* was soon dropped. Secretary of State Cordell Hull sounded out Ottawa on July 19 regarding the new name and won Canadian government approval. "The government of the United States believes that the name suggested by Mr. Dimond is suitable and in harmony with popular usage," said Hull.[9]

Alcan Highway had never been a popular name. Some soldiers derisively called it the Oil Can Highway, in part because it was littered with empty oil and gas drums, and the All Can Highway. One Canadian journalist wrote, "What a name. Reminds me of the town dump."[10] Others called it just the Road or the Army Road. Some people in Fairbanks called it the Negro Road because the black 97th Regiment had built the Alaska portion. The *Toronto Star* suggested International Friendship Trail.[11] Lt. Col.

Albert L. Lane, commander of the 341st Regiment, referred to the highway as the Long Trail. Writers variously called it America's Burma Road, the Road to Tokyo, the Tokyo Turnpike, the Frozen Pathway to Tokyo and the Continent's Mystery Road. One person who didn't favor the name change was Brig. Gen. Ludson D. Worsham, then commanding officer of the Northwest Division of the Corps of Engineers. "The Alcan Highway was the glamour girl of 1942," he said. "In 1943, however, even her name was changed to the Alaska Highway."[12]

Lt. Clyde S. Deal, commanding officer of Company "D" of the 93rd Regiment, recalled how he and his men, working at Judith Creek, about fifty miles south of Whitehorse, learned that the Alaska Highway had been opened. "One day we were building away when we heard an unusual horn blast," he said. "Everyone rushed out to the road to see what was going on. Coming over the flat was a Greyhound bus heading to Whitehorse. Until then we hadn't known — but now we did — that the road was open."[13] The Army chartered two dozen buses to carry troops and authorized personnel on the seventy-two-hour run between Dawson Creek and Fairbanks; ordinary citizens could not use the buses. Each bus had two drivers who spelled each other. The Army recruited the drivers from Greyhound runs in western Canada.

By late 1943, the Army had a fleet of 1,500 trucks operating on the highway. The 477th Quartermaster Trucking Regiment was brought in to replace the engineers who had previously been driving trucks on the highway once their construction work had been completed. During the winter, the American military police patrolled the highway twenty-four hours a day in winterized Dodge weapons carriers, carrying hot coffee and spare parts. They had two tow trucks at their posts, located fifty miles apart.

Those who saw the black regiments in action were laudatory of their work. "The Negro troops have distinguished themselves," said Col. John W. Wheeler, an Army engineer from Northern Sector headquarters in Whitehorse. "Working under severe handicaps of subzero weather and moving ahead so rapidly that their living quarters were primitive and sketchy, they have nevertheless constructed a highway through some of the most rugged wilderness on the North American continent. The interest they display in the accomplishment of their tasks is remarkable."[14]

Allen Raymond of the *New York Herald Tribune* interviewed some white Army engineers in a beer parlor in Whitehorse. "You want to see the road?" one asked. "We surveyed it. My outfit. A pretty rugged outfit. We kept just ahead of the Negroes, and, boy, they're pretty rugged too. They're good if you ask me."[15]

Referring to the black regiments, civilian engineer Kenneth J. Deacon, of Baltimore, said, "The men came from farms, factories, and ranks of the unemployed; from the countryside, small towns, and urban slums and tenements. Having been brought up during the Depression, most of them lacked the education or opportunities to show their stuff in the workaday world. But now, besides building a difficult road, they would make an honorable niche for themselves in history."[16]

Richard Neuberger, General O'Connor's public relations officer, declared, "When

Soldiers repair a tire from an Army carryall truck (courtesy William E. Griggs).

some people decry the passing of American spirit, I think of the boys who hacked a road through a wilderness as trackless as that crossed by the covered wagons which went to Oregon in 1850. I think of the Negro soldiers from the Deep South who drove trucks at forty-five degrees below zero."[17]

J. Lance Rumble, an executive of General Motors of Canada who had been on loan to the Northwest Service Command, said, "Some of these regiments had never seen snow before, particularly those who came from the big cities of the South. The colored troops especially deserve great credit."[18]

Elsdon Gladwin, the first Canadian officer to drive the Alaska Highway, said, "If you weren't there, you just couldn't understand it. I saw fellows so tired they were ready to drop in their tracks. It was rush-rush-rush! Fellows were doing eighteen to twenty hours a day on bulldozers. One was up to his neck in ice water repairing timbers in subzero weather. God, I admired them! Most were southerners — they'd never experienced cold like that."[19]

Author/adventurer Herbert C. Lanks went so far as to say, "The heroic work of those Army engineer regiments, nearly half of which were Negro troops, has never been equaled by any armed service in the world. Their record is as glorious as that of any combat unit on the fighting front, for here, too, men suffered and died in a battle of the wilderness so that America might be made safe."[20]

The black soldiers themselves realized they had done something special. "We showed that black soldiers did their duty no matter how horrible the circumstances," said Fred Spencer of Sneads, Florida, a member of the 93rd Regiment.[21] Jessie Weeke, motor pool sergeant of the 97th from Moore Haven, Florida, also said, "I worked on that highway and I'm proud of it."[22] William E. Griggs of the 97th, a native of Baltimore, agreed, "We took great pride in what we were doing."[23]

Otis E. Lee of the 95th, born in Virginia, stated, "We were segregated but proud. Because whatever we were doing, we were doing it for our country. Somebody had to do it to prove to the world that they were wrong and we were not all dumb. And that we loved this country."[24] Wesley Davis, a member of the 95th from Winter Haven, Florida, said, "I was a young man who felt he had a job to do and did it."[25]

E.C. Marshall of the 95th, a native of the Washington, D.C., suburbs, additionally reported, "We put the pioneer road in."[26] Alexander Powell of the 97th, a native of Quincy, Florida, said, "We worked very hard in the fight for freedom along with soldiers of all races."[27] And Paul W. Francis of the 93rd said, "This tremendous project, though necessary, was undertaken amidst racism by white officers against black soldiers."[28]

Was the Alaska Highway a great feat of construction? "The building of 1,671 miles of highway in itself does not seem impressive to Americans familiar with our own vast highway system," said Army headquarters in Alaska. "But there were two factors which made this particular task an almost impossible feat: one was the necessity for speed, the other was inaccessibility. The road had to go through in one summer, and in the North the summer is brief."[29]

What was this inaccessible land like? "The best description that I ever heard of the terrain through which the highway runs came from one of the Negroes at Fort Nelson," said Canadian war correspondent Peter Stursberg. "'Brother,' he said to me, 'this country am nothin' but miles and miles of nothin' but miles an' miles.' It was a little unfair, this remark of his, but I think it does give you an idea of the vastness of this northern wilderness, a vastness that you can never really grasp until you have been up there and traveled through it."[30]

Was the construction of the Alaska Highway comparable to that of the Panama Canal? "From a logistics standpoint the building of the Alcan was a major offensive that rivaled the construction of the Panama Canal," said military historian Jonathan M. Nielson.[31] "It bids fair to be the greatest piece of roadmaking yet undertaken by man," said Britain's high commissioner to Canada, Malcolm MacDonald.[32]

Even as the troops and civilian workers were leaving the Far North, General O'Connor defended the need for the Alaska Highway. "As it stands, this road is a sword pointed at our enemies in Japan," he said. "It isn't a boulevard. Some folks would like to see us make it that, even with a war on. But we set out to build a military road, and that's what it is. The main thing is that trucks can go through — even if they get through with a few squeaks in the springs."[33]

Canadian military historian, C.P. Stacey, dismissed the Alaska Highway. "As a military route carrying supplies to Alaska, the highway was completely insignificant," he said.[34] "Apart from its utility in connection with the airway, there was no real military requirement whatever for the Alaska Highway."[35]

The Corps of Engineers History Office made a more reasoned assessment of the construction: "The highway project was not a miracle, nor was any great engineering skill needed for its accomplishment; it was, however, one of the outstanding demonstrations of the fortitude, perseverance, and indomitable spirit of the American soldier. Long hard hours of work, under the worst possible conditions of living, were the primary reasons for the successful accomplishment of the mission. All possible credit for the task should go to the soldier in the field, who, without complaining, often not too well fed or clothed, cooperated with his fellows in hewing out the highway by brute strength."[36]

The House Roads Committee under the chairmanship of Representative Will Robinson of Utah conducted a four-month investigation of the Alaska Highway and concluded that a "splendid job" had been done. "If Japan had taken advantage of the situation during 1942 it is the opinion of high military leaders it could have fully occupied the territory," said the committee report. "There was some evidence of overbuying of certain supplies. However, this cannot be too severely criticized because there was no precedent in road construction in a remote and virtually unexplored wilderness."[37]

The Canol project was not as blessed as the highway when a Senate committee chaired by Senator Harry S Truman investigated it. If one man's reputation was burnished by the Canol pipeline, it was that of Harry S Truman, a World War I veteran who had been an unsuccessful haberdasher back in Kansas City, Missouri. If one man's reputation was tarnished, it was that of Brig. Gen. Brehon B. Somervell, head of the War Department's Services of Supply, whose face had graced the cover of *Time* magazine a year earlier. Ironically, it was Somervell who was originally touted as a possible vice-presidential running mate for President Roosevelt in the 1944 election, or even an eventual presidential candidate himself. Truman became that person, in great part because of the publicity he received through chairing an investigation of the Canol pipeline. He had none of the polish or background of Somervell, whose grandfather had voted for Tennessee to secede from the Union. But as president, Truman probably provided as many opportunities to young black American males as Roosevelt did for their parents during the Great Depression. Yet black newspapers and civil rights leaders believed President Roosevelt selected Truman as his running mate in 1944 to appease Southerners, especially those in Congress.[38]

The U.S. Senate Special Committee Investigating the National Defense Program, commonly known as the Truman Committee, was set up in 1941 at the senator's request. When it began its investigation of the Canol project in September 1943, private contractors had only partially laid pipes from the Norman Wells oilfield to Whitehorse.

James H. Graham, the Somervell aide whose one-page memo was the basis of the Canol project, emphasized the wartime need for oil up north. "Gentlemen, there was a war going on and there still is a war going on," he told the committee. "I've been taught not to consider costs in time of war."[39] Undersecretary of War Robert P. Patterson said in his testimony, "The project was initiated at a time when there was imminent danger of a Japanese attack on Alaska and possible control of coastal waters in that area, to ensure an overland supply of petroleum near the base of operations. There was no time for long investigation of resources and costs. The project was a military operation, pure and simple."[40]

Somervell himself was one of the last witnesses called, testifying just before Christmas of 1943. He told the senators that the new wells drilled in the Norman Wells field represented the biggest discovery of oil in North America in fifteen years. "If it was a crime to discover it," a defiant Somervell said, "then we are guilty." Republican Senator Edward H. Moore, an Oklahoma oil man, challenged Somervell, saying there'd been a score of similar-sized finds. "It is a reckless man indeed who questions the strategy that has pulled us up and is going to lead us to victory," Somervell replied.[41]

Somervell did concede that the Canol project was costly. "It was justified on the grounds of military necessity alone," he said. "As an economic proposition, the whole thing was cockeyed from the beginning." The general received understanding support from Senator Carl A. Hatch, a Democrat of New Mexico. "To summarize," Hatch said to Somervell, "we were at war, we needed oil, shipping was short, and you faced a desperate situation, so you ascertained that there was oil there and you decided to develop it. You took a chance, made the decision yourself and passed the buck to no one." "That's it," said Somervell.[42]

Truman, who as president had a "buck stops here" sign on his desk, would have closed down the Canol project immediately if he'd had his way. "This is a bad, bad project undertaken without any estimate of its cost and the time required to complete it," Truman said after Somervell had completed his testimony.[4e] Although Interior Secretary Harold Ickes was Roosevelt's oil czar, he told the committee that the Canol project was launched without his approval and continued over his objection. "The whole thing ought to be scrapped—junked—right now," he said.[44] Both Canada's Imperial Oil and Standard Oil of California had doubts about the worth of the project. The Navy Department, which had never been consulted about the project, recommended it be abandoned. So did the War Production Board. Maj. Gen. Thomas M. Robins, the deputy chief of the Corps of Engineers, said a few oil barges could take to Alaska ten times the amount of oil to be carried by the Canol pipeline at one-tenth of the cost. But Somervell enjoyed the support of the Joint Chiefs of Staff, who recommended complete funding of the pipeline project through to its completion, regardless of the diminished threat from Japan. The additional cost to complete the project was estimated at $30 million.

As a result, the Truman Committee condemned the project but agreed it should be completed. "What has been done has been done," said the committee report issued on January 8, 1944. "It is too late to go back and rectify. The Canol project was undertaken without adequate consideration or study. It should not have been undertaken." It conceded, however, that "there may be some slight excuse for General Somervell's original hasty decision in view of the tremendous pressure on him at the time."[45] When President Roosevelt weighed in, he appeared sympathetic to Somervell. "It looked like there might be a lot of activity up around Alaska at that time, and I would have approved anything to get more oil up there," he said.[46]

The War Department met with the Canadian government and Imperial Oil to revise the Canol agreement, which had been one of the recommendations of the Senate committee. The oil company agreed to lower the cost to the Army of the crude produced and to the post-war purchase for $3 million of the drilling equipment provided by the United States. Basically, the Canadian government replaced the Army as developer of the oil field. "The Army wishes publicly to express its appreciation of the spirit of cooperation shown by the Government of Canada and Imperial Oil Limited in working out the principles of this mutually satisfactory agreement," said Undersecretary of War Patterson.[47]

On February 16, 1944, the pipeline crew working north from Whitehorse met the crew working south from Camp Canol, across the Mackenzie River from the Norman Wells oil field. The linking up of the 595-mile-long pipeline was called the "golden weld," after the gold spike used to signify completion of railroad lines. Given the publicity of the Truman hearing, there was no celebration ceremony, as there had been for completion of the Alcan Highway. Truck drivers, bulldozer operators and other civilian workers witnessed the weld. The pipeline was completed twenty-two months and four days after the route was determined in the flyover of the region.

The first oil from the field reached Whitehorse on April 16, 1944, but it was just placed in one of the storage tanks until the refinery was officially opened two weeks later. "Canol stands as one more example of United States–Canadian cooperation," said Prime Minister Mackenize King.[48] "The gasoline that flows from the refinery is proof enough that you have accomplished what so many doubters called impossible," said General Somervell in a message to those who laid the Canol pipeline. "You have every right to be proud of the outstanding engineering and construction accomplishment in the Far North."[49]

The life of the pipeline was short. On June 30, 1945, six weeks before the surrender of Japan, the Army officially closed the refinery. By then, sixty-one wells had gone into production in the Norman Wells field. The refinery processed nearly one million barrels of oil from them. But the four-inch pipes carrying the oil were only designed for 4,000 barrels a day, a figure criticized by the Truman Committee as being too low for the money being spent.

One of the most knowledgeable defenders of the Canol project was Canadian journalist Richard Finnie. Steven Bechtel, president of the lead Canol construction company, had hired Finnie as a northern specialist. After a year, the Army Corps of Engineers hired him as an advisor on the Canol project and the Alaska Highway. Finnie wrote:

The Canol Project did fuel the Alaska Highway and its airplanes, and it's been widely criticized, but one thing to remember, in the light of today's problems, [is that] the Canol project was the granddaddy of all large construction projects to take oil and move it in the Arctic and sub–Arctic. It was done by trial and error, and some dreadful mistakes were made, but it was an extraordinary project.

Mistakes? Same as the Alaska Highway. Ignorance, mostly.[50]

A contemporary report asked a series of questions:

Why was the refinery built at Whitehorse, in Canada, instead of Fairbanks, Alaska, where it would have been better placed for the war against Japan? Why did General Somervell rely on a one-page memorandum from a technical advisor in deciding to start the project and why did the Joint Chiefs of Staff, as late as the fall of 1943, refuse to turn over to the Truman committee their confidential file on the undertaking? Why was Ickes not consulted in advance? Why did Somervell ignore the pipeline route advised by the noted Arctic explorer Vilhjalmur Stefansson, who Patterson said had fathered the Canol idea and who told the *St. Louis Post Dispatch* that his simpler, lesser route would have placed the refinery in Alaska? Why was a four-inch pipeline built from Norman Wells to Whitehorse instead of a pipeline of greater capacity? ...

In retrospect it becomes painfully clear that Canol was ill conceived and ill executed, and that responsible War Department officials clung stubbornly to their mistake. Even as the sponge is tossed in, with the announcement that operations will cease in June, there is no confession that a staggering blunder was made, and persisted in, despite repeated warnings by the Truman Committee, by Ickes, and even by the Navy Department, which frowned on the undertaking from the start.[51]

Said Pierre Berton, a native of the Yukon and Canada's foremost author on the Far North: "The Canol project was a boondoggle that gobbled tax money to no great purpose and was allowed to fall into disrepair after the war."[52] And according to Lt. Col. Lyman L. Woodman, public affairs officer of the Army Corps of Engineers, Alaska Division, "The Canol served no great practical purpose as a logistical aid in World War II, and to many it seemed a visionary, unnecessary, and expensive undertaking."[53]

After the war, the *New York Times* said that the reason the Joint Chiefs of Staff continued to press for completion of the pipeline was to befuddle the Japanese: "It was felt that to abandon the project, a large-scale and physically visible signal to the enemy which could be hidden from his agents neither in progress nor in suspense, would be to inform him that our plans were turning elsewhere."[54]

While the Truman Committee questioned the Canol pipeline, the Canadian government had reservations about both it and the highway. The American military presence in the Yukon and the Northwest Territories marked the first time since the War of 1812 that foreign troops were stationed on Canadian soil. For the most part, Canadians didn't resent the Americans in their midst, although some were upset at the greater wages paid to American workers doing the same job as Canadians on the Alaska Highway and the Canol pipeline. Nor did it help that some operators at the Northwest Service Command in Whitehorse said "Army of Occupation" when answering the telephone, or that when they ran up the Stars and Stripes beside the Union Jack, the Canadian flag was flown upside down.[55]

Prime Minister King was leery of American military ambitions in Canada — he did not initially favor the Alaska Highway or the Canol pipeline — even though he and President Roosevelt could be considered friends. He noted some of his preoccupation with the United States in a March 18, 1942, entry in his personal diary: "It was not without some concern that ... I viewed the Alaskan [sic] Highway and some other things growing out of the war, which was clear to my mind that America has had as her policy, a western hemispheric control which would mean hemispheric immunity, if possible, from future wars but [with] increasing control by the U.S."[56] Three days later, the British high commissioner to Canada, Malcolm MacDonald, saw King after returning from the first of two trips he was to make to the Yukon and Northwest Territories. "Says Americans sending 46,000 workers to construct another highway along Mackenzie River," King told his diary. "I said to him that we were going to have a hard time after the war to prevent the U.S. attempting control of some Canadian situations. He said already they speak jokingly of their men as an Army of Occupation."[57]

Among those who shared MacDonald's view of the United States was his opposite number in London, Canadian High Commissioner Vincent Massey, destined to be Canada's first native-born governor general. "The American government clearly have in mind the use of the air routes for commercial purposes," he said. "All they have to do is to repaint their planes and change the clothes of their crews and they will have their civil routes in being directly peace is declared."[58]

What galled the Canadian government was American reluctance to tell them what was happening in the Northwest, especially on the Canol project, the existence of which had been a closely guarded secret for more than a year. Even before the government was notified of U.S. intentions to lay the pipeline, American Army Air Forces planes had photographed 160,000 square miles of the Northwest Territories, extending as far as the Arctic Ocean, in an attempt to identify sources of oil.[59] Not until the United States negotiated a new Canol agreement with Canada in 1944 as a result of the Truman Committee's intervention did the Army reveal its oil finds. "What is going on in northwest Canada?" M.J. Coldwell, the leader of the Co-operative Commonwealth Federation, Canada's socialist party, demanded of a government that wasn't quite sure of the answer.[60]

15

Identifying Problems

"We got the bottom of the bucket."

Even if the Army had wanted to assign black officers to the four black regiments deployed up north, it couldn't have done so: none were available. At that time, the only black officers were the chaplains, who held the rank of captain, and the father and son pair of Benjamin O. Davis and his son, Benjamin Jr. (the first a brigadier general and the latter a lieutenant colonel). The Army's Officer Candidate Schools, which accepted black candidates, only became operational in mid–1942 when the troops were already at work on the Alaska Highway and Canol pipeline. An appointment to West Point to become an officer was a rarity for blacks. The younger Davis earned one in 1932 from the only black congressman at the time, Oscar S. De Priest, a Republican from Illinois, but fellow cadets shunned Davis during his four years at the military academy. He was not assigned a roommate and took his meals alone. He graduated thirty-fifth out of 276 in his class.[1]

The Army assigned mainly Southern officers to the 93rd, 95th, 97th and 388th Regiments in the belief that they would be more culturally attuned to dealing with black enlisted men. Many white officers felt that a colleague assigned to a black unit must have earned the wrath of his superior and was being punished. "Well, what did you do to get sent here?" was a common greeting to a new white officer upon arriving at a black post.[2] Black enlisted men also questioned the qualifications of white officers. "Most of the officers weren't qualified to go to a white unit so they sent them to take care of the black soldiers," said Joseph Haskin of the 93rd. "We got the bottom of the bucket."[3] Haskin's commander, Lt. Col. James L. Lewis, recognized the complaints. "Officers of mediocre caliber and with no ability to handle Negroes were too frequently placed in isolated places to work men and equipment under very trying circumstances," he said. "The unfortunate assignment of unqualified officers has provoked some racial feelings. Most Negro soldiers acknowledge the situation exists and take a realistic view that they are soldiers in the Army of the United States and that winning the war and getting home again are more important."[4] The War Department had been advised about the quality of white officers assigned to command black units. Ulysses Lee, the official Army historian, wrote in 1942, "A special inspector reported to the War Department that there was a tendency to assign white officers of mediocre caliber to Negro units and that leadership in many units was therefore deficient."[5] There were pitfalls for those white officers who did a good job. "Once you get a Negro outfit and are reputed to handle it effectively, you are stuck with it," said a lieutenant colonel from the 95th.[6] White officers were obviously in short supply because the 388th Regiment deployed in Canada's Northwest Territories had only twenty-six, half the number assigned to the three black regiments working on the Alaska Highway.

One white lieutenant, Joseph J. Sincavage of Company "A" of the 95th, showed his sympathy for the black troops in a letter to his wife that she never received because it had been censored. Such letters were released years later:

> We have a few officers in our company that's getting money under false pretenses. We have a few officers in our company that are a disgrace to the service. As a result of higher education, they were given commissions without any trial....
>
> I saw in my own tent an officer lying in bed and giving his platoon sergeant orders for the day while the lazy scum lolled in bed. They won't eat the same food that is dished out to the men. The cooks prepare what they demand, and if their pork chop is cold, they won't eat it....
>
> Strange as it seems, these dastardly punks are southerners. The Army works for them, and the colored man is still a slave. I'd like to line them up against a stone wall and then convert them into fertilizer. If this despicable corruption was in the enlisted ranks, they'd spend their life on the "bull gang."[7]

(A member of a bull gang usually labored in heavy construction.)

One of the white officers to whom Sincavage, a Northerner, was alluding was Lt. Lloyd B. Lee of Virginia, acting platoon commander of "A" Company of the 95th. "As company clerk, I saw Lieutenant Lee every day," said Pfc. James F. Jones. "He was a racist."[8] "Lieutenant Lee treated us the way people did where he came from," said Pfc. Nathaniel Dulin of "A" Company. "He was hard to get along with."[9] Dulin once witnessed an incident between the two lieutenants when Lee swore at Sincavage. "I thought I told you to keep those men out on the road," Lee told him. Sincavage struck Lee, knocking him to the ground. "It took them sergeants on each side of him [to keep him] from stomping Lee," Dulin said. No charges were brought against Sincavage.[10]

Another white officer on the 95th was the colonel demoted to major because he refused to salute General Davis when he visited the regiment at Fort Belvoir. "The boys really hate him," said Sgt. Henry Roberts.[11]

One of the perks that many of the white officers enjoyed up north was a black orderly, a manservant to look after their needs, a throwback to the nineteenth-century military and probably not in use in the Army anywhere else during the war.[12] One such officer was Lt. Donald J. ("Smitty") Schmitt of "D" Company of the 93rd Regiment. His and his tent mate's orderly was Pvt. Charlie Knowles: "Charlie prepared our breakfast and his respectful, 'Your breakfast is served, sirs,' was always welcome. He started the fire in our tent on the cold mornings."[13] All the officers in the 97th had orderlies. Capt. James C. Coleman of "C" Company, born and raised in Bridgeport, West Virginia, said of his orderly, "He moved my tent and gear, washed clothes, kept my equipment in good shape."[14]

The Southern enlisted men tended to accept segregation in the Army as being a continuation of civilian life. "The white officers were just the way they were in the States," said Anthony Mouton of the 95th. "They weren't really ugly to us, but they just let us know that they were in charge. We just accepted that as part of the Army."[15] Quoting black soldiers on the Alaska Highway, the *Chicago Defender* newspaper reported, "Some white officers in the colored units went out of their way to make it as unpleasant for us as possible."[16] Treatment of the enlisted men by white officers varied from company to company. According to Fred Spencer of the 93rd, "Most of our officers were from the South and they knew how to get along with black people. So we had no problem with them, at least in my outfit."[17] There was some anecdotal evidence that the Army assigned a few Jewish officers to the regiments up north on the assumption that they would be less biased toward black soldiers.[18]

One white officer based in the Yukon complained, in a letter stopped by censors, about two black chaplains — Capt. Edward G. Carroll of the 95th and his counterpart with the 93rd, a minister named Austin. "First they wanted to live in the same barracks with us," the unidentified officer wrote. "That was too much, so I told them that as long as they were working up here with me, no colored officers would live with any whites.... Pretty soon expect to be called before the Colonel but I'll be damned if I am going to live with any Niggers."[19]

Maj. Thomas Arnold said, "I don't like my assignment because I don't trust Negroes. White officers who work with them have to work harder than with white troops."[20] For Floyd A. Bishop, born in Cheyenne, Wyoming, serving up north as a lieutenant with Company "D" of the 93rd Regiment was not what he had wanted to do in the Army. "I'd hardly ever seen a black man before," he said. "It was an education. They're different, all right. Most of them were pretty good. There were a few eight balls in the outfit, but that's true in any outfit."[21] After the 93rd was assigned to the Aleutians, Bishop was accepted in the Army Air Forces, where he always wanted to be. Captain Coleman, commander of "C" Company in the 97th Regiment, said, "We worked hard, we worked well together, we had no problems."[22] Coleman, who retired as a lieutenant colonel, commanded two other black units after leaving the 97th: the 855th Engineer Aviation Battalion and the 1872nd Engineer Aviation Battalion.[23]

About the only way for black enlisted men to become officers was to take a test for admission to the Officer Candidate School. Many black non-commissioned officers, including those from the 93rd, 95th, 97th and 388th, applied once the program started accepting applicants in 1942. But the Army found ways to thwart black applicants, such as Jesse Balthazar of the 97th. "I passed the test when I was in Alaska and I had an appointment to go to the school, but I couldn't go right away," he said. "When I got back to the States, I was told I couldn't attend because I had changed theaters. I had passed it in Alaska and they said it didn't count."[24] The application of Charles Gardener of Savannah, Georgia, suffered a similar fate. A member of the 93rd with one year of college, Gardener easily passed the test while at Camp Claiborne, but his application was ignored when he left for the Far North.[25]

One black officer who kept an eye on the schools was General Davis. "No colored soldiers were admitted to Officer Candidate School until I checked and found some with proper qualifications," he said. "Of the fourteen candidates selected, all graduated."[26] One of those helped by Davis was 1st Sgt. Herbert Tucker of the 95th, who had passed the test but not been accepted. He had enlisted in May of 1941, three weeks before receiving a Bachelor of Science degree from Virginia State, where he won letters in football, basketball and track. The first time he took the test, in the spring of 1942, he narrowly missed passing. Crossing the Peace River when the temperature was fifty below zero, he said to himself, "If I have to pass that test to get out of here, that's what I'm going to do."[27] He passed it shortly afterward and attended school (thanks to Davis's interest), and became a second lieutenant. Tucker remained in the Army and rose to the rank of lieutenant colonel. By the end of World War II, there were thirty-four black colonels. Davis was the only general. Tucker would later say that his most difficult wartime assignment was helping to build the Alaska Highway.[28]

Sgt. Herbert Tucker of Washington, D.C., a member of the 95th Regiment who qualified for Officer Candidate School, made lieutenant and retired from the Army as a lieutenant colonel (courtesy Thelma Tucker).

As chaplain of the 95th, Captain Carroll encouraged enlisted men to apply for officer school. When he learned that the regiment's white officers were not forwarding applications, he wrote a letter to Judge William H. Hastie, black civilian aide to Secretary of War Henry L. Stimson, and an investigation was started. Carroll said he was summoned by the regimental commander — he didn't say whether it was David L. Neuman, Heath Twichell or Albert L. Lane, all of whom held the post at various times in 1942–1943 — and was upbraided. "Chaplain," the commander said, "you have violated Army rules. You have to show reason why you shouldn't be thrown out." Carroll said his chaplain superior told him, "Well, you did violate the rules, but I think you did it for a good cause."[29] He recommended Carroll be transferred. His eventual punishment: being sent to Scotland and assigned to a port battalion. The chaplain was delighted!

Because of the expense of having separate schools for black candidates, the Army decided to integrate the Officer Candidate Schools. After service on the Alaska Highway,

Sgt. William E. Griggs, the 97th's photographer, passed the test and was accepted at the Army's school at Monmouth, New Jersey. He was the only black candidate in a class of twenty-seven for the twelve-week course. "The commandant at Monmouth was racially tolerant and put off-limits all establishments that denied service to blacks," he said.[30] As a lieutenant, he rejoined the 97th when it was assigned to the Pacific theater.

Those black enlisted men who went to school in the South weren't always as well received as was Sergeant Griggs up north. A sign was found on a fence of the school at Fort Benning, Georgia, that read, "Nigger, read this and run. If you can't read it, run anyway." Away from the post, they were referred to as "Niggers," "Snow Balls," and members of the "Black African Army."[31]

Two unlikely white women raised the question of white officers commanding black troops. One was Jean Byers, a native of Somerville, Massachusetts, who developed an interest in social justice and civil rights while attending Smith College, a woman's college in Northampton, Massachusetts. She was a member of the college's Factory Follies, a student musical troupe whose star was the future first lady Nancy Reagan. Upon graduating at twenty-one, Byers joined *Time* magazine as a writer. But the NAACP asked her to become a "special researcher" and write a report on blacks in the military. She was one of only three white employees on a staff of sixty-one. A headline in the *New York Amsterdam News* said "WHITE GIRL DOING NEGRO WAR STORY."[32]

The other woman was Ruth Gruber, a Brooklyn native who earned her Ph.D. from Germany's Cologne University at age twenty. Having written a book titled *I Went to the Soviet Arctic*, she told Harold Ickes, the interior secretary, that she'd like to work in Alaska. "Dr. Gruber is a very attractive young woman and is quite good looking," said Ickes, who was known for having a keen eye for the ladies. "I could not quite make out whether she is Jewish or not, but she may be. Anyhow, I confess that I fell for her line and decided that I would like her to go to Alaska."[33] At the time Gruber traveled, the three black regiments were working on the Alcan Highway, so Ickes asked her to report on how they were treated, a decision he probably regretted later.

Byers was given access to the records of various military branches. She also interviewed personnel from privates to generals. Although it was the NAACP that commissioned her report, the Defense Department (formerly the War Department) published it. Writing about the officer corps in the report, *A Study of the Negro in Military Service*, she noted:

> A completely false standard was used by the Army in the selection of white officers for colored units. Instead of securing officers who had proved themselves unbiased and willing to consider Negroes as soldiers, the Army often chose men with exactly the opposite qualities. One of the principal prerequisites for the assignment of a white officer to a colored unit seemed to be that he was born and reared in the South....
>
> It was assumed that by reason of his birthplace, a southern officer was more competent to exercise command of colored troops. In many instances, the fact that a white officer was from the South really handicapped him in the command of colored units, especially when

such units were made up of Negroes who lived in other parts of the United States. The majority of Southern white officers refused to think of the Negro as a soldier; they could think of him only as a laborer, a buffoon, a servant, a helpless child.[34]

Gruber made her report to Ickes in a memo dated June 11, 1943. Titled "Negro Discrimination in Alaska and Along the Alaska Highway," it said:

> Two [sic] Negro regiments were sent to Alaska and Canada to help build the Highway. They were told that as soon as they built the road they would be sent home. They worked like Trojans; they drove tractors, cut timber, barged trucks; in forty-two hours [sic] they built a bridge over a wide swift mountain stream. Morale was superb. Even the Southern officers spoke of them with praise. "The Negroes were better soldiers and builders than the whites. They put our gold-bricks to shame. We never had a bit of trouble with them; they policed themselves. If one of the Negroes got out of line about ten others would get around him right away and yell: 'Everybody's been good to us. We don't want no bad Nigger spoiling things for us.'"
>
> Uncomplainingly, the Negroes worked all summer in the mosquito-infested areas, eating, as the white soldiers did, only Spam and Vienna Sausage. When winter came, early and severe, they lived in tents. The cold was hard on them; in Whitehorse alone, according to some reports, there were three dozen amputations of frost-bitten arms and legs. Morale began to crumble a little. Yet they hardly complained, for as soon as the road was built, they were going home.
>
> They finished the job ahead of schedule. There was great publicity and rejoicing. But instead of going home, one regiment was sent to the Aleutians and the other to Livengood, north of Fairbanks, to build the pipeline road. There [sic] were shocked and furious. Tension ran so high that some of the white officers slept fearfully with guns at their sides.
>
> The regiment bound for the Aleutians was sent to Chilkoot Barracks to be re-equipped. Here they were said to have wrecked buildings; some of them had to be loaded into transports at the point of machine guns. Twelve Negroes are said to be still in chains at Whitehorse. [Author's note: She was referring to the members of the 97th Regiment who were court-martialed for refusing to ride in the back of a truck at thirty degrees below zero.]
>
> At Fairbanks and Livengood the picture is not much prettier. The only way to handle Negroes, according to certain groups in the community and the Army, is by segregation and suppression. The tragic thing is that Fairbanks has been the least offender in Alaska in race discrimination; its attitude toward its Indians and Eskimos was comparatively civilized and intelligent. Now many of the people are beginning to talk in the idiom of the South — "the flower of American womanhood is in danger; white girls aren't safe on the street; the Niggers are getting out of hand." In the same cheerful spirit, one of the most respectable women in Fairbanks telephoned the military police while I was there, demanding that they come right away; three Negro soldiers were consorting with an Indian girl on her lawn. The MPs discovered the small but amusing fact that the woman had been standing at her window for some time crinkling in the whole picture before she telephoned.
>
> What Is Being Done to Solve the Problem?
>
> In Fairbanks, so far as I could judge, nothing was done except to declare the city out of bounds for most of the Negro troops. Many of the officers sincerely regretted doing this, but they felt it was the only way to prevent trouble.
>
> At Whitehorse in the Canadian Yukon Territory, a few genuine attempts are being made to alleviate the problem. Several of the more prejudiced white officers have been removed. The food situation has been improved. For some time, according to one report, the Negro went without meat and even bread; now they are said to be the only ones who are given

Birdseye Frozen Foods. An honest, but questionably effective effort is being made to entertain them; but in a Territory which has few recreational facilities for white soldiers, the Negroes know the grim truth that they are unwanted and openly ostracized.

Suggestions:

1. An immediate and thorough investigation should be conducted by the Army or any agency not likely to whitewash or evade the problem. If the story beings [sic] to leak, Congress may decide to make its own investigation, backed by the Negro organizations in the States.

2. Establish a fixed and comprehensive Governmental policy toward Negro soldiers in the Army which might outlaw Jim Crowism toward all minorities.

3. Send recreational directors to establish a full program with mental as well as physical objectives for Negroes and whites. Enlarge the recreational facilities. Stress education in race tolerance.

The War has awakened the aspirations of the Negroes. They are eager to fight; they have proved along the Highway how capable they are. But we are corroding their faith in us, ripening them for Nazi propagandists, and preparing the soil for more race riots, willfully spreading raced hatred wherever we go, whether it be England, Australia or north of the 60th parallel, in the frontiers where men are supposed to be free.

(signed) Ruth Gruber,
Field Representative[35]

Ickes forwarded Gruber's report to the assistant secretary of war, John J. McCloy, on June 14, 1943. Four days later, Maj. Gen. Thomas T. Handy, assistant chief of staff, replied, "The memorandum is not believed to be factually accurate and is being forwarded to the Commanding General, Armed Service Forces, for investigation and report."[36] On the Fourth of July, an unnamed officer wrote, "Suspected subversion by (Dr.) Ruth Gruber (representative of Interior), who criticized Army's treatment of colored troops used in constructing Alcan."[37] A memo from the Office of the Quartermaster General said, "Her allegations apparently never saw print beyond the confidential military report that denied mistreatment and hinted that Gruber was a communist sympathizer."[38] This memo could not be located at the National Archives. Gruber said in 2008 that she never heard back from Ickes or anyone from the War Department or Army.[39]

(Ickes was one of Roosevelt's cabinet ministers who most opposed racial injustice in the United States. Abe Fortas, then Ickes' undersecretary and a future justice of the Supreme Court, once summarily fired a young black elevator operator who didn't know the floor on which his office was located. Word got to Ickes, who called the still weeping operator into his office. She was promptly rehired and told the job was hers as long as she wanted it.)[40]

A third woman who defended the rights of black soldiers was Eleanor Roosevelt. Said Baltimore's *Afro American* newspaper in its coverage of a speech at a local black church: "Mrs. Franklin D. Roosevelt, of whose liberality and magnanimity on the race question there is no doubt, used glowing terms in describing the work colored troops are doing on the Alcan Highway and in transportation in England and North Africa."[41]

Mrs. Roosevelt likewise addressed a meeting in the African Methodist Episcopal Zion Church of America in Salisbury, North Carolina, much to the displeasure of most of the local residents, and reviewed black troops from Camp Sutton led by white officers. "We must have patience and we must try with all our might to bring about recognition of the fact that man must have equal opportunity to get any job he is capable of filling," she said in her remarks.[42]

Mrs. Roosevelt also wrote to Secretary of War Stimson about how Southerners were "indignant to find that the Negro soldiers were not looked upon with terror by the girls" in other countries. "I think we will have to do a little educating among our Southern white men and officers, emphasizing the fact that every effort should be made to prevent marriages during this period but that normal relationships with groups of people who do not have the same feeling that they have about the Negro cannot be prevented and that it is important for them to recognize that in different parts of the world, certain situations differ and have to be treated differently."[43] She wrote to Stimson's undersecretary, McCloy, after black lyric tenor Roland Hayes was beaten by police in Rome, Georgia, after he sat in the white section of a shoe store. "The feeling among the colored people is very sad and I think they should be given a chance to prove their mettle," she said. "I feel they have something to gain in the war."[44]

The War Department itself undertook the biggest study in history of its personnel in wartime, blacks and whites alike. The Research Branch of the Information and Education Division of the War Department carried out the survey in March of 1943, making the results immediately available to military planners but not the public. It commissioned a companion study three months later regarding public opinion, both black and white, of the role of blacks in the war. The conclusion of the studies: white Americans were unaware of the depth of black resentment of racial discrimination in the military and in civilian life; despite this, the loyalty of blacks to the United States never wavered.

The Research Branch queried 3,000 black soldiers and 4,800 white soldiers. The black soldiers also posed questions of their own to the researchers:

"Will I as a Negro share this so-called democracy after the war?"
"Will it make things better for the Negro?"
"Will colored people be given a fair chance of employment?"
"Will colored people be continually subjected to the humiliation of Jim Crow segregation as before the war?"
"Will the South treat Negroes like human beings?"
"Will lynching cease?"
"Why do white people hate the Negro when they hire them to cook & wash & care for their children?"
"Why aren't Negro troops allowed to fight in combat as much as white troops?"

"If the white & colored soldiers are fighting and dying for the same thing, why can't they train together?"

"Why is there discrimination even in the Army?"

"Why aren't Negro soldiers given the same chance of advancement as white soldiers?"

"I would like to know what have we got to fight for?"

"Why must I fight for freedom when there is no such thing for a Negro?"

"If it's not going to benefit our race, why should we be called to shed our blood?"[45]

Commenting on the questions, the report said:

> The concern expressed in these comments is hardly consonant with the view that most Negroes were satisfied with the status of their group. Yet two-thirds of the Southern white soldiers and over half of the Northern white soldiers expressed this opinion in response to the question: Do you think that most Negroes in this country are pretty well satisfied or do you think most of them are dissatisfied? This apparent lack of awareness on the part of whites of attitudes which are rather widespread in the Negro group tends, in part, to result from cultural isolation which minimizes personal contacts between races and thereby reduces opportunities for whites to learn the thoughts and feelings of Negroes.[46]

The researchers additionally found that a majority of black soldiers from the North had attended high school, compared to only 14 percent during World War I. However, only 33 percent of black soldiers from the South had any high school education, compared to just 3 percent in the earlier war. "The illiterate plantation hand from the cotton belt was no longer the typical Negro," the report said, although there were many soldiers from Louisiana and Mississippi on the Alaska Highway and Canol projects who couldn't read or write. "But the Northern Negro fell below the Northern white and, especially, the Southern Negro fell far below the Southern whites."[47]

The War Department's Army General Classification Tests (AGCT) scores were broken down into five categories. Those in groups I and II were eligible to apply to Officer Candidate School.

AGCT	Black	White
I	1%	6%
II	6%	32%
III	14%	32%
IV	45%	23%
V	28%	3%
Unknown	6%	4%
	100%	100%

Inferior schooling for blacks, especially in the South, was generally considered the cause of their lower scores.

Black and white soldiers were also asked if they thought they were being given a fair chance to do as much as they could to help win the war:

	Black	White
YES	35%	76%
NO	54%	12%
UNDECIDED	11%	12%
	100%	100%[48]

This reflected the fact that the vast majority of black soldiers were assigned to service units, like the 93rd, 95th, 97th and 388th regiments, while most white soldiers were placed in combat units.

The black soldiers were asked if they thought they'd be treated better or worse by white people after the war than they were before the war:

BETTER	30%
ABOUT THE SAME	44%
WORSE	8%
UNDECIDED	18%
	100%[49]

Did the survey show that black troops were less loyal than whites? "There is no evidence that Negroes, in overt behavior, were less loyal than whites—for example, that they were draft evaders, or political conscientious objectors or allies of enemy agents more often than were whites."[50]

Troops in five parts of the world were asked if they ever had the feeling that the war was not worth fighting:

	Black	White
U.S.	36%	51%
European Theater	47%	43%
Mediterranean	40%	44%
Pacific	40%	46%
India/Burma	37%	47%

A soldier based in England commented on his experience: "Here in England a few of the narrow minded possibly white Southern American soldiers have already poisoned the mind of a few of the British people toward us. We were 'bears without tails,' wild, sex crazy maniacs." The researchers explained, "As these comments imply, Americans transported their values as well as their troops overseas. There was so much friction between white and Negro soldiers, and outbreaks of violence, usually arising in English towns when men were off duty and Negro men were seen associating with English girls, and were frequent enough so that the Army felt called upon to act. The solution adopted was in the American pattern of enforcing racial separation."[51]

Did the black troops support the war? "Negroes dissatisfied with the prevailing system of race relations and their inferior status were less likely than whites to accept official formulations of war aims and to view the war as of central concern to them. For Negroes there were two struggles—the war which preoccupied the nation and their own endeavor to achieve higher status in that nation."[52] Some of the comments from the black soldiers were as follows: "I am colored and friendless; we don't have anything so it's not our war"; "The white man brought us here and he should do the fighting if he does not want us"; "I don't have a country."[53]

The researchers said in their conclusion:

> On the one hand, a concept of the average Negro as a happy, dull, indifferent creature, who was quite contented with his status in the social system as a whole and in the military segment of that social system, finds little support in this study....
>
> On the other hand, the Negroes were not revolutionaries plotting the overthrow of the present social system. They were Americans in spirit. They accepted the moral values of the American creed and they protested where the discrepancies between creed and practice put them in a disadvantaged position.[54]

After the war, the Social Science Research Council funded the publication of the survey results in two volumes. The authors described the work as "one of the largest social science projects in history."[55]

Another survey in 1943 was done for the War Department by the National Opinion Research Center, then located at the University of Denver. Questions were asked of 800 blacks and 800 whites in five cities: Birmingham, Alabama; Raleigh, North Carolina; Oklahoma City; Chicago; and Detroit. Among their conclusions were the following:

> "Negroes express many grievances and dissatisfactions, yet the majority of whites think Negroes are generally satisfied."
>
> "Negroes do not think they have enough opportunity to play their part in winning the war — and again white opinion largely takes the opposite view."
>
> "Negro opinion opposes segregation in the Armed Forces, but white respondents strongly support it, not only there but in the wider social sphere."
>
> "In sum, there is little indication of white willingness to accommodate in respect to Negro demands for increased participation."

Some comments from blacks who were interviewed are listed below:

> "We don't have the chance to get jobs like we should."
>
> "A lot of Negroes are qualified for good jobs and the white man won't give them."
>
> "Our boys in camps [are] being treated so bad."
>
> "We can't go places like whites do."
>
> "You gotta beg 'em to let us help fight, or do anything else to help win the war."
>
> "Colored folks is being ignored and mistreated."
>
> "They fight together on the battlefield, why shouldn't they be trained together?"
>
> "This is supposed to be a colored man's country too."
>
> "We could end the war quicker if democracy was working here."
>
> "Clean up our own house first before we clean up somebody else's."

"Democracy must work here before the rest of the world would accept it."
"During the war, whites are learning how much the Negro can do, and will have a better attitude after the war."[56]

Based in part on the results of these studies, the War Department in 1944 issued three manuals designed to help white officers in charge of black enlisted men: "Command of Negro Troops," "Leadership and the Negro Soldier" and "Army Service Forces Manual M5." "The very material differences between white and Negro soldiers in terms of knowledge and skills important to the Army is illustrated by their comparative performances on the Army General Classification Test," noted "Command of Negro Troops." "This test, given to all selectees at reception centers, is a roughly accurate measure of what the new soldier knows, what skills he commands, and of his aptitude in solving problems. It is not a test of inborn intelligence."[57]

On the causes of black resentment in the Army, "Command of Negro Troops" said:

> Most Negroes resent any word or action which can be interpreted as evidence of a belief that they are by birth inferior in ability to members of other races. Since the Army is concerned only with individual soldiers as functioning members of military organizations, there is never any occasion to make such uncomplimentary references. When the training and assignment of Negro troops varies from that of whites, the only sound justification is in the varying distribution of individuals in terms of educational levels, skills, and experience. Many people who do not mean to be insulting use terms, tell jokes, and do things which are traditionally interpreted by Negroes as derogatory. Such words as "boy," "Negress," "darky," "uncle," "Mammy," "aunty," and "Nigger" are generally disliked by Negroes. There is also dislike of the pronunciation of the word "Negro" as though it were spelled "Nigra," because it seems to be a sort of genteel compromise between the hated word "Nigger" and the preferred term "Negro."[58]

"Leadership and the Negro Soldier" was written by black academic Ulysses Lee, an education officer at the Army Service Forces Headquarters. Some points he made in the manual were as follows:

> Negroes have been alleged to be lazy and slow moving. Certain studies have shown that they are slower in speed of reaction than whites. When one analyzes the mode of life and the environmental backgrounds of each group however, it is seen that the cultural pattern rather than the racial predisposition is the outstanding reason for manifested differences in speed. Life in rural areas does not require speed. But in large cities, where speed is more essential, both Negroes and whites react more quickly....[59]
>
> Some officers made the mistake of coddling and pampering Negro soldiers in the way they would not treat white troops, because they feel this is the way to make Negroes happy. While this practice may succeed in making a few Negroes happy, it will antagonize the great majority....[60]
>
> In civilian life every Negro, at one time or another, has been told, or has read, or has been made to feel that he is considered inferior by the majority of white people. The limited status that he has acquired in civilian life from the fact he was born with a darker skin than other Americans has influenced most of his thinking and behavior from infancy.... His entrance into the Army, like that of most soldiers, was not a matter of free choice. But

more Negro enlisted men than white enlisted men have doubts as to whether this war is their affair and whether the United States is fighting to give everybody a fair chance for a decent living.[61]

The other manual, titled "Army Service Forces Manual M5," was part of a ten-course training session for officers commanding black troops. Marked "Restricted," it said, "War Department concern with the Negro is focused directly and solely on the problem of the most effective military use of colored troops. It is essential that there be a clear understanding that the Army has no authority or intention to participate in social reform as such but does view the problem as a matter of efficient troop utilization."[62]

The manual singled out the black regiments that helped build the Alaska Highway and worked on the Canol pipeline: "American Negro soldiers are now serving in every region where there are American soldiers — regions where climates range from Arctic cold to the steaming heat of equatorial jungles. They have shown excellent adaptability to all sorts of climatic conditions.

"When the Alcan Highway was cut through, it was a Negro engineer soldier bulldozing down from the north who met and shook hands with a white engineer soldier working from the south as the two sections of this vital military artery were joined."[63]

Such feats, however, seldom had resonance in the American news media.

16

News Coverage of Black Troops Suppressed

"Here lies a black man killed fighting a yellow man for the glory of a white man."

The photograph of the black soldier from the 97th Regiment shaking hands with the white soldier from the 18th, an act that marked the completion of the Alaska Highway, was an anomaly: it showed a black soldier in a positive light. Coming less than a year after the United States entered World War II, the photograph was one of the first published in the United States of a black soldier serving abroad. There would not be many more. Southern Congressmen, some business leaders and some government officials considered "emphasis on African American achievements a threat to national unity" during the war.[1] For that reason, many Southern newspapers refused to publish such photos to avoid offending readers and elected officials. Army censors often withheld the photos from the black press for fear that the newspapers would overemphasize and distort the role of the black soldiers. One historian said, "Picturing black men in uniform could serve a positive function in the black press, but in the white press it could arouse anger, particularly among southerners, who linked black military service to the unraveling of the racial status quo."[2]

The mainstream media in the United States covered the construction of the Alaska Highway, but most stories ignored the fact that more than one-third of the troops involved were black. Had a magazine or newspaper wished to write about the black troops helping to build the Alaska Highway, the reporter would have had difficulty locating them, as they were always posted to inaccessible areas. The Army did not give press credentials to reporters from black newspapers until the highway had been completed. This lack of coverage bothered members of the black regiments up north, for they wanted their relatives and friends back home to see proof that they were contributing to the war effort.

The Army manual "Leadership and the Negro Soldier" noted that white Americans received very little information in the news media about the role of blacks in the war effort. "That being the case, it is not very surprising that many Americans feel that Negroes are not doing their share in winning the war," it said. "Negroes themselves feel this absence of news as a refusal to tell the whole story, and the result intensifies whatever strained feeling already exists between the two groups."[3] Journalist Lael Morgan, who researched the subject years later, said, "With the exceptions of a feature on the 95th in *Yank* magazine (February 10, 1943), a wire service photo of a black heavy equipment operator from the 97th shaking hands with a white counterpart from the 18th when the pioneer road was completed (October 20, 1942), and a twenty-second mention in a Hollywood-produced documentary called *The Negro Soldier* (1942), black builders of the Alcan received virtually no press."[4]

J. Edgar Hoover, director of the Federal Bureau of Investigation, was one of many top government — and military — officials who were angered by the critical role assumed by the black news media during the war. Hoover sent FBI agents to the *Pittsburgh Courier*, the largest black newspaper in the country, to complain about a series of articles on the suppression of black voting rights in the South. He also tried (unsuccessfully) to have Postmaster General Frank Walter punish black newspapers by canceling their second-class mailing privileges. He was more successful with Attorney General Francis Biddle, who invited publishers of the major black newspapers to a conference in Washington. When they arrived, they saw issues of the *Courier, Chicago Defender, Norfolk Journal and Guide* and Baltimore's *Afro American*, among others, laid out on a table. The newspapers contained articles about clashes in April 1942 between black soldiers and white police and citizens in Fort Dix, New Jersey, and Tuskegee, Alabama, that left three dead and many injured. Biddle told the publishers that they were doing a disservice to the war effort by publishing such articles, and warned he was "going to shut them all up" on grounds of sedition if they did not desist.[5] The FBI in September published a 714-page "Survey of Racial Conditions in the United States During World War II" in which it listed forty-three black newspapers it said had negative coverage, thirteen of them with communists on their staffs.[6]

The War Department's Maj. Gen. W.D. Styer sent a memo to Brig. Gen. James A. O'Connor, head of the Northwest Service Command in Whitehorse, about the "Colored situation" at Fort Dix. "Although it cannot be definitely proven, it is believed that one of the sources of agitation emanates from persons in the employ, either regularly or on a part-time basis, of the colored newspapers," he said. "These men follow the trend set by the colored press which is to the effect that with the country at war the Negro race has an opportunity for social gains, and that every possible active discrimination should be played up and promptly reported."[7] At the time, there were 33,302 white enlisted men and 8,820 blacks at Fort Dix; they were commanded by 2,767 white officers and just sixty-one black officers.

Maj. Gen. George V. Strong, assistant to Army Chief of Staff George Marshall, attacked the black newspapers:

> Certain sections of the Negro press in the United States have seized the opportunity provided by the need for unity in war to press their demands for greater equality and the remedying of alleged injustices....
> Some influential papers as the *Pittsburgh Courier*, the *Chicago Defender*, and certain members of the *Afro American* chain, have published articles caustically criticizing the Army and

its administration. Under the guise of agitation for better conditions for Negro troops these papers at times have been extremely bitter, and could not be considered as influencing their readers toward high allegiance to the Army. As long as these papers carry on their efforts for the purpose of racial betterment they cannot be termed as subversive organs. They do, however, at times appear to achieve the same result as outright subversive publications.[8]

His recommendation: "All possible steps should be taken to reduce and control the publication of inflammatory and vituperative articles in the colored press."[9] Secretary of War Henry L. Stimson agreed, saying, "The attitudes and opinions advanced by most Negro newspapers, too, were shockingly biased and unreliable."[10]

President Roosevelt told NAACP director Walter White that the Justice Department was under pressure to indict the publishers for sedition and to deny the newspapers scarce newsprint. White met with the publishers in January 1943 and encouraged them to form the Negro Newspaper Publishers Association, which then adopted a code of ethics to curb what they termed sensationalism.

The newspaper that drew the most ire was the *Pittsburgh Courier*, which launched on February 7, 1942, what became known as the "Double V" campaign. Suggested by a reader, the campaign grew out of the "V for Victory" made by the index and middle fingers that was British Prime Minister Winston Churchill's rallying symbol during the early years of the war, adopted by the United States as well after Pearl Harbor. For the newspaper, there were two victories to be won — the defeat of the Axis Powers abroad and the defeat of racism at home: "The first V for victory over our enemies from without, the second V for victory over our enemies from within."[11] The *Courier* designed a poster ("Double V — victory abroad — at home") that was sent to the newspaper's distributors throughout the country for local display. Other black newspapers immediately joined the campaign. Then civil rights leaders adopted the "Double V" as *their* rallying cry.

Among the targets of the campaign was the Army's policy of consigning most black troops to service regiments like those that worked on the construction projects in Alaska and Canada's Northwest. The reasoning went like this: "If blacks did not win the fight for the right to fight, then after the war the attitude of the majority race would be: 'After all, boy, you didn't do any of the fighting, you just stayed behind the line and drove trucks.'"[12] "The Negro reporter is a fighting partisan," wrote Percival L. Prattis, editor of the *Courier*, which then had a circulation of 350,000. "He has an enemy. That enemy is the enemy of his people. The people who read his newspaper, or read after him, expect him to put up a good fight for them."[13] Prattis upset the military shortly after assuming the editorship of the newspaper in 1940. He published a letter from thirteen black seamen on the light cruiser USS *Philadelphia* who complained of the Navy's racial policy. When the Navy jailed the black sailors pending a court-martial, Prattis and the newspaper took up their cause and got all charges against them dropped, although they were given bad conduct or undesirable conduct discharges.

The *Courier's* George Schuyler, who was considered the leading black columnist in the United States, was always critical of the Army and supportive of its black troops. "Our war is not against Hitler in Europe, but against Hitler in America," he once wrote. "Our war is not to defend democracy, but to get a democracy we have never had."[14]

The influence of the black press could not be ignored. By the end of the war, weekly circulation of black newspapers had reached nearly two million. It was estimated that one-third of the urban black population subscribed to a black newspaper.[15] The newspapers' questioning of the Army's racial policy and the treatment of blacks generally resonated with the public. A saying attributed to a black draftee was, "Here lies a black man killed fighting a yellow man for the glory of a white man."[16] Harlem leader Charles Williams said, "If we don't fight for our rights during this war, while the government needs us, it will be too late after the war."[17]

Critics of the black press were emboldened in their attacks by two of President Roosevelt's executive orders: the establishment of an Office of Censorship shortly after Pearl Harbor and of the Office of War Information in June 1942. The director of the latter office was the poet Archibald MacLeish, who urged the black newspaper publishers to back off the "Double V" campaign. They declined his request. Others thought the president's executive orders gave them leeway to initiate their own policies. Lt. Buel A. Williamson ordered the cancellation of subscriptions to five black newspapers received at Camp Forest, Georgia. Other officers simply confiscated the newspapers at their camp post offices. The War Department finally issued a directive that no newspaper or magazine that enjoyed mailing privileges could be banned at Army posts.[18] "Some officers have made the mistake of forbidding Negro newspapers on the Post out of fear that they would lower the morale of the men," said the Army. "Such action is against Army policy and is unwise."[19]

Renowned syndicated columnist Westbrook Pegler, an ultra-conservative and fierce critic of President Roosevelt's New Deal, weighed in, saying of the black newspapers that "in their obvious, inflammatory bias in the treatment of news they resemble such one-sided publications as the Communist Party's *Daily Worker*." The column so infuriated the Negro Newspaper Publishers Association that it ordered a study of 2,270 news items published in the five largest black newspapers, including the *Pittsburgh Courier*. "The five weeklies came out with a clean bill of health except for minor aberrations here and there. Specifically [it was] found that the Negro papers support the basic democratic tenets of the United States but are critical of the practices of the American social system."[20]

Black newspapers were not made available to the troops working on the Alaska Highway and the Canol pipeline, although at least one soldier subscribed for himself—Sgt. John A. Bollin of "F" Company of the 93rd Regiment. "I had the *Afro American* follow me the whole time I was in the Army," he said. "It came by mail. I was the only one in the company to receive a newspaper."[21] A commander of the 93rd, Lt. Col. James L. Lewis, was well aware of the interest in news from home. He wrote in a report on his experience with the regiment:

> Newspapers and periodicals published by Negroes are widely read and discussed. The race riots and disputes in the United States are most frequently discussed. Treatment of Negro soldiers by the civilians has not always been conducive to high morale or good feelings....
>
> Radical newspapers and magazines for Negroes are read with growing racial consciousness. It is believed the same interest would be shown in a service newspaper for Negro soldiers similar to *Yank* [magazine]. Coverage of music, sports and hometown news should be stressed. Activities of prominent Negro leaders in the Army should be featured. Such a newspaper would be definitely worthwhile as a means of giving adequate news coverage to Negro outfits.[22]

The *Pittsburgh Courier* even tackled Hollywood after Paramount Pictures brought out the movie *Alaska Highway*, starring Richard Arlen, in 1943. It was as much a love story as wartime construction saga about a private contractor and his workers seconded by the Army's Corps of Engineers. "Pushing themselves and their equipment to the limit in the rough Canadian wilderness, the men must pull together to survive the brutal cold and natural disasters they encounter," said a blurb. "To keep up morale, the crew entertain themselves with practical jokes, dreaming of warmer days, romantic affairs and an electric blanket." The *Courier* headline over its story of the movie said, "HOLLYWOOD MISSES BOAT: MOVIE MOGULS IGNORE PART PLAYED BY NEGRO ENGINEERS." "A lily-white Paramount version of Pan-American history has been released, but it is an example to show what Hollywood did not do to show democracy in its real sense," the newspaper declared. "After promising leading Americans that Negroes would be given decent roles in the forthcoming film, Hollywood turned out 'Alaska Highway' without including a single Negro face."[23] Cpl. Refines Sims, the black catskinner who met up with his white counterpart from the 18th Regiment at Beaver Creek to complete the highway, was portrayed by a white actor. Much of the movie was filmed in the province of Alberta; actual newsreel footage was also used.

It wasn't as if blacks weren't getting roles in movies. They were. About one of four wartime feature films had parts for blacks, but they portrayed domestic servants, entertainers or poor people. Black Army historian Ulysses Lee faulted these roles. "The failure to portray the Negro in films and other information channels as an ordinary, normal American with a dark skin, has contributed heavily to what the psychologists call a 'stereotype,'" he said. "By this, they mean a fixed mental picture. When the Negro is portrayed in the movies, or elsewhere, as a lazy, shiftless, no-good, slew-footed, happy-go-lucky, razor-toting, tap-dancing vagrant, a step has been taken in the direction of fixing this mental picture of the Negro in the minds of whites."[24]

As the black troops had already left, or were preparing to leave the Alaska Highway in 1943, the *Chicago Defender* obtained permission to send reporter Albert G. Barnett up north to write an article it would have preferred to have published months earlier. He started his report by calling the Alaska Highway "the world's greatest monument to Negro labor, an enduring, indestructible highway of sand and gravel, steel and concrete — snatched from virgin jungle and mountain fastness and christened with the sweat from 4,000 black brows."[25] He added, "A force of nearly 4,000 Negroes worked through the tough, frigid Arctic season, seven days a week, without complaint or remonstrance. Demonstrating the faith, loyalty and patriotism of black Americans for flag and country, they carried through to the glorious finale."

Epilogue

1943

When Staff Sgt. Clifton B. Monk, born and raised in Newton Grove, North Carolina, returned to the lower forty-eight states from Alaska with the 97th Regiment, he found little had changed in the eighteen months he'd been away. "We were on the train going back south to Camp Sutton," he recalled. "When we crossed the Mason-Dixon Line around Washington, the train stopped. They blew a whistle and made us line up in a big old field where there weren't any houses or buildings. Then they related about that segregation business. We would have to live like we lived before we left. We had been sitting anywhere we wanted to on the train, but now we was back in segregation. We loaded up and got into separate cars. It sounded ignorant and foolish then, and now too. I didn't feel good about it."[1]

The 97th reached the camp in North Carolina on September 18, 1943; seven months later, after being re-outfitted, it arrived at Milne Bay, New Guinea. Its new assignment: more roadwork. "We went from the coldest place in the world to the hottest," said Jesse Balthazar, born in McIntosh, Louisiana. "We were moving all the time in Alaska, but at least in New Guinea we stayed in one place."[2] Lee Young, a native of Engelhard, North Carolina, witnessed an incident unlike anything he had seen in Alaska. "We had a battalion commander — he was a major then — he was from Mississippi," he said. "He got into trouble when we got to New Guinea. We didn't have stockades there and he tied one of the black soldiers to a tree. A white lieutenant came by and reported this. They sent the commander back to the States right quick."[3]

The 95th Regiment left Dawson Creek in a snowstorm. "The snow was up to the hood of the jeep and it was still snowing," said Sgt. Otis E. Lee, born in Virginia and raised in Trenton, New Jersey. "They took us down to Louisiana and we still had our heavy clothes on."[4] When the 95th got to Camp Claiborne, Louisiana, the troops were in for an indignity. Fearing possible violence, camp authorities denied the enlisted men the use of knives at meals in the mess hall. "We were one of the largest black units in Louisiana and they thought we were going to tear up the town," said Pfc. James F. Jones.[5] When they did go into nearby Alexandria, they were hassled by police, so they kept to the black district. During the regrouping of the 95th, Pvt. Richard E. Trent from the Pittsburgh area received a pass to visit his family. Not used to segregation back home, he waited in the white line for the train instead of the black one. By the time he realized his mistake, the black coach had filled up. "I didn't get home," he said. "I kept thinking of all the people who came out to cheer our troop train in Canada."[6]

The 95th worked on flood control on the White River in Arkansas before being assigned to Camp Shanks in New York, the port of embarkation for Europe, where their resentment was said to have boiled over. "They threatened to kill their Southern officers and a riot broke out," said one report.[7] By August of 1943 the troops were in Britain, building camps and hospitals for the invasion that was coming. After D-Day the following year, they were on the continent and involved in road and rail construction. They cleared debris and did street reconstruction in the Cherbourg area and rehabilitated railroad tracks elsewhere in France.

1944

The 93rd Regiment shipped out to Burma where it worked on the Ledo Road (although not on construction, as it was nearly complete when the troops arrived). As it did on the Alaska Highway, the 93rd provided truck drivers to move supplies and ammunition on the road. "When we got to Burma it was 115 degrees, 120 some days," said Fred Spencer, born in Grande Ridge, Florida. "It was very humid. During the monsoon season, you'd lay in your cot and you'd be soaking wet."[8] After finishing a tour on the road, the 93rd moved to India, where it built hangars.

The 388th arrived in France on July 5, where it did construction work during the Normandy and northern France campaigns. It sailed from Marseilles, France, on July 16, 1945, bound for the Philippines.

On August 12, President Roosevelt arrived by Navy ship in Adak in the Aleutian Islands on his last military trip, eight months before his death. He had lunch with 125 enlisted men, of whom twenty-three were black soldiers, plus a handful of black naval messmen. He had said he did not want to have lunch with officers. Press reports did not say whether the black enlisted men were obliged to eat at tables by themselves.[9]

1945

The officer opposed to the black regiments being deployed up north, Simon Bolivar Buckner, Jr., was promoted to lieutenant general and given command of the 10th Army during the battle for Okinawa. On June 22, a shell hit the mountaintop from which the general was observing action. When it exploded, the shell drove a piece of rock into Buckner's chest, killing him. He was the highest-ranking American officer killed by enemy fire during the war.

Lt. Gen. Brehon Somervell, the man responsible for the Canol pipeline, remained in Washington until the end of the war, organizing and directing the worldwide supply lines for the Army. He announced his retirement in December 1945.

Brig. Gen. James A. O'Connor, the commander who oversaw construction of the highway and pipeline projects, completed his service up north in 1944 and was named commandant of the Army's training center at Fort Devens, Massachusetts. The following year he was named chief engineer of Army units in the China-Burma-India theater, once again having the 93rd and 97th Regiments under his command.

Some members of the other two black regiments that served up north, the 95th and the 388th, became involved in the same European operation as Brig. Gen. William M. Hoge, the first head of the Alaska Highway project: the Battle of the Bulge. Adolf Hitler had ordered the German army to make a last stand in the Ardennes mountain region of Belgium, concentrating on American troops in the belief that Americans back home would flinch at the casualties. The American losses totaled 19,000 dead, making it the single deadliest battle in U.S. history. After the battle, Hoge, who commanded troops from the 9th Armored Division, was awarded the Distinguished Service Medal for his defense of the town of St. Vith, delaying the German advance.

Since the Army desperately needed reinforcements during the Battle of the Bulge, Lt. Gen. John C. H. Lee, the Service and Supplies commander responsible for supplying troops, recommended asking members of the black service units like the 95th and the 388th to volunteer for combat. They would fight alongside white troops, effectively desegregating the Army. Gen. Dwight D. Eisenhower, the supreme Allied commander, approved the plan and passed it along to Washington. But Gen. George C. Marshall, the Army's chief of staff, disliked the racial integration aspect. His office approved the plan provided the black troops were kept in their own platoons, not in desegregated, mixed units.[10] General Lee sent a letter to commanders of black troops: "This opportunity to volunteer will be extended to all soldiers without regard to color or race."[11] Some 4,000 black enlisted men answered the call to fight and 2,221 were selected. One of these was Otis Lee of the 95th, who voluntarily gave up his sergeant's stripes and served as a private.[12] "A lot of guys from my outfit went," said Pvt. Henry Easter, also of the 95th. "One of them got killed. I was close enough to hear the guns go off."[13] Others from the 388th volunteered.[14] In one company, 171 out of 186 men volunteered for combat.[15] Black and white soldiers ate and slept together and used the same sanitary facilities, effectively desegregating the Armed Forces for the first time since the American Revolution, even if the Army high command disapproved.[16]

The most storied black participants in the Battle of the Bulge were members of the 761st Tank Battalion, known as the Black Panthers. Landing at Omaha Beach on October 10, 1944, the 761st was once in combat for 183 consecutive days, a period that included the Battle of the Bulge and later crossing the Rhine River. It was said that the 761st was denied fuel at the close of fighting so it couldn't be the first unit to meet up with Russian forces, leaving that honor to a white unit. When the 761st was assigned to Gen. George Patton, he told them, "Men, you're the first Negro tankers to ever fight in the American Army. I would never have asked for you if you weren't good."[17]

"They said we couldn't even operate the mechanized equipment," said Floyd Dade, who was a twenty-year-old private in the Battle of the Bulge. "But we were the best."[18]

Once the Battle of the Bulge and cleanup operations ended, the black soldiers were sent back to their segregated service units, just as their predecessors had been returned to their slave owners following the War of Independence.

Why did these men volunteer for combat? "We figured, 'Well, let's fight. It's what we're here for,'" said Milton S. Hale of Pell City, Alabama, member of a black service unit.[19] "I was young, adventurous, looking for excitement," said Matthew S. Brown of Savannah, Georgia. "I wanted to do something meaningful."[20] According to Pfc. George Freeman of Dunn, North Carolina, "I came into the Army to fight, not to labor. That's why I volunteered."[21] The explanation of James Smith, who earned a Bronze Star during his time in combat: "In case people ever said, 'You boys didn't do anything over there.'"[22]

1946

The most popular piece of legislation passed by Congress for veterans, both black and white, was the GI Bill, under which returning veterans could obtain a free university education. Proportionally, more black GIs than whites wanted to attend a university. But the blacks faced a problem: finding where to enroll. There were only 112 black universities and colleges, which soon were filled to capacity, while Southern universities were all-white. A native of Baltimore, William E. Griggs would have preferred to attend the University of Maryland for his Master's degree, but it barred blacks. He obtained his degree at New York University and returned home to Baltimore, where he taught math for thirty-seven years in the city's school system. He was not the only GI to look for a university in the more tolerant North.

Hayward Oubre, a native of New Orleans and also of the 97th, obtained a Master of Fine Arts degree from the University of Iowa under the GI Bill. He became a well-known sculptor and art teacher at several universities.

George A. Owens of the 93rd Regiment, a native of Bolton, Mississippi, obtained his Master's in business administration from Columbia University in New York and returned to his alma mater, Tougaloo College, a historical black institution near Jackson, Mississippi, founded in 1869. He served as its president from 1964 to 1984.

What did some of the others quoted in this book do once back in civilian life? Herbert L. Tucker of the 95th, a native of Washington, retired from the Army in 1961 with the rank of lieutenant colonel and later held various posts in the District of Columbia, including that of director of the Solid Waste Management Administration.

Chaplain Edward G. Carroll of the 95th, a native of Wheeling, West Virginia, became a Methodist Church bishop for New England. General O'Connor once sent Carroll a letter complimenting him on his sermons.

Nehemiah Atkinson of the 97th became supervisor of the recreation department in New Orleans, where he was born and raised. He taught tennis and was a ranked senior player, competing against white greats such as Bobby Riggs and Gardner Mulloy.

Joseph Prejean became a famous chef in New Orleans.

Jesse Balthazar, Joseph Haskin, Irving Smith and Henry Easter had long careers in the postal service.

Otis E. Lee, Albert E. France and James F. Jones were railroad employees, while Fred Spencer worked in construction and John A. Bollin started a travel agency.

Alexander Powell started Powell Bridal and Rental Service in Quincy, Florida, and Wesley Davis became a circus foreman.

Anthony Mouton played one year of baseball in a California Negro league, finished high school and entered a university before leaving to work in business, whereas Lee Young stayed in the Army until 1961, then went into construction, and Reginald Beverly resumed teaching high school science and math.

On January 26, 1946, a three-man War Department board studying the utilization of Negro manpower in the post-war Armed Forces noted the success of mixed white and black units used during the Battle of the Bulge.[23] Among those who initially opposed post-war integration were Generals Dwight D. Eisenhower, George C. Marshall and Mark W. Clark.[24]

On April 3, the United States officially transferred the Alaska Highway to Canada in a ceremony held in Whitehorse. General Hoge returned to his old northern headquarters for the event, at which Canada was represented by its minister of national defense, retired general A.G.L. MacNaughton, who had commanded Canadian troops in the European theater. The Canadian Army assumed management of the highway and opened it to the public in 1948.

On April 27, a three-member military commission headed by Lt. Gen. Alvan C. Gillen, Jr., recommended better use of blacks in the Armed Services but stopped short of outright desegregation.

On July 25, the last mass lynching in the United States occurred near Monroe, Georgia, where a mob hanged black Army veteran George W. Dorsey, his wife, Mae, and another black couple, Roger and Dorothy Malcom. A member of the mob cut Mrs. Malcom's unborn child from her womb.

On December 5, President Truman, prompted by a spate of lynchings, appointed a President's Committee on Civil Rights to investigate racial abuses in the United States. A fifteen-man commission, it was chaired by Charles E. Wilson, president of General Electric.

1947

On February 13, Imperial Oil's Leduc No. 1 produced a gusher, marking the discovery of a large oil field just outside of Edmonton, Alberta. The Canol refinery at Whitehorse was dismantled and moved to Alberta.

On April 15, a black war veteran named Jack Roosevelt Robinson, once court-martialed in Texas for refusing to move to the back of a bus, broke the color barrier in major league baseball with the Brooklyn Dodgers.

On October 29, the Committee on Civil Rights submitted its report to President Truman. Among the issues raised was the fact that blacks served in the military under discriminatory conditions.

1948

On July 26, President Truman, acting on the findings of the Committee on Civil Rights, issued Executive Order No. 9981, officially desegregating the U.S. military. It says in part, "There shall be equality of treatment and opportunity for all persons in the armed services without regard to race, color, religion or national origin." The president also created the Committee of Equality of Treatment and Opportunity in the Armed Forces to ensure that the goals of desegregation in the military were met. The committee consisted of three white and two black members.

1949

On March 28, Gen. Omar Bradley, chief of staff, told the Committee of Equality that "a system of complete integration might seriously affect morale and thus affect battle efficiency."

On April 1, the secretary of the Army, Kenneth Claiborne Royall, was forced into retirement for refusing to desegregate the Army. A native of Goldsboro, North Carolina, Royall was a brigadier general in World War II.

1954

On September 30, Secretary of Defense Charles Wilson announced that the last all-black Army unit had been abolished.

1963

On July 26, Secretary of Defense Robert S. McNamara issued a directive under which military commanders were empowered to declare off-limits any establishments that discriminated against black servicemen.

1993

Alaskan journalist Lael Morgan and the Black Archives Research Center at Florida A&M University mounted an exhibit marking the fiftieth anniversary of the deployment of black soldiers to work on the Alaska Highway. The exhibit opened at the University of Alaska Museum in Fairbanks and later spent six months at the Pentagon. Gen. Colin Powell, the first black chairman of the Joint Chiefs of Staff, said on April 14, "I had no idea black men had done anything like this."[25] On June 14, a group of veterans from the 93rd, 95th and 97th Regiments visited the Pentagon. The previous month, the Alaska State Legislature had named the bridge over the Gerstle River in Alaska between Delta Junction and Tok the Black Veterans Recognition Bridge.

1996

The Alaska Highway was cited as an international landmark by the International Historical Engineering Landmark Commission.

1997

On January 17, President Bill Clinton awarded seven Congressional Medals of Honor to black soldiers, the only ones given to any of the 1,154,720 who served in World War II; the only living recipient was Vernon Baker of St. Maries, Idaho, who, as a second lieutenant with the 370th Infantry, singlehandedly destroyed three German machine-gun nests, an observation post and a dugout and killed nine enemy soldiers.

2005

On January 4, Congress passed a joint resolution that recognized the role played by the 93rd, 95th, 97th and 388th Regiments in construction in the Far North and in the integration of the Armed Forces:

> Whereas the bombing of Pearl Harbor necessitated constructing an overland route between Alaska and the lower 48 States for military purposes;
> Whereas on February 11, 1942, President Franklin Delano Roosevelt authorized the construction of the Alaska-Canada Highway (Also known as the "Alcan Highway");
> Whereas construction of the Alcan Highway, a 1,552-mile long road from Dawson Creek, Canada, to Fairbanks, Alaska, was an engineering feat of enormous challenge;
> Whereas the Alcan Highway was constructed by approximately 10,000 United States troops through rugged, unmapped wilderness and extreme temperatures, ranging from 80-degrees-below to 90-degrees-above zero;

Alcan's Black Engineers

When America needed a highway through
The lads of Black all dressed in brown
Carved out a road from frozen ground
From Dawson Creek to Delta Junction
They hacked and chopped and froze their toes
To save America from its foes.

Many a night they went to bed
With bodies black and blue and red
Mosquitoes, Black flies, No see'ums too
Had bitten their clothes and gotten through.
In muck and mire, brimstone and fire
They bulldozed their way and didn't tire.

Without shellfire or any belle
They came through many swamps of hell.
Missing grits and American fries
They made the mighty  lifeline
Of the Alcan Highway rise.

Then tanks, guns and aiplane crews
Could roll this highway to pay their dues.
In spring, summer, winter and fall
Sometimes with no day or sun at all
These Black guys answered their countries call.

Kept the Alcan open, made it work.
A monster challenge they did not skirk.
The black soldier and his crew
Saw this great endeavor through.

The Alcan Highway is now history
And will remain into eternity.
North to the future in this state
That's a cut above the forty eight.

Epilogue

Whereas the Corps of Engineers units assigned to construct the Alcan Highway were segregated by race;

Whereas the 93rd, 95th, and 97th Regiments and the 388th Battalion of the Corps of Engineers, part of a group known as the "Black Corps of Engineers," were African American units assigned to the Alcan Highway project, and these units comprised one-third of the total engineering workforce on the project;

Whereas despite severe discriminatory policies, and abominable living and social conditions, the soldiers of the Black Corps of Engineers performed notably and unselfishly on the project;

Whereas on November 20, 1942, the Alcan Highway was completed in an astonishing 8 months and 12 days, becoming one of the Nation's greatest public works projects in the 20th century;

Whereas the Alcan Highway became the only land route that strategically linked the northern territory to the remainder of the continental United States and facilitated the construction of airstrips for refueling planes and vital supply routes during World War II;

Whereas although considerable praise was bestowed upon soldiers for exemplary work in constructing the Alcan Highway, the soldiers of the Black Corps of Engineers were seldom recognized; and

Whereas despite enduring indignities and double standards, the soldiers of the Black Corps of Engineers contributed unselfishly to the western defense in World War II and these contributions helped lead to the subsequent integration of the military: Now, therefore, be it

Resolved by the House of Representatives (the Senate concurring), that Congress honors the soldiers of the Army's Black Corps of Engineers for their contributions in constructing the Alaska-Canada highway during World War II and recognizes the importance of these contributions to the subsequent integration of the military.

The author of the resolution was Eddie Bernice Johnson, then a seventy-year-old black Democratic congresswoman from Waco, Texas, who, like Colin Powell, had been unaware of the presence and role of the black troops up north. "Regretfully, since 1942, their contributions toward this country's Western defense during World War II and subsequent integration of the military have been excluded from many of the footnotes of history," she said.[26]

Sixty years after the end of World War II, she decided to do something about it.

Opposite: Peggy D'Orsay, librarian at the Yukon Archives in Whitehorse, recalled J. Roscoe Hurst as a "nice-looking black man" who appeared to be in his late sixties when he showed up at the Archives in late 1992. He spent five minutes there, said he had been a soldier working on the Alaska Highway during the World War II, and he had a poem he wanted to leave. He never returned. Efforts by the author to locate him were fruitless. The Archives later posted the poem on its Web site (courtesy Yukon Archives).

Chapter Notes

Introduction

1. Robert Platt Boyd, Jr., *Me and Company "C"* (Self-published, Library of Congress Catalog Card #92-90656, 1992), p. 62.
2. *The Atlanta Journal-Constitution*, June 21, 1991.
3. Master Sgt. George H. Burke, quoted in Harold Griffin, *Alaska and the Canadian Northwest: Our New Frontier* (New York: W.W. Norton, 1944), p. 119.
4. *Chicago Defender*, March 6, 1943.
5. Kenneth S. Coates and William R. Morrison, "Soldier-Workers: The U.S. Army Corps of Engineers and the Northwest Defense Projects 1942–46," *The Pacific Historical Review*, Vol. 62, No. 3 (August 1993), p. 294.
6. *Ibid.*
7. Patricia A. McCormack to author, e-mail April 1, 2008.
8. Joseph Driscoll, *War Discovers Alaska* (New York: J.B. Lippincott, 1943), p. 28.
9. Gen. Simon Bolivar Buckner, Jr., to Brig. Gen. Clarence L. Sturdevant, letter, April 20, 1942, Historical Division, Chief of Engineers, Fort Belvoir, Va.
10. Memo, June 17, 1942, from the Military Intelligence Division of the War Department to the assistant chief of staff of the Army, Brig. Gen. Thomas T. Handy, OPD291.21 Section 10, NA RG165.
11. The city of Fort St. John in British Columbia took the first step in February of 2010 when it passed a resolution to support historical status for the highway.
12. Waldo G. Bowman, *Bulldozers Come First: The Story of U.S. War Construction in Foreign Lands* (New York: McGraw-Hill, 1944), p. 119.
13. Richard Finnie, *Canol: The Sub-Arctic Pipeline and Refinery Project Constructed by Bechtel-Price-Callahan for the Corps of Engineers United States Army 1942–44* (San Francisco: Ryder & Ingram, 1945), p. 2.

Chapter 1

1. Pierre Berton, *Klondike: The Life & Death of the Last Great Gold Rush* (Toronto: McClelland & Stewart, 1958), p. 417.
2. The 1900 and 1901 censuses in the U.S. and Canada, respectively, showed 168 blacks in Alaska and ninety-nine in the Yukon, most of them in the Dawson City area.
3. Berton, *Klondike*, p. 395.
4. *Dawson Daily News*, February 2, 1903.
5. George Harper Collection, "Blacks in Alaska History," Box 1, Folder 13, Archives and Special Collections, Consortium Library, University of Alaska, Anchorage.
6. *Ibid.*
7. Vincent Massey, *What's Past Is Prologue: The Memoirs of the Right Honourable Vincent Massey* (Toronto: University of Toronto Press, 1963), p. 396.
8. Lyman L. Woodman, "Building the Alaska Highway: A Saga of the Northland," *The Northern Engineer*, Vol. 8, No. 2 (1976), p. 15.
9. Harold Griffin, *Alaska and the Canadian Northwest: Our New Frontier* (New York: W.W. Norton, 1944), p. 103.
10. Jean Potter, *Alaska Under Arms* (New York: Macmillan, 1942), p. 75.
11. "The Alaska Highway 1942–49," produced by Alaska Public Telecommunications, Inc., Channel 7, 1992.
12. Bryr Ludington, "Pioneer of the Alaska Highway," *Alaska*, October 2008.
13. Canadian Press, Ottawa, November 13, 1941.
14. *Globe and Mail*, Toronto, August 18, 1940.
15. Richard G. Bucksar, "The Alaska Highway: Background to Decision," *The Arctic Institute of North America*, Vol. 21, No. 4 (1968), p. 215.

Chapter 2

1. Philip H. Godsell, *The Romance of the Alaska Highway* (Toronto: The Ryerson Press, 1944), p. 139.
2. Jean Potter, *Alaska Under Arms* (New York: Macmillan, 1942), p. 78.
3. Phyllis Lee Brebner, *The Alaska Highway: A Personal & Historical Account of the Building of the Alaska Highway* (Erin, Ontario: The Boston Mills Press, 1985), p. 10.
4. Gregory A. Johnson, "Strategic Necessity or Military Blunder? Another Look at the Decision to Build the Alaska Highway," *CCI Occasional Publication*, No. 38 (1996), Canadian Circumpolar Institute, p. 5.
5. Alden P. Armagnac, "Six-Month's Miracle:

How U.S. Army Engineers Conquered Bogs and Forests in One of the Greatest Road-Building Jobs of Our Day," *Popular Science* (February 1943), p. 100.

6. V.H. Jorgensen, Jr., "Our New Land and Air Route to Alaska," *Saturday Evening Post*, November 7, 1942.

7. John Schmidt, *This Was No ----- Picnic: 2.4 Years of Wild and Woolly Mayhem in Dawson Creek* (Hanna, Alberta: Gorman & Gorman, 1991), p. 40.

8. *Ibid.*

9. Ronald A. Keith, *Bush Pilot with a Briefcase: The Happy-Go-Lucky Story of Grant McConachie* (Toronto: Doubleday Canada, 1972), p. 238.

10. Godsell, *The Romance of the Alaska Highway*, p. 146.

11. Canadian Press, Washington, March 2, 1942.

12. C.L. Sturdevant, "The Alaska Military Highway," *Engineering Journal*, Vol. 26 (1943), p. 117.

13. Canadian Press, Ottawa, April 22, 1942.

14. Col. K.B. Bush Papers, Yukon Archives, Whitehorse, Yukon Territory.

15. U.S. Congress, Senate Investigation of the National Defense Program, Part 13, 78th Congress, January 8, 1944, Appendix II.

16. Richard Finnie, "The Epic of Canol," *Canadian Geographical Journal*, March 1947.

17. John Sibley Butler, "Affirmative Action in the Military," *Annals of the American Academy of Political and Social Science*, Vol. 523 (September 1992), p. 198.

18. Earl Brown, "American Negroes and the War," *Harper's* (April 1942), p. 546.

19. Ulysses Lee, *The Employment of Negro Troops* (Washington, D.C.: U.S. Government Printing Office, 1963), p. 88.

20. Philip A. Klinkner and Rogers M. Smith, *The Unsteady March: The Rise and Decline of Racial Equality in America* (Chicago: University of Chicago Press, 1999), p. 149.

21. Lee, *The Employment of Negro Troops*, p. 45.

22. Henry L. Stimson Diary, September 22, 1941, Yale University Library, New Haven, Conn.

23. Lee, *The Employment of Negro Troops*, p. 48.

24. Bruce Bartlett, *Wrong on Race: The Democratic Party's Buried Past* (New York: Palgrave Macmillan, 2008), p. 118.

25. Ronald Takaki, *Double Victory: A Multicultural History of America in World War II* (New York: Little, Brown, 2000), p. 39.

26. Daniel Kryder, *Divided Arsenal: Race and the American State During World War II* (New York: Cambridge University Press, 2000), p. 27.

27. *Ibid.*, p. 29.

28. Phillip McGuire, *He, Too, Spoke for Democracy: Judge Hastie, World War II, and the Black Soldier* (New York: Greenwood Press, 1988), p. 4.

29. Klinkner and Smith, *The Unsteady March*, p. 152.

30. Nat Brandt, *Harlem at War: The Black Experience in WWII* (Syracuse: Syracuse University Press, 1996), p. 70.

31. AG 291.21 (10-9-40) M-A-M. October 16, 1940.

32. Morris J. MacGregor and Bernard C. Nalty, *Blacks in the United States Armed Forces: Basic Documents* (Wilmington, DE: Scholarly Resources, 1977), p. 109.

33. *The Crisis*, October 9, 1940.

34. Robert W. Mullen, *Blacks in America's Wars: The Shift in Attitudes from the Revolutionary War to Vietnam* (New York: Monad Press, 1973), p. 54.

35. Kryder, *Divided Arsenal*, p. 33.

Chapter 3

1. *New York Amsterdam News*, November 2, 1940.

2. Ulysses Lee, *The Employment of Negro Troops* (Washington, D.C.: U.S. Government Printing Office, 1963), p. 80.

3. Earl Brown, "American Negroes and the War," *Harper's* (April 1942), p. 552.

4. Lee Finkle, "The Conservative Aims of Militant Rhetoric: Black Protest during World War II," *The Journal of American History*, Vol. 60, No. 3 (December 1973), p. 692.

5. Philip A. Klinkner and Rogers M. Smith, *The Unsteady March: The Rise and Decline of Racial Equality in America* (Chicago: University of Chicago Press, 1999), p. 159.

6. *Ibid.*, p. 157.

7. Nat Brandt, *Harlem at War: The Black Experience in WWII* (Syracuse: Syracuse University Press, 1996), p. 56.

8. Phillip McGuire, *He, Too, Spoke for Democracy: Judge Hastie, World War II, and the Black Soldier* (New York: Greenwood Press, 1988), p. 31.

9. Brown, "American Negroes," p. 549.

10. *Ibid.*

11. *Ibid.*

12. "The Negro's War," *Fortune*, June 1942.

13. Morris J. MacGregor and Bernard C. Nalty, *Blacks in the United States Armed Forces: Basic Documents* (Wilmington, DE: Scholarly Resources, 1977), p. 98.

14. McGuire, *He, Too, Spoke for Democracy*, p. 57.

15. American Red Cross statement of policy regarding Negro blood donors, January 21, 1942.

16. Walter White, "What the Negro Thinks of the Army," *Annals of the American Academy of Political and Social Sciences* (September 1942).

17. Hastie to Stimson, letter, January 8, 1942, Subject File, 1940–1947, NA RG 107.

18. MacGregor and Nalty, *Blacks in the United States Armed Forces*, p. 281.

19. *Ibid.*, p. 139.

20. Albert E. Williams, *Black Warriors: The Legacy World War II* (Haverford, PA: Infinity, 2002), p. 30.

21. W. Y. Bell, Jr., "The Negro Warrior's Home Front," *Phylon*, Vol. 5, No. 3 (3rd Qtr. 1944), p. 271.

22. Charles C. Spellman, "The Black Press: Setting the Political Agenda During World War II," *Negro History Bulletin* (December 1993).

23. Phillip McGuire, "Judge Hastie, World War II, and Army Racism," *The Journal of Negro History*, Vol. 62, No. 4 (October 1977), p. 351.

24. P.L. Prattis, "The Morale of the Negro in the Armed Services of the United States," *The Journal of Negro Education*, Vol. XII, No. 3 (Summer 1943), p. 355.

25. MacGregor and Nalty, *Blacks in the United States Armed Forces*, p. 15.

26. War Department, Operations and Training Division, OPD291.21 Section 10, NA RG165.

27. MacGregor and Nalty, *Blacks in the United States Armed Forces*, p. 164.

28. *Ibid.*

29. Lee, *The Employment of Negro Troops*, p. 146.

30. *Ibid.*, p. 145.

31. *Ibid.*, p. 114.

32. *Ibid.*, p. 142.

33. *Ibid.*

34. MacGregor and Nalty, *Blacks in the United States Armed Forces*, p. 178.

35. Henry L. Stimson and McGeorge Bundy, *On Active Service in War and Peace* (New York: Harper & Brothers, 1947), p. 461.

36. Henry L. Stimson Diary, January 17, 1942, Yale University Library, New Haven, Conn.

Chapter 4

1. Anthony Mouton to author, interview January 14, 2009.

2. *Miles and Miles: Honoring Black Veterans Who Built the Alcan Highway*, The University of Alaska Museum, Fairbanks, Alaska, Feb. 1–March 15, 1992.

3. Joseph Schiffman, "The Education of Negro Soldiers in World War II," *The Journal of Negro Education*, Vol. 18, No. 1 (Winter 1949), p. 28.

4. Phillip McGuire, "Desegregation of the Armed Forces: Black Leadership, Protest and World War II," *The Journal of Negro History*, Vol. 68, No. 2 (Spring 1983), p. 147.

5. Ira Katznelson. When Affirmative Action Was White: An Untold History of Racial Inequality in Twentieth-Century America (New York: W.W. Norton & Company Ltd., 2005), p. 100.

6. Henry L. Stimson Diary, Yale University Library.

7. John Hope Franklin, interview, "All Things Considered," National Public Radio, rebroadcast 25 March 2009.

8. Jean Byers. *A Study of the Negro in Military Service* (Washington, D.C.: Department of Defense 1947), p. 15.

9. *Leadership and the Negro Soldier* (Headquarters, Army Services Forces, Oct. 1944), p. 31.

10. Wilbert L. Jenkins. Climbing Up to Glory: A Short History of African Americans During the Civil War and Reconstruction (New York: Rowman & Littlefield Publishers, Inc., 2002), p. 175.

11. Lanier Philips, interview, "All Things Considered," National Public Radio, September 3, 2002.

12. Byers. A Study of the Negro in Military Service, p. 36.

13. Henry L. Stimson and McGeorge Bundy. *On Active Service in War and Peace* (New York: Harper & Brothers 1947), p. 463.

14. John E. Bollin to author, interview November 19, 2008.

15. "Reports re Opns Alaska," World War II Unit Operations Reports, Entry 427 ENRG-93-3.0 Box 19550. 270:62/18/6, NA RG407.

16. Lee Young to author, interview June 24, 2007.

17. Walter Parsons to Lael Morgan, interview January 20, 1992. Lael Morgan Papers, Acc. #99-080, Box 1, Alaska and Polar Regions Collection, Rasmuson Library, University of Alaska Fairbanks.

18. Earl Brown and George R. Leighton. *The Negro and the War* (New York: AMS Press, 1962), p. 14.

19. *Ibid*, p. 11

20. Harvard Sitkoff, "Racial Militancy and Interracial Violence in the Second World War," *The Journal of American History*, Vol. 58, No. 3 (Dec. 1971), p. 676.

21. Philip A. Klinkner and Rogers M. Smith, *The Unsteady March: The Rise and Decline of Racial Equality in America* (Chicago: University of Chicago Press, 1999), p. 180.

22. Brown and Leighton. *The Negro and the War*, p. 11.

23. Lee Young to author, interview June 24, 2006.

24. Nathaniel Dulin to author, interview October 28, 2008.

25. Fred Spencer to author, interview June 2, 2007.

26. Joseph Haskin to author, interview June 30, 2007.

27. Nolan Hamilton, letter to James N. Eaton, 14 Aug. 1990 Meek-Eaton Southeastern Regional Black Archives, Florida A&M University, Tallahassee, Fla.

28. Jesse Balthazar to author, interview July 14, 2007.

29. Otis E. Lee to author, interview April 22, 2007.

30. John E. Bollin to author, interview April 22, 2007.

31. James F. Jones to author, interview June 13, 2009.

32. Wansley Hill to author, interview 4 Nov. 2008.
33. Reginald Beverly to author, interview 24 June 2007.
34. Hayward Oubre, Jr., to Lael Morgan, interview 22 Feb. 1992. Lael Morgan Papers, Acc. #99-080, Box 1, Alaska and Polar Regions Collection, Rasmuson Library, University of Alaska Fairbanks.
35. Washington City Paper, 8 Oct. 1993.
36. Richard E. Trent to Lael Morgan, interview 20 Jan. 1992. Lael Morgan Papers, Acc. #99-080, Box 1, Alaska and Polar Regions Collection, Rasmuson Library, University of Alaska Fairbanks.
37. Leadership and the Negro Soldier, p. 8.
38. McGuire, "Desegregation of the Armed Forces," p. 147.
39. *Pittsburgh Courier*, 18 April 1942.
40. Walter Mason to Lael Morgan, undated interview. Lael Morgan Papers, Acc. #99-080, Box 1, Alaska and Polar Regions Collection, Rasmuson Library, University of Alaska Fairbanks.
41. Lauren Rebecca Sklaroff, "Constructing G.I. Joe Louis: Cultural Solutions to the 'Negro Problem' During World War II," *The Journal of American History* (Dec. 2002), p. 975.
42. Richard Bak, *Joe Louis: Great Black Hope* (Cambridge, Mass.: Da Capo Press, 1998), p. 206.
43. Chris Mead, *Joe Louis: Black Hero in White America* (New York: Penguin, 1986), p. 274.
44. P.L. Prattis, "The Morale of the Negro in the Armed Services of the United States," *The Journal of Negro Education*, Vol. XII, No. 3 (Summer 1943), p. 355.
45. William E. Griggs to author, interview 21 April 2007.
46. Lee Young to author, interview 19 March 2009.
47. Ulysses Lee, *The Employment of Negro Troops* (Washington, D.C.: U.S. Government Printing Office, 1963), p. 100.
48. *Ibid.*, p. 104.
49. Dallas Morning News, 4 Nov. 1941.
50. Lee, The Employment of Negro Troops, p. 104.
51. Lee Finkle, *Forum for Protest: The Black Press During World War II* (Cranbury, N.J.: Associated University Presses, 1975), p. 166.
52. Lucille B. Milner, "Jim Crow in the Army," *The New Republic*, Vol. 110 (13 March 1944) p. 339.
53. Harvard Sitkoff, "Racial Militancy and Interracial Violence in the Second World War," *The Journal of American History*, Vol. 58, No. 3 (Dec. 1971), p. 670.
54. Alton Post to author, interview 4 May 2009.
55. Mary Penick Motley, *The Invisible Soldier: The Experience of the Black Soldier in World War II* (Detroit: Wayne State University Press, 1975), p. 163.
56. Sitkoff, "Racial Militancy and Interracial Violence in the Second World War," p. 668.
57. Motley, The Invisible Soldier, p. 47.
58. Jean Byers, *A Study of the Negro in Military Service* (Washington, D.C.: Department of Defense, 1947), p. 67.
59. Daniel Kryder, *Divided Arsenal: Race and the American State During World War II* (New York: Cambridge University Press, 2000), p. 71.
60. Byers, A Study of the Negro in Military Service, p. 65.
61. *Ibid.*, p. 68.
62. Sitkoff, "Racial Militancy and Interracial Violence in the Second World War," p. 670.
63. Ibid.
64. Philip A. Klinkner and Rogers M. Smith, *The Unsteady March: The Rise and Decline of Racial Equality in America* (Chicago: University of Chicago Press, 1999), p. 182.
65. Joseph Haskin to author, interview 9 Jan. 2009.
66. John E. Bollin to author, interview 7 Jan. 2009.
67. Morris J. MacGregor and Bernard C. Nalty, *Blacks in the United States Armed Forces: Basic Documents* (Wilmington, Del.: Scholarly Resources, 1977), p. 270.
68. *Leadership and the Negro Soldier* (Headquarters, Army Services Forces, October 1944), p. 55.
69. Robert Platt Boyd, Jr., *Me and Company "C."* Self-published. Library of Congress Catalog Card #92-90656 1992, p. 52.
70. Henry L. Stimson and McGeorge Bundy, *On Active Service in War and Peace* (New York: Harper & Brothers, 1947), p. 462.
71. Byers. A Study of the Negro in Military Service, p. 69.

Chapter 5

1. Civilian Aide to the Secretary of War Subject File, 1940–47, NA RG107.
2. Walter White, "Behind the Harlem Riot of 1943," *New Republic*, August 16, 1943, p. 22.
3. Ira Katznelson, *When Affirmative Action Was White: An Untold History of Racial Inequality in Twentieth-Century America* (New York: W.W. Norton, 2005), p. 91.
4. *The Call and Post*, Cleveland, December 3, 1943.
5. Mary Penick Motley, *The Invisible Soldier: The Experience of the Black Soldier in World War II* (Detroit: Wayne State University Press, 1975), p. 68.
6. *Afro American*, Baltimore, June 26, 1943.
7. *Pittsburgh Courier*, October 28, 1942.
8. Phillip McGuire, *Taps for a Jim Crow Army: Letters From Black Soldiers in World War II* (Lexington: University of Kentucky Press, 1983), p. 135.
9. *Ibid.*, p. 106.
10. Henry Easter to author, interview, June 5, 2009.
11. Motley, *The Invisible Soldier*, p.162.

12. Anthony Mouton to author, interview February 3, 2009.
13. Lucille B. Milner, "Jim Crow in the Army," *The New Republic*, Vol. 110 (March 13, 1944), p. 339.
14. Joseph Schiffman. "The Education of Negro Soldiers in World War II," *The Journal of Negro Education*, Vol. 18, No. 1 (Winter 1949), p.22.
15. Robert Shogan and Tom Craig, *The Detroit Race Riot: A Study in Violence* (Philadelphia: Chilton Books, 1964), p. 89.
16. "The Negro's War," *Fortune*, June 1942.
17. *Ibid.*
18. Morris J. MacGregor and Bernard C. Nalty, *Blacks in the United States Armed Forces: Basic Documents* (Wilmington, DE: Scholarly Resources, 1977), p. 273.
19. *Ibid.*, p. 326.
20. Robert Platt Boyd, Jr., *Me and Company "C"* (Self-published, Library of Congress Catalog Card #92-90656, 1992), p. 44.
21. Heath Twichell, *Northwest Epic: The Building of the Alaska Highway* (New York: St. Martin's Press, 1992), p.144.
22. McGuire, *Taps for a Jim Crow Army*, p. 106.
23. Reginald Beverly to author, interview, June 24, 2007.
24. Boyd, *Me and Company "C,"* p. 5.
25. Winnie Boyd to author, interview, November 12, 2009.
26. *The Atlanta Journal-Constitution*, June 21, 1991.
27. John A. Bollin to author, interview, November 19, 2008.
28. Letter, August 3, 1990, to James N. Eaton, Sr., Director, Southeastern Regional Black Archives Research Center and Museum, Florida A&M University, Tallahassee, Fla.
29. Anthony Mouton to author, interview, June 29, 2007.
30. *Ibid.*
31. John A. Bollin to author, interview, November 3, 2008.
32. Wansley Hill to author, interview, November 4, 2008.
33. *The Fayetteville Observer*, February 20, 1994.

Chapter 6

1. Froelich Rainey, "Alaska Highway and Engineering Feat," *National Geographic* (February 1943).
2. Philip H. Godsell, *The Romance of the Alaska Highway* (Toronto: The Ryerson Press, 1944), p. 149.
3. Richard Finnie, "A Route to Alaska Through the Northwest Territories," *Geographical Review*, Vol. 32, No. 3 (July 1942), p. 409.
4. United Press, Washington, March 11, 1942.
5. *Peace River Block News*, Dawson Creek, February 26, 1942, and March 19, 1943.

6. Godsell, *The Romance of the Alaska Highway*, p. 114.
7. *Alaska Daily Empire*, May 8, 1943.
8. Don Menzies, *The Alaska Highway* (Edmonton, Alberta: Stuart Douglas, 1943), 44.
9. *Peace River Block News*, Dawson Creek, February 26, 1942.
10. Walter Mason to Lael Morgan, undated interview, Lael Morgan Papers, Acc. #99-080, Box 1, Alaska and Polar Regions Collection, Rasmuson Library, University of Alaska, Fairbanks.
11. Ulysses Lee, *The Employment of Negro Troops* (Washington, D.C.: U.S. Government Printing Office, 1963), p. 254.
12. *Ibid.*, p. 255.
13. Lt. Gen. John L. DeWitt to the House Naval Affairs Subcommittee, April 13, 1943.
14. Memo to Chief of Staff Marshall, OPD291.21 Section 10, NA RG165.
15. www.alaskool.org/projects/native_gov/recollections/peratrovich/Gruening_Letter.htm.
16. A. Russell Buchanan, *Black Americans in World War II* (Santa Barbara: Clio Books, 1977), p. 89.
17. Lee, *The Employment of Negro Troops*, p. 617.
18. Pat Lawler, "Taking the Territory by Storm: Buckner and his boys invade Alaska!" *Alaska Journal*, 2 (1981), p. 85.
19. Sturdevant/Buckner exchange, OCE Box 14/20, NA RG77.
20. *Ibid.*
21. Lawler, "Taking the Territory by Storm," p. 95.
22. *Ibid.*
23. Ernest Gruening, *Many Battles: The Autobiography of Ernest Gruening* (New York: Liveright Press, 1973), p. 48.
24. Walter Mason to Lael Morgan, undated interview.
25. Robin W. Winks, *The Blacks in Canada: A History* (Montreal: McGill-Queen's University Press, 1997), p. 422.
26. Walter Muir to author, e-mail, March 3, 2009.
27. Lee, *The Employment of Negro Troops*, p. 439.
28. *Edmonton Capital*, April 25, 1911.
29. The Applied History Research Group, University of Calgary, 1997.
30. Winks, *The Blacks in Canada*, p. 325.
31. The Applied History Research Group.
32. Kenneth W. Tingley, ed., *For King and Country: Alberta in the Second World War* (Edmonton, Alberta: Reidmore Books, 1995), p. 174.
33. *Globe and Mail*, Toronto, March 13, 1943.

Chapter 7

1. Harold Griffin, *Alaska and the Canadian Northwest: Our New Frontier* (New York: W.W. Norton, 1944), p. 119.

Notes — Chapter 7

2. *Peace River Block News*, Dawson Creek, March 12, 1942.
3. *Ibid.*
4. John Schmidt, *This Was No — Picnic: 2.4 Years of Wild and Woolly Mayhem in Dawson Creek* (Hanna, Alberta: Gorman & Gorman, 1991), p. 42.
5. *Ibid.*
6. *Ibid.*, p. 43
7. Walter Mason to Lael Morgan, undated interview, Lael Morgan Papers, Acc. #99-080, Box 1, Alaska and Polar Regions Collection, Rasmuson Library, University of Alaska Fairbanks.
8. *The Frederick Post*, Frederick, Md., April 25, 1942.
9. Sid Navratil, John K. Lloyd, Helen Navratil and Stan R. Caldwell, *Alcan Trail Blazers* (Pittsburgh: 648th Memorial Fund, 1992), p. 1.
10. *Modern Marvels*, "The Alcan Highway," The History Channel, 2000/2001.
11. *Peace River Block News*, March 12, 1942.
12. *Washington City Paper*, October 8, 1993.
13. *Ibid.*
14. Nathaniel Dulin to author, interview, October 15, 2008.
15. *Washington City Paper*, October 8, 1992.
16. Dulin to author.
17. Jim Christy, *Rough Road to the North: Travels Along the Alaska Highway* (New York: Doubleday, 1980), p. 123.
18. Canadian Press, Dawson Creek, March 17, 1942.
19. Anthony Mouton to author, interview, February 2, 2009.
20. John A. Bollin to author, interview, August 4, 2007.
21. Robert Platt Boyd, Jr., *Me and Company "C"* (Self-published, Library of Congress Catalog Card #92-90656, 1992), p. 67.
22. Joseph Haskin to author, interview, January 29, 2009.
23. Anthony Mouton to author, interview, June 29, 2007.
24. P.L. Prattis, "The Morale of the Negro in the Armed Services of the United States," *The Journal of Negro Education*, Vol. XII, No. 3 (Summer 1943), p. 355.
25. Jean Byers, *A Study of the Negro in Military Service* (Washington, D.C.: Department of Defense, 1947), p. 71.
26. Boyd, *Me and Company "C,"* p. 69.
27. Author asked them if they had heard about the rape.
28. Corps of Engineers History Office, History of the Whitehorse Section of Alcan Highway X Box 9 Folder 8.
29. Willis R. Grafe, *An Oregon Boy in the Yukon: A Story of the Alaska Highway* (Albany, OR: Chesnimus Press, 1992), p. 101.
30. William E. Griggs, *The World War II Black Regiment That Built the Alaska Military Highway* (Jackson: University Press of Mississippi, 2002).
31. Griggs to author, interview, April 21, 2007.
32. Walter Parsons to Lael Morgan, interview, January 20, 1992, Lael Morgan Papers, Acc. #99-080, Box 1, Alaska and Polar Regions Collection, Rasmuson Library, University of Alaska, Fairbanks.
33. Walter Mason to Lael Morgan, undated interview.
34. *American Legacy* (Fall 2005).
35. Heath Twichell, *Northwest Epic: The Building of the Alaska Highway* (New York: St. Martin's Press, 1992), p. 145.
36. Wansley Hill to author, interview, November 4, 2008.
37. *Ibid.*, February 3, 2009.
38. Phillip McGuire, *Taps for a Jim Crow Army: Letters From Black Soldiers in World War II* (Lexington: University of Kentucky Press, 1983), p. 116.
39. Kenneth S. Coates and William R. Morrison, "Soldier-Workers: The U.S. Army Corps of Engineers and the Northwest Defense Projects 1942–46," *The Pacific Historical Review*, Vol. 62, No. 3 (August 1993), p. 295.
40. *Ibid.*
41. Memo, June 17, 1942, for the assistant chief of staff of the Operations Division of the War Department, Entry 118, Box 472 Dir. Plans & Operations, NA RG165.
42. Engineers Memoirs, EP870-1-25, Office of History, U.S. Army Corps of Engineers, Alexandria, Va., p. 88.
43. Schmidt, *This Was No — Picnic*, p. 53.
44. Peter Stursberg, *Journey Into Victory: Up the Alaska Highway and to Sicily and Italy* (London: George G. Harrap, 1944), p. 14.
45. Philip H. Godsell, *The Romance of the Alaska Highway* (Toronto: The Ryerson Press, 1944), p. 159.
46. Les McLaughlin, "North to Alaska," *Legion Magazine*, CanVet Publications, September/October 2002.
47. *Chicago Daily Tribune*, January 10, 1943.
48. Malcolm MacDonald, *Down North: A View of Northwest Canada* (New York: Farrar & Rinehart, 1943), p. 237.
49. *Winnipeg Evening Tribune*, November 17, 1942.
50. Don Menzies, *The Alaska Highway* (Edmonton, Alberta: Stuart Douglas, 1943), p. 31.
51. Pacific Lutheran University, Tacoma, Wash., documentary, *Building Connections*, 2007.
52. David A. Remley, *Crooked Road: The Story of the Alaska Highway* (New York: McGraw-Hill, 1976), p. 69.
53. *The Atlanta Journal-Constitution*, June 21, 1991.
54. Otis E. Lee to author, interview, April 22, 2007.

Chapter 8

1. Karl C. Dod, *The Corps of Engineers: The War Against Japan* (Washington, D.C.: Office of the Chief of Military History, 1966), p. 276.
2. George L. MacGarrigle, *Aleutian Islands: The U.S. Army Campaigns of World War II* (Washington, D.C.: U.S. Army Center of Military History, 2003), p. 67.
3. Report of Subcommittee of Foreign Relations Committee Having Under Consideration Senate Resolution 253, 17 June 1942, p. 93.
4. Edgar Snow, "The Most Valuable Ground on Earth," *Saturday Evening Post,* July 4, 1942.
5. Engineers Memoirs, EP870-1-25, Office of History, U.S. Army Corps of Engineers, Alexandria, Va., p. 92.
6. *Chicago Daily Tribune,* July 23, 1943.
7. *Seattle Post-Intelligencer*, September 23, 1943.
8. Alaska Highway Complete Report, Headquarters Northwest Service Command, April 6, 1945, 625.7 US, Yukon Archives, Whitehorse, Yukon Territory.
9. Heath Twichell, *Northwest Epic: The Building of the Alaska Highway* (New York: St. Martin's Press, 1992), p. 207.
10. Engineers Memoirs, EP870-1-25, Office of History, U.S. Army Corps of Engineers, Alexandria, Va., p. 87.
11. Froelich Rainey, "Alaskan Highway an Engineering Feat," *National Geographic,* February 1943.
12. Pacific Lutheran University, Tacoma, Wash., documentary, *Building Connections,* 2007.
13. Harold W. Richardson, "Alcan-America's Glory Road: Part II — Supply, Equipment and Camps," *Engineering News-Record* (December 31, 1942), p. 36.
14. Richard L. Neuberger, "Highballing at Sixty Below," *Saturday Evening Post,* November 27, 1943.
15. Barry Broadfoot, *Six War Years 1939–1945: Memories of Canadians at Home and Abroad* (Toronto: Doubleday Canada, 1974), p. 218.
16. Reginald Beverly to author, interview, June 24, 2007.
17. Otis E. Lee to author, interview, March 25, 2008.
18. Thomas Riggs to Brig. Gen. Clarence Sturdevant, letter, March 21, 1942, file 50-39, 72-A-3173, ACE, U.S. Army Military History Institute, Carlisle, Penn.
19. Historical Record of Task Force 2600, p. 14, Box 4 Folder 2, Office of History, U.S. Army Corps of Engineers, Alexandria, Va.
20. John Schmidt, *This Was No — Picnic: 2.4 Years of Wild and Woolly Mayhem in Dawson Creek* (Hanna, Alberta: Gorman & Gorman, 1991), p. 48
21. *Ibid.*
22. Broadfoot, *Six War Years,* p. 219.
23. *Yukon News,* June 16, 1982.
24. Richard E. Trent, undated letter to James N. Eaton, Meek-Eaton Southeastern Regional Black Archives, Florida A&M University, Tallahassee, Fla.
25. *The Fayetteville Observer,* February 20, 1994.
26. "Building the Alaska Highway," *American Experience,* PBS, 2005.
27. www.upress.state.ms.us.
28. *The News-Journal,* Daytona Beach, Fla., December 3, 1991.
29. Historical Record of Task Force 2600, p. 21, Box 4 Folder 2, Office of History, U.S. Army Corps of Engineers, Alexandria, Va.
30. Engineers Memoirs, EP870-1-25, Office of History, U.S. Army Corps of Engineers, Alexandria, Va., p. 93.
31. Robert Platt Boyd, Jr., *Me and Company "C"* (Self-published, Library of Congress Catalog Card #92-90656, 1992), p. 80.
32. Peter Stursberg, *Journey Into Victory: Up the Alaska Highway and to Sicily and Italy* (London: George G. Harrap, 1944), p. 42.
33. William E. Griggs to author, interview, April 21, 2007.
34. Casey McLaughlin to author, interview, October 16, 2008.
35. Boyd, *Me and Company "C"* p. 81.
36. *Chicago Defender,* December 4, 1943.
37. *The Sun,* Baltimore, July 4, 1992.
38. History of the Whitehorse Section of Alcan Highway, Box 9, Folder 8, Office of History, U.S. Army Corps of Engineers, Alexandria, Va.
39. *Ibid.*
40. Richard E. Trent, undated letter to James N. Eaton.
41. Philip H. Godsell, *The Romance of the Alaska Highway* (Toronto: The Ryerson Press, 1944), p. 161.
42. Ulysses Lee, *The Employment of Negro Troops* (Washington, D.C.: U.S. Government Printing Office, 1963), p. 439.
43. William Morrison, "Uncle Sam's Warpath," *Horizon Canada,* August 1986.
44. William E. Griggs to author, interview, April 21, 2007.
45. *The Atlanta Journal-Constitution,* June 21, 1991.
46. *Ibid.*
47. Chester L. Russell, *Tales of a Catskinner: A Personal Account of Building the Alcan Highway, the Winter Trail, and Canol Pipeline Road in 1942–43* (Fort Nelson, B.C.: Autumn Images, 1999), p. 32.
48. Otis E. Lee to author, interview, April 22, 2007.

Chapter 9

1. Robert Platt Boyd, Jr., *Me and Company "C"* (Self-published, Library of Congress Catalog Card #92-90656, 1992), p. 103.

2. *Ibid.*
3. RCMP report dated June 9, 1942, www.alaskahighwayarchives.ca.
4. Anthony Mouton to author, interview, June 29, 2007.
5. John A. Bollin to author, interview, April 21, 2007.
6. Anthony Mouton to author, interview, June 29, 2007.
7. World War II Unit Operations Reports Box 19550 270:62/18/6, ENRG-93-3.0, Entry 427, NA RG407.
8. *Ibid.*
9. Kenneth Coates, *North to Alaska: Fifty Years on the World's Most Remarkable Highway* (Fairbanks: University of Alaska Press, 1992), p. 103.
10. John A. Bollin to author, interview, April 21, 2007.
11. *Ibid.*
12. Boyd, *Me and Company "C,"* p. 94.
13. History of the 93rd Regiment, Box 19554 File ENGR. 93-3.0, NA RG407.
14. Judith L. Bellafaire, ed., *The U.S. Army and World War II: Selected Papers from the Army's Commemorative Conferences* (Washington, D.C.: Center of Military History United States Army, 1998), p. 174.
15. Fern Chandonnet, ed., *Alaska at War 1941–1945: The Forgotten War Remembered* (Fairbanks: University of Alaska Press, 2008), p. 278.
16. 93rd Reg. Box 19549 ENRG-93-0.7, NA RG407.
17. Boyd. *Me and Company "C,"* p. 119.
18. 93rd Reg. Box 19549 ENRG-93-0.7, NA RG407.
19. *The Anchorage Daily News*, February 23, 2009.
20. Bellafaire, *The U.S. Army and World War II*, p. 173.
21. Fred Spencer to author, interview, June 2, 2007.
22. Historical Diaries, Box 19950 File 910-2.1, NA RG407.
23. Anthony Mouton to author, interview, January 15, 2009.
24. "Notes on Service with the Ninety-third 1944," Box 19550 ENRG 93-0.7, NA RG407.
25. Joseph Haskin to author, interview, June 30, 2007.
26. Fred Spencer to author, interview, March 18, 2009.
27. *Ibid.*
28. Walter Mason to Lael Morgan, undated interview, Lael Morgan Papers, Acc. #99-080, Box 1, Alaska and Polar Regions Collection, Rasmuson Library, University of Alaska, Fairbanks.
29. 95th Reg. Report of Operations, Box 19553 ENRG 95-0.1, NA RG407.
30. Henry Easter to author, interview, June 5, 2009.
31. Edward Carroll to Lael Morgan, interview, January 20, 1992, Lael Morgan Papers, Acc. #99-080, Box 1, Alaska and Polar Regions Collection, Rasmuson Library, University of Alaska, Fairbanks.
32. Papers of Brig. Gen. William M. Hoge, Box 2, U.S. Army Military History Institute, Carlisle, Penn.
33. *The Atlanta Journal-Constitution*, June 21, 1991.
34. Pacific Lutheran University, Tacoma, Wash., *Building Connections* documentary, 2007.
35. James F. Jones to author, interview, June 13, 2009.
36. J.G. MacGregor, *The Land of Twelve-foot Davis: A History of the Peace River Country* (Edmonton, Alberta: Applied Art Products Limited, 1952), p. 187.
37. Froelich Rainey, "Alaskan Highway an Engineering Feat," *National Geographic*, February 1943.
38. Harold Griffin, *Alaska and the Canadian Northwest: Our New Frontier* (New York: W.W. Norton, 1944), p. 119.
39. *Ibid.*
40. Nathaniel Dulin to author, interview, October 28, 2008.
41. Phillip McGuire, *Taps for a Jim Crow Army: Letters from Black Soldiers in World War II* (Lexington: University of Kentucky Press, 1983), p. 118.
42. 95th Reg. Report of Operations, Box 19553 ENRG 95-0.1, NA RG407.
43. Engineers Memoirs, EP870-1-25, Office of History, U.S. Army Corps of Engineers, Alexandria, Va., p. 100.
44. Dulin interview, November 12, 2008.
45. "Building the Alaska Highway," *American Experience*, PBS, 2005.
46. Dulin interview, March 4, 2009.
47. *Ibid.*, September 30, 2008.
48. *Yank* magazine, February 10, 1943.
49. Edward Carroll to Lael Morgan, undated interview.
50. Dulin interview, March 4, 2009.
51. Reginald Beverly to author, interview, June 24, 2007.
52. Lee Young to author, interview, June 24, 2007.
53. *Chicago Defender*, February 20, 1943.
54. Col. K.B. Bush Papers, Box 6, U.S. Army Military History Institute, Carlisle, Penn.
55. *Yank*, February 10, 1943.
56. *Ibid.*
57. Norman Rosten, *The Big Road* (New York: Rinehart, 1946), p. 134.

Chapter 10

1. Fern Chandonnet, ed., *Alaska at War 1941–1945: The Forgotten War Remembered* (Fairbanks: University of Alaska Press, 2008), p. 278.
2. Lyman L. Woodman, *Duty Station Northwest:*

The U.S. Army in Alaska and Western Canada, Volume Two 1918–1945 (Anchorage: The Alaska Historical Society, 1997), p. 187.

3. *News & Observer*, Raleigh, N.C., February 22, 1994.

4. Hayward Oubre to Lael Morgan, interview, February 22, 1992, Lael Morgan Papers, Acc. #99-080, Box 1, Alaska and Polar Regions Collection, Rasmuson Library, University of Alaska, Fairbanks.

5. William E. Griggs to author, interview, May 11, 2009.

6. William E. Griggs, *The World War II Black Regiment That Built the Alaska Military Highway* (Jackson: University Press of Mississippi, 2002), p. 93.

7. *Cleveland Plain Dealer*, October 25, 1992.

8. Judith L. Bellafaire, ed., *The U.S. Army and World War II: Selected Papers from the Army's Commemorative Conferences* (Washington, D.C.: Center of Military History United States Army, 1998), p. 173.

9. *Fayetteville Observer*, February 20, 1994.

10. Philip H. Godsell, *The Romance of the Alaska Highway* (Toronto: The Ryerson Press, 1944), p. 131.

11. Harold Griffin, *Alaska and the Canadian Northwest: Our New Frontier* (New York: W.W. Norton, 1944), p. 156.

12. James C. Coleman to author, interview, June 5, 2009.

13. Lee Young to author, interview, June 24, 2007.

14. *Fayetteville Observer*, February 20, 1994.

15. William E. Griggs to author, interview, April 21, 2007.

16. "Building the Alaska Highway," *American Experience*, PBS, 2005.

17. Lee Young to author, interview, June 24, 2007.

18. Walter Mason to Lael Morgan, undated interview, Lael Morgan Papers, Acc. #99-080, Box 1, Alaska and Polar Regions Collection, Rasmuson Library, University of Alaska, Fairbanks.

19. H. Milton Duesenberg, *Alaska Highway Expeditionary Force: A Roadbuilder's Story* (Clear Lake, IN: H&M Industries, 1994), p. 25.

20. Lee Young interview, March 19, 2009.

21. *News & Observer*, Raleigh, N.C., February 22, 1994.

22. Heath Twichell, *Northwest Epic: The Building of the Alaska Highway* (New York: St. Martin's Press, 1992), p. 211.

23. James C. Coleman to author, interview, June 5, 2009.

24. *Ibid.*, letter, June 8, 2009.

25. Harold W. Richardson, "Alcan-America's Glory Road: Part II — Supply, Equipment and Camps," *Engineering News-Record*, December 31, 1942, p. 134.

26. Woodman, *Duty Station Northwest*, p. 195.

27. Donna Blasor-Bernhardt, *Pioneer Road: Anthology of the Alaskan Highway* (Las Vegas: ArcheBooks, 2004), p. 28.

28. Twichell, *Northwest Epic*, p. 213.

29. Lee Young to author, interview, March 19, 2009.

30. Karl C. Dod, *The Corps of Engineers: The War Against Japan* (Washington, D.C.: Office of the Chief of Military History, 1966), p. 311.

31. Canadian Press, Whitehorse, Yukon Territory, November 4, 1942.

32. Diary of E.L. ("Gene") Telgmann of the 18th Regiment, Corps of Engineers, MacBride Museum of Yukon History, Whitehorse, Yukon Territory.

33. *Yank*, February 10, 1943.

34. Douglas Coe, *Road to Alaska: The Story of the Alaska Highway* (New York: Julian Messner, 1943), p. 163.

35. Walter Parsons to Lael Morgan, interview, January 20, 1992, Lael Morgan Papers, Acc. #99-080, Box 1, Alaska and Polar Regions Collection, Rasmuson Library, University of Alaska, Fairbanks.

36. Peter Stursberg, *Journey Into Victory: Up the Alaska Highway and to Sicily and Italy* (London: George G. Harrap, 1944), p. 38.

37. War Department press release, October 29, 1942.

38. Lee Young interview, March 19, 2009.

39. *Yank*, February 10, 1943.

40. Canadian Press, Kluane Lake, Yukon Territory, November 23, 1943.

41. Raw tapes, Canadian Broadcasting Corporation, November 1942.

42. Twichell, *Northwest Epic*, p. 215.

43. *Ibid.*

44. John Schmidt. *This Was No — Picnic: 2.4 Years of Wild and Woolly Mayhem in Dawson Creek* (Hanna, Alberta: Gorman & Gorman, 1991), p. 213.

45. Raw tapes.

46. *Ibid.*

47. *Ibid.*

48. Ulysses Lee, *The Employment of Negro Troops* (Washington, D.C.: U.S. Government Printing Office, 1963), p. 6.

49. Walter R. Borneman, *Alaska: Saga of a Bold Land* (New York: HarperCollins, 2003), p. 339.

50. Twichell, *Northwest Epic*, p. 145.

51. Woodman, *Duty Station Northwest*, p. 195.

Chapter 11

1. Richard J. Diubaldo, "The Canol Project and Canadian-American Relations," *Historical Papers*, Vol. 12, No. 1 (1977), p. 180.

2. Karl C. Dod, *The Corps of Engineers: The War Against Japan* (Washington, D.C.: Office of the Chief of Military History, 1966), p. 322.

3. Alex Hemlock, former Imperial Oil engineer

at Norman Wells, speech at the Petroleum History Society, Calgary, Alberta, April 25, 2001.

4. Richard Finnie, *Canol: The Sub-Arctic Pipeline and Refinery Project Constructed by Bechtel-Price-Callahan for the Corps of Engineers United States Army 1942–44* (San Francisco: Ryder & Ingram, 1945), p. 123.

5. Hemlock speech.

6. *Time*, October 15, 1945.

7. John Schmidt, *This Was No — Picnic: 2.4 Years of Wild and Woolly Mayhem in Dawson Creek* (Hanna, Alberta: Gorman & Gorman, 1991), p. 48.

8. Harold Griffin, *Alaska and the Canadian Northwest: Our New Frontier* (New York: W.W. Norton, 1944), p. 73.

9. www.nnsl.com/frames/newspapers/1996-10/oct21_96trail.html.

10. Wansley Hill to author, interview, November 4, 2008.

11. *Canol 1945*, Public Relations Branch of the Northwest Service Command, Col. K.B. Bush Papers, Box 6, U.S. Army Military History Institute, Carlisle, Penn.

12. Ibid.

13. Historical Record of Task Force 2600, p. 17, Box 4 Folder 2, Office of History, U.S. Army Corps of Engineers, Alexandria, Va.

14. Philip H. Godsell, *The Romance of the Alaska Highway* (Toronto: The Ryerson Press, 1944), p. 195.

15. William A. Leising, *Arctic Wings* (Garden City, NY: Doubleday, 1959), p. 82.

16. Ibid.

17. Godsell, *The Romance of the Alaska Highway*, p. 195.

18. Ibid., p. 172.

19. *Canol 1945*, Col. K.B. Bush Papers.

20. Franklin J. Brehon to Lael Morgan, interview, January 20, 1992, Lael Morgan Papers, Acc. #99-080, Box 1, Alaska and Polar Regions Collection, Rasmuson Library, University of Alaska, Fairbanks.

21. Malcolm MacDonald, *Down North: A View of Northwest Canada* (New York: Farrar & Rinehart, 1943), p. 223.

22. *Canol 1945*, Col. K.B. Bush Papers.

23. Historical Record of Task Force 2600, p. 21, Box 4 Folder 2, Office of History, U.S. Army Corps of Engineers, Alexandria, Va.

24. Ibid., p. 17.

25. Ibid., p. 27.

26. *Hamilton Spectator*, September 30, 1943.

27. Richard Finnie, "Canol Blitx," *Maclean's*, August 15, 1943.

28. Philip L. Fradkin, "The First and Forgotten Pipeline," *Audubon*, November 1, 1977, p. 68.

29. *Canol 1945*, Col. K.B. Bush Papers.

30. Richard J. Diubaldo, "The Canol Project and Canadian-American Relations," *Historical Papers*, Vol. 12, No. 1 (1977), p. 183.

31. Department of External Affairs Records, External Affairs Archives, file 4349-40C, Hugh Keenleyside to Norman Robertson, October 6, 1942.

32. House of Commons Debates, 1942, Vol. 3, 2486.

33. Franklin J. Brehon to Lael Morgan, interview, January 20, 1992, Lael Morgan Papers, Acc. #99-080, Box 1, Alaska and Polar Regions Collection, Rasmuson Library, University of Alaska, Fairbanks.

34. Ibid.

35. Robert Platt Boyd, Jr., *Me and Company "C"* (Self-published, Library of Congress Catalog Card #92-90656, 1992), p. 107.

36. Phillip McGuire, *Taps for a Jim Crow Army: Letters From Black Soldiers in World War II* (Lexington: University of Kentucky Press, 1983), p. 121.

37. Fradkin, "The First and Forgotten Pipeline," p. 67.

38. P.S. Barry, *The Canol Project: An Adventure of the U.S. War Department in Canada's Northwest* (Edmonton, Alberta: Self-published, 1985), p. 3.

39. Alaska Defense Command, Periodic Intelligence Report No. 52, 22 May 1943, File 910-2.1, Box 7, NA RG407.

40. Associated Press, Washington, June 20, 1943.

41. Wansley Hill to author, interview, March 17, 2009.

42. Ibid., March 26, 2009.

43. Ibid.

44. Ibid., January 6, 2009.

45. Lyman L. Woodman, "CANOL: Pipeline of Brief Glory," *The Northern Engineer*, Vol. 9, No. 2 (1977), p. 20.

46. Chester L. Russell, *Tales of a Catskinner: A Personal Account of Building the Alcan Highway, the Winter Trail, and Canol Pipeline Road in 1942–43* (Fort Nelson, B.C.: Autumn Images, 1999), p. 98.

47. Leising, *Arctic Wings*, p. 87.

48. Richard Finnie, "Canol Blitz," *Maclean's*, August 15, 1943.

49. *Canol 1945*, Col. K.B. Bush Papers.

Chapter 12

1. Harry Yost, "Building the Alaska Highway," *The Alaska Journal* (Autumn 1985), p. 23.

2. Engineers Memoirs, EP870-1-25, X Box 4 Folder 2, Office of History, U.S. Army Corps of Engineers, Alexandria, Va.

3. Ken Coates, *North to Alaska: Fifty Years on the World's Most Remarkable Highway* (Fairbanks: University of Alaska Press, 1992), p. 104.

4. Historical Record of Task Force 2600, p. 39, Box 4 Folder 2, Office of History, U.S. Army Corps of Engineers, Alexandria, Va.

5. Ibid., p. 36.

6. Franklin J. Brehon to Lael Morgan, interview, January 20, 1992, Lael Morgan Papers, Acc. #99-

080, Box 1, Alaska and Polar Regions Collection, Rasmuson Library, University of Alaska, Fairbanks.

7. Harold Griffin, *Alaska and the Canadian Northwest: Our New Frontier* (New York: W.W. Norton, 1944), p. 119.

8. Walter Parsons to Lael Morgan, interview, January 20, 1992, Lael Morgan Papers.

9. William E. Griggs to author, interview, April 21, 2007.

10. H. Milton Duesenberg, *Alaska Highway Expeditionary Force: A Roadbuilder's Story* (Clear Lake, IN: H&M Industries, 1994), p. 98.

11. Boulton B. Miller, *A Hand on My Shoulder*, www.boultonmiller.com/Handonsh3.htm (self-published, 2001).

12. *News & Observer*, Raleigh, N.C., February 22, 1994.

13. *Winston-Salem Journal*, July 4, 1993.

14. Records of the Office of the Quartermaster General, Box 5, 333.1, 183, NA RG62.

15. Frank C. Lee. *Alaska Highway Poems* (Mason City, IA: Klipto, 1944).

16. John Schmidt, *This Was No — Picnic: 2.4 Years of Wild and Woolly Mayhem in Dawson Creek* (Hanna, Alberta: Gorman & Gorman, 1991), p. 88.

17. George Young to author, interview, April 29, 2009.

18. Sid Navratil, John K. Lloyd, and Helen Navratil and Stan R. Caldwell, *Alcan Trail Blazers* (Pittsburgh: 648th Memorial Fund, 1992), p. 3.

19. Reginald Beverly to author, interview, June 24, 2007.

20. Nathaniel Dulin to author, interview, October 15, 2008.

21. Otis E. Lee to author, interview, April 22, 2007.

22. Lee Young to author, interview, June 24, 2007.

23. *Ibid.*

24. Robert Platt Boyd, Jr., *Me and Company "C"* (Self-published, Library of Congress Catalog Card #92-90656, 1992), p. 81.

25. *Washington City Paper*, October 8, 1993.

26. Anthony Mouton to author, interview, June 29, 2007.

27. Paul W. Francis, letter, November 14, 1991, to James N. Eaton, Meek-Eaton Southeastern Regional Black Archives, Florida A&M University, Tallahassee, Fla.

28. Jesse Balthazar to author, interview, July 14, 2007.

29. Navratil, Lloyd, Navratil and Caldwell, *Alcan Trail Blazers*, p. 57.

30. Capt. Richard Neuberger talk for the BBC, Col. K.B. Bush Papers, Box 6, U.S. Army Military History Institute, Carlisle, Penn.

31. Maj. T.L. Ferguson, G-4 Periodic Report, January 16, 1943, Northwest Service Command, Whitehorse, Yukon Territory.

32. World War II Unit Operations Reports Box 19550, ENRG-93-3.0 Entry 427 Reports on Opns Alaska, NA RG407.

33. Boyd, *Me and Company "C,"* p. 79.

34. *Chicago Daily Tribune*, January 17, 1943.

35. David A. Remley, *Crooked Road: The Story of the Alaska Highway* (New York: McGraw-Hill, 1976), p. 72.

36. *Afro American*, Baltimore, May 1, 1943.

37. "Notes on Service with the Ninety-third 1944," Box 19550 ENRG 93-0.7, NA RG407.

38. Neuberger talk for the BBC.

39. Anthony Mouton to author, interview June 29, 2007.

40. Jesse Balthazar to author, interview, July 14, 2007.

41. *Chicago Defender*, December 4, 1943.

42. Otis E. Lee to author, interview, April 22, 2007.

43. William E. Griggs to author, interview, April 21, 2007.

44. Neuberger talk for the BBC.

45. *Los Angeles Times*, January 5, 1992.

46. Schmidt, *This Was No — Picnic,* p. 84.

47. "The Alaska Highway ... the First 50 Years," Public Works Canada video, 1991, Yukon Archives, Whitehorse, Yukon Territory.

48. *The Atlanta Journal-Constitution*, June 21, 1991.

49. Coates, *North to Alaska*, p.104.

50. www.livinglandscapes.bc.ca/prnr/alaska/chester_russel.htm.

51. *Modern Marvels*; "The Alcan Highway," The History Channel, 2000/2001.

52. Lee Young to author, interview, June 24, 2007.

53. Teaching Equity, Florida A&M University, Tallahassee (February 1992).

54. George Young to author, interview, July 14, 2007.

55. *The Atlanta Journal-Constitution*, June 21, 1991.

56. *St. Petersburg Times*, January 20, 1992.

57. *Chicago Defender*, March 6, 1943.

58. *Houston Post*, September 19, 1990.

59. *Fayetteville Observer*, February 20, 1994.

60. Joseph Haskin to author, interview, June 30, 2007.

61. Jesse Balthazar to author, interview, July 14, 2007.

62. Walter Tatum to All Unit Commanders, Whitehorse Sector, Alcan Highway, November 7, 1942, NWSC, HD 350.5, Box 15A, Entry 54B, RG112, BC.

63. Philip H. Godsell, *The Romance of the Alaska Highway* (Toronto: The Ryerson Press, 1944), p. 161.

64. *New York Herald Tribune*, November 11, 1942.

65. Remley, *Crooked Road*, p. 72.

66. Peter Stursberg, *Journey Into Victory: Up the*

Alaska Highway and to Sicily and Italy (London: George G. Harrap, 1944), p. 31.

67. Donna Blasor-Bernhardt, *Pioneer Road: Anthology of the Alaskan Highway* (Las Vegas: ArcheBooks, 2004), p. 20.

68. *Chicago Defender*, October 23, 1943.

69. John A. Bollin to author, interview, April 21, 2007.

70. Anthony Mouton to author, interview, June 29, 2007.

71. Hayward Oubre, Jr., to Lael Morgan, interview February 22, 1992, Lael Morgan Papers, Acc. #99-080, Box 1, Alaska and Polar Regions Collection, Rasmuson Library, University of Alaska, Fairbanks.

72. *Ibid.*

73. Fred Spencer to author, interview, June 2, 2007.

74. Record of Trial, Lael Morgan Papers, Acc. #99-080, Box 1, Alaska and Polar Regions Collection, Rasmuson Library, University of Alaska, Fairbanks.

75. *Ibid.*

76. Lael Morgan, "Unsung Heroes," *Anchorage Daily News*, August 9, 1992.

77. Lael Morgan Papers, Acc. #99-080, Box 1, Alaska and Polar Regions Collection, Rasmuson Library, University of Alaska, Fairbanks.

78. *The Atlanta Journal-Constitution*, June 21, 1991.

79. Sturdevant memorandum for Commanding General, Services of Supply, enclosure to memo, May 2, 1942, Documents May–June, box 15, 72-A-3173, Fort Belvoir, Va., ACE.

80. *Faculty of Engineering*, University of Alberta (Fall 2004).

81. Kenneth S. Coates and William R. Morrison, *The Alaska Highway in World War II: The U.S. Army of Occupation in Canada's Northwest* (Norman: University of Oklahoma Press, 1992), p. 200.

82. *Afro American*, Baltimore, November 10, 1942.

Chapter 13

1. *Dawson Daily News*, November 5, 1942.
2. *Fayetteville Observer*, February 20, 1994.
3. *Winston-Salem Journal*, July 4, 1993.
4. *American Legacy*, (Fall 2005).
5. Nathaniel Dulin to author, interview, October 15, 2008.
6. Henry Easter to author, interview, June 5, 2009.
7. Joseph Haskin to author, interview, February 4, 2009.
8. *Cleveland Plain Dealer*, October 25, 1992.
9. *The Atlanta Journal-Constitution*, June 21, 1991.
10. *Ibid.*
11. Haskin to author, interview, June 30, 2007.
12. Allen W. Sowden to author, interview, July 2010.
13. William E. Griggs to author, interview, April 21, 2007.
14. *The Sun*, Baltimore, July 4, 1992.
15. Otis E. Lee to author, interview, April 22, 2007.
16. World War II Unit Operations Reports, Box 19550 270:62/18/6, ENRG-93-3.0, Entry 427, NA RG407.
17. *Ibid.*
18. Associated Negro Press, September 5, 1942.
19. Records of the U.S. Army Service Forces World War II, Box 2, NND 947500, NA RG160.
20. John Schmidt, *This Was No — Picnic: 2.4 Years of Wild and Woolly Mayhem in Dawson Creek* (Hanna, Alberta: Gorman & Gorman, 1991), p. 78.
21. Kenneth S. Coates and William R. Morrison, *The Alaska Highway in World War II: The U.S. Army of Occupation in Canada's Northwest* (Norman: University of Oklahoma Press, 1992), p. 140.
22. Dorthea Calverley, *Creek Disaster: A Personal Account of the Explosion and Fire*. www.calverley.ca/Part05-Dawson%20Creek/5-024.html.
23. Canadian Press, Ottawa, February 19, 1943.
24. Calverley, *The Dawson Creek Disaster*.
25. Operation Report, 95th Regiment, February 15, 1943, Entry 427, ENRG-93-0.20, NA RG407.
26. Heath Twichell, *Northwest Epic: The Building of the Alaska Highway* (New York: St. Martin's Press, 1992), p. 295.
27. *Chicago Defender*, May 15, 1943.
28. Records of the U.S. Army Service Forces World War II, Box 2, NND 947500, NA RG160.
29. Schmidt, *This Was No — Picnic*, p. 149.
30. Letter to Brig. Gen. James A. O'Connor, April 26, 1943, Lael Morgan Papers, Acc. #99-080, Box 1, Alaska and Polar Regions Collection, Rasmuson Library, University of Alaska, Fairbanks.
31. Operation Reports, G-2 File 91 Box 32, NA RG407.
32. *Chicago Defender*, July 3, 1943.
33. *Ibid.*
34. *Ibid.*
35. *Ibid.*
36. Ulysses Lee, *The Employment of Negro Troops* (Washington, D.C.: U.S. Government Printing Office, 1963), p. 439.
37. Sheila Dodds and Spence Hill to author, interviews, August 28, 2008.
38. Sister Cecile Montpetit to author, interview, September 5, 2008.
39. Coates and Morrison, *The Alaska Highway in World War II*, p. 137.
40. www.nnsl.com/frames/newspapers/1996-10/oct21_96trail.html.
41. Burwash Walking Tour, Folder Blacks 1/2, Yukon Archives, Whitehorse, Yukon Territory.
42. *American Legacy* (Fall 2005).

43. Fred Spencer to author, interview, March 18, 2009.
44. *Afro American*, Baltimore, November 10, 1942.
45. Malcolm MacDonald, *Down North: A View of Northwest Canada* (New York: Farrar & Rinehart, 1943), p. 224.
46. Pacific Lutheran University, Tacoma, Wash., documentary, *Building Connections*, 2007.
47. William E. Griggs to author, interview, April 21, 2007.
48. Walter Mason to Lael Morgan, undated interview, Lael Morgan Papers, Acc. #99-080, Box 1, Alaska and Polar Regions Collection, Rasmuson Library, University of Alaska, Fairbanks.
49. Jesse Balthazar to author, interview, July 14, 2007.
50. Barry Broadfoot, *Six War Years 1939–1945: Memories of Canadians at Home and Abroad* (Toronto: Doubleday Canada, 1974), p. 221.
51. *Los Angeles Times*, January 5, 1992.
52. Peter Stursberg, *Journey Into Victory: Up the Alaska Highway and to Sicily and Italy* (London: George G. Harrap, 1944), p. 42.
53. Laurence Bergreen, "Irving Berlin: This Is the Army," *Prologue*, Vol. 28, No. 2 (Summer 1996).
54. Joseph Haskin to author, interview, June 30, 2007.
55. Otis E. Lee to author, interview, April 22, 2007.
56. Walter Mason to Lael Morgan.
57. *American Legacy* (Fall 2005).
58. Griggs interview.
59. Donna Blasor-Bernhardt, *Pioneer Road: Anthology of the Alaskan Highway* (Las Vegas: ArcheBooks, 2004), p. 28.
60. Ralph McManus to author, interview, July 4, 2007.
61. Lee interview.
62. Haskin interview.
63. Untitled Col. K.B. Bush Papers, Box 6, U.S. Army Military History Institute, Carlisle, Penn.
64. *American Legacy* (Fall 2005).
65. Dulin interview.
66. Blasor-Bernhardt, *Pioneer Road*, p. 18.
67. Box 7 353.8 Special Service, NA338.
68. "Leadership and the Negro Soldier." Headquarters, Army Service Forces (October 1944), p. 18.
69. *Edmonton Journal*, August 15, 1942.
70. Stursberg, *Journey Into Victory*, p. 28.
71. *Yank*, February 10, 1943.
72. Robert Platt Boyd, Jr., *Me and Company "C"* (Self-published, Library of Congress Catalog Card #92-90656, 1992), p. 114.

Chapter 14

1. Theodore J. Karamanski, "The Canol Project: A Poorly Planned Pipeline," *The Alaska Journal* (Autumn 1979), p. 17.
2. Nat Brandt, *Harlem at War: The Black Experience in WWII* (Syracuse: Syracuse University Press, 1996), p. 4.
3. Galen Roger Perras, "Canada as a Military Partner: Alliance Politics and the Campaign to Recapture the Aleutian Island of Kiska," *The Journal of Military History*, Vol. 56, No. 3 (July 1992), p. 423.
4. Karl C. Dod, *The Corps of Engineers: The War Against Japan* (Washington, D.C.: Office of the Chief of Military History, 1966), p. 317.
5. Col. K.B. Bush Papers, Memo 21 June 1943, Box 6, U.S. Army Military History Institute, Carlisle, Penn.
6. John Schmidt. *This Was No — Picnic: 2.4 Years of Wild and Woolly Mayhem in Dawson Creek* (Hanna, Alberta: Gorman & Gorman, 1991), p. 70.
7. War Department press release, April 16, 1943.
8. Associated Press, Washington, March 10, 1943.
9. *Vancouver Sun*, July 22, 1943.
10. *Globe and Mail*, Toronto, November 16, 1942.
11. *Toronto Star*, April 2, 1942.
12. *Edmonton Bulletin*, July 11, 1943.
13. Donna Blasor-Bernhardt. *Pioneer Road: Anthology of the Alaskan Highway* (Las Vegas: ArcheBooks, 2004), p. 84.
14. *Chicago Daily Tribune*, January 17, 1943.
15. *New York Herald Tribune*, November 11, 1942.
16. *Engineer Update*, April 1986.
17. Capt. Richard Neuberger talk for the BBC, Col. K.B. Bush Papers, Box 6, U.S. Army Military History Institute, Carlisle, Penn.
18. *Hamilton Spectator*, February 16, 1945.
19. http://www.airhighways.com/advroads.htm.
20. Herbert C. Lanks, *Highway to Alaska* (New York: D. Appleton-Century, 1944), p. 24.
21. *The Atlanta Journal-Constitution*, June 21, 1991.
22. Jessie Weeke, letter, August 28, 1990, James N. Eaton, Meek-Eaton Southeastern Regional Black Archives, Florida A&M University, Tallahassee, Fla.
23. *Modern Marvels*, "The Alcan Highway," The History Channel, 2000/2001.
24. Maryland Public Television, June 27, 2007.
25. *St. Petersburg Times*, January 20, 1992.
26. *Washington City Paper*, October 8, 1993.
27. *Houston Post*, September 19, 1990.
28. Letter to Lael Morgan, November 14, 1991, Lael Morgan Papers, Acc. #99-080, Box 1, Alaska and Polar Regions Collection, Rasmuson Library, University of Alaska, Fairbanks.
29. "Building Alaska with the United States Army, 1867–1965," Headquarters, United States Army Alaska October 1, 1965, US, Yukon Archives, Whitehorse, Yukon Territory.
30. Peter Stursberg, *Journey Into Victory: Up the Alaska Highway and to Sicily and Italy* (London: George G. Harrap, 1944), p. 32.

31. Jonathan M. Nielson, *Armed Forces on a Northern Frontier: The Military in Alaska's History, 1867–1987* (New York: Greenwood Press, 1988), p. 138.

32. Malcolm MacDonald, *Down North: A View of Northwest Canada* (New York: Farrar & Rinehart, 1943), p. 236.

33. Morley Cassidy, North American Newspaper Alliance, Inc., June 26, 1943.

34. Stanley W. Dziuban, *Military Relations Between the United States and Canada, 1939–1945* (Washington, D.C.: Office of the Chief of Military History, 1959), p. 383.

35. Kenneth W. Tingley, ed., *For King and Country: Alberta in the Second World War* (Edmonton, Alberta: Reidmore Books, 1995), p. 178.

36. History of the Whitehorse Section of Alcan Highway, Box 9, Folder 8, Office of History, U.S. Army Corps of Engineers, Alexandria, Va.

37. Associated Press, Washington, March 21, 1946.

38. William E. Leuchtenburg, *The White House Looks South: Franklin D. Roosevelt, Harry S. Truman, Lyndon B. Johnson* (Baton Rouge: Louisiana State University, 2005), p. 160.

39. U.S. Special Committee Investigating the National Defense Program, 78th Congress, Report No. 10, Part 14, known as the Truman Committee, Testimony, November 22, 1943.

40. *Ibid.*, November 23, 1943.

41. *Ibid.*, December 20, 1943.

42. *Ibid.*

43. *Ibid.*

44. *Ibid.*, November 22, 1943.

45. Truman Committee report, January 9, 1944.

46. *New York Times,* December 20, 1943.

47. War Department press release, May 5, 1944.

48. Associated Press, Whitehorse, May 1, 1944.

49. *Globe and Mail*, Toronto, May 1, 1944.

50. Richard Finnie, "The Epic of Canol," *Canadian Geographical Journal* (March 1947).

51. Edward A. Harris, "Canol: The War's Epic Blunder," *Nation* (May 5, 1945), p. 513.

52. Pierre Berton, *Prisoners of the North: Portraits of Five Arctic Immortals* (New York: Carroll & Graf, 2004), p. 119.

53. Lyman L. Woodman, "CANOL: Pipeline of Brief Glory," *The Northern Engineer*, Vol. 9, No. 2 (1977), p. 27.

54. *New York Times*, October 8, 1946.

55. Richard J. Diubaldo, "The Canol Project and Canadian-American Relations," *Historical Papers*, Vol. 12, No. 1 (1977), p. 184.

56. NAC, Mackenzie King Diaries, March 18, 1942, p. 243.

57. *Ibid.*, March 21, 1942.

58. Vincent Massey, *What's Past Is Prologue: The Memoirs of the Right Honourable Vincent Massey* (Toronto: University of Toronto Press, 1963), p. 371.

59. P.S. Barry, "The Prolific Pipeline: Finding Oil for Canol," *Dalhousie Review*, No. 57 (2) (1977), p. 205.

60. P.S. Barry, "The Canol Project: An Adventure of the U.S. War Department," *NeWest Review*, Vol. 4, No. 8 (April 1976).

Chapter 15

1. Benjamin O. Davis, Jr., *Benjamin O. Davis, Jr.* (Washington, D.C.: Smithsonian Institution Press, 1991), p. 24.

2. Richard M. Dalfiume, *Desegregation of the United States Armed Forces* (Columbia: University of Missouri Press, 1969), p. 71.

3. Joseph Haskin to author, interview, December 11, 2008.

4. "Notes on Service with the Ninety-third 1944," Box 19550 ENRG 93-0.7, NA RG407.

5. Ulysses Lee, *The Employment of Negro Troops* (Washington, D.C.: U.S. Government Printing Office, 1963), p. 188.

6. Letter to a friend, September 8, 1944, Lael Morgan Papers, Acc. #99-080, Box 1, Alaska and Polar Regions Collection, Rasmuson Library, University of Alaska, Fairbanks.

7. OCE Box 15/20 Accession 72A3173, Folder 50-26, NA RG77.

8. James F. Jones to author, interview, June 13, 2009.

9. Nathaniel Dulin to author, interview, September 30, 2008.

10. *Ibid.*, November 14, 2008.

11. Phillip McGuire, *Taps for a Jim Crow Army: Letters From Black Soldiers in World War II* (Lexington: University of Kentucky Press, 1983), p. 106.

12. Michael Broadhead, History Office, Army Corps of Engineers, Alexandria, Va., e-mail, May 9, 2009.

13. Donna Blasor-Bernhardt, *Pioneer Road: Anthology of the Alaskan Highway* (Las Vegas: ArcheBooks, 2004), p. 15.

14. James C. Coleman to author, e-mail, June 20, 2009.

15. Anthony Mouton to author, interview, June 29, 2007.

16. *Chicago Defender*, March 6, 1943.

17. Fred Spencer to author, interview, December 12, 2008.

18. Gordon W. Weil, *America Answers a Sneak Attack: Alcan and Al Qaeda* (Los Angeles: The Americas Group, 2005), p. 75.

19. Ken Coates, *North to Alaska: Fifty Years on the World's Most Remarkable Highway* (Fairbanks: University of Alaska Press, 1992), p.104.

20. Morris J. MacGregor and Bernard C. Nalty, *Blacks in the United States Armed Forces: Basic Documents* (Wilmington, DE: Scholarly Resources, 1977), p. 491.

21. Floyd A. Bishop to author, interview, June 8, 2009.
22. Coleman interview, June 5, 2009.
23. Coleman to Jack Sigler, interview, April 23, 2003.
24. Balthazar to author, July 14, 2007.
25. Heath Twichell, *Northwest Epic: The Building of the Alaska Highway* (New York: St. Martin's Press, 1992), p. 141.
26. MacGregor and Nalty, *Blacks in the United States Armed Forces*, p. 335.
27. Lael Morgan, "Miles and Miles ... Remembering Black Troops Who Built the Alcan Highway," *CCI Occasional Publication,* No. 38, 1996, Canadian Circumpolar Institute, p. 149.
28. *Lincoln Clarion*, Jefferson City, Mo., October 18, 1950.
29. Edward Carroll to Lael Morgan, interview, January 20, 1992, Lael Morgan Papers, Acc. #99-080, Box 1, Alaska and Polar Regions Collection, Rasmuson Library, University of Alaska, Fairbanks.
30. William E. Griggs to author, interview, April 21, 2007.
31. Maggi M. Morehouse, *Fighting Jim Crow in the Army: Black Men and Women Remember World War II* (Lanham, MD: Rowman & Littlefield, 2000), p. 117.
32. *New York Amsterdam News*, February 23, 1946.
33. Harold L. Ickes, *The Secret Diary of Harold L. Ickes: The Lowering Clouds 1939–1941* (New York: Simon & Schuster, 1954), p. 475.
34. Jean Byers, *A Study of the Negro in Military Service* (Washington, D.C.: Department of Defense, 1947), p. 51.
35. OPD 291.21 Section 2, NA RG165.
36. Dir. Plans & Operations, Entry 118, Box 472, NA RG165.
37. Entry 427, Box 6, 91-DC1-2.1, NA RG407.
38. Records of the Office of the Quartermaster General, Box 5, 333.1, 183, NA RG92.
39. Ruth Gruber to author, e-mail, May 31, 2008. "Unfortunately, I do not have any reply to my report on the conditions of African-American soldiers in Alaska. But I am not surprised."
40. *Ibid.*, e-mail, June 1, 2008.
41. *Afro American*, Baltimore, March 20, 1943.
42. *Chicago Defender*, August 24, 1942.
43 MacGregor and Nalty, *Blacks in the United States Armed Forces*, p. 170.
44. *Ibid.*, p. 299.
45. Samuel A. Stouffer, Edward A. Suchman, Leland C. DeVinney, Shirley A. Star and Robin M. Williams, Jr., *The American Soldier: Adjustment During Army Life*, Vol. 1 (Princeton, N.J.: Princeton University Press, 1949), p. 504.
46. *Ibid.*, p. 506.
47. *Ibid.*, p. 492.
48. *Ibid.*, p. 511.
49. *Ibid.*, p. 515.
50. *Ibid.*, p. 509.
51. *Ibid.*, p. 544.
52. *Ibid.*, p. 525.
53. *Ibid.*, p. 510.
54. *Ibid.*, p. 595.
55. *Ibid.*, Introduction.
56. MacGregor and Nalty, *Blacks in the United States Armed Forces*, p. 187.
57. "Command of Negro Troops" (Washington, D.C.: War Department, February 29, 1944).
58. *Ibid.*
59. "Leadership and the Negro Soldier," Headquarters, Army Service Forces (October 1944), p. 28.
60. *Ibid.*, p. 22.
61. *Ibid.*, p. 12.
62. "Armed Service Forces Manual M5" (Washington, D.C.: War Department, October 1, 1944).
63. *Ibid.*

Chapter 16

1. George H. Roeder, *The Censored War: American Visual Experience During World War Two* (New Haven: Yale University Press, 1993), p. 77.
2. Lauren Rebecca Sklaroff, "Constructing G.I. Joe Louis: Cultural Solutions to the 'Negro Problem' During World War II," *The Journal of American History* (December 2002), p. 968.
3. "Leadership and the Negro Soldier," Headquarters, Army Service Forces (October 1944), p. 72.
4. Lael Morgan, "Miles and Miles ... Remembering Black Troops Who Built the Alcan Highway," *CCI Occasional Publication,* No. 38 (1996), Canadian Circumpolar Institute, p. 160.
5. Nat Brandt, *Harlem at War: The Black Experience in WWII* (Syracuse: Syracuse University Press, 1996), p. 96.
6. Robert A Hill, ed., *The FBI's Racon: Racial Conditions in the United States During World War II* (Hanover, N.H.: Northeastern University Press, 1995), p. 124.
7. Memo dated September 8, 1943, Lael Morgan Papers, Acc. #99-080, Box 1, Alaska and Polar Regions Collection, Rasmuson Library, University of Alaska, Fairbanks.
8. Director Plans and Operations, Entry 118, Box 472, NA RG165.
9. *Ibid.*
10. Henry L. Stimson and McGeorge Bundy, *On Active Service in War and Peace* (New York: Harper & Brothers, 1947), p. 464.
11. *Pittsburgh Courier*, February 7, 1942.
12. Lee Finkle, *Forum for Protest: The Black Press During World War II* (Cranbury, NJ: Associated University Presses, 1975), p. 121.
13. P.L. Prattis, "The Role of the Negro Press in

Race Relations," *Phylon*, Vol. 7, No. 3 (3rd Qtr. 1946), p. 273.

14. Harvard Sitkoff, *A New Deal for Blacks: The Emergence of Civil Rights as a National Issue—The Depression Decade* (Oxford: Oxford University Press, 1978), p. 301.

15. Lee Finkle, "The Conservative Aims of Militant Rhetoric: Black Protest during World War II," *The Journal of American History*, Vol. 60, No. 3 (December 1973), p. 692.

16. Edwin R. Embree, "Julius Rosenwald Fund: Review for the Two-year Period 1942–1944" (Chicago, 1944).

17. Charles Williams, "Harlem at War," *Nation* (16 Jan. 1943), p. 88.

18. Finkle, *Forum for Protest*, p. 82.

19. "Leadership and the Negro Soldier," p. 23.

20. Armistead S. Pride, "The Negro Press Re-examined," *The Journal of Negro History*, Vol. 45, No. 1 (January 1960), p. 51.

21. John A. Bollin to author, interview, March 22, 2008.

22. Notes on Service with the Ninety-third 1944, Box 19550 ENRG 93-0.7, NA RG407.

23. Lael Morgan Papers, Acc. #99-080, Box 1, Alaska and Polar Regions Collection, Rasmuson Library, University of Alaska, Fairbanks.

24. "Leadership and the Negro Soldier," p. 67.

25. *Chicago Defender*, February 6, 1943.

Epilogue

1. *Fayetteville Observer*, February 20, 1994.

2. Jesse Balthazar to author, interview, December 15, 2008.

3. Lee Young to author, interview, June 24, 2007.

4. Otis E. Lee to author, interview, April 22, 2007.

5. James F. Jones to author, interview, June 30, 2009.

6. *The Atlanta Journal-Constitution*, June 21, 1991.

7. Gordon W. Weil, *America Answers a Sneak Attack: Alcan and Al Qaeda* (Los Angeles: The Americas Group, 2005), 77.

8. Fred Spencer to author, interview, December 12, 2008.

9. Herbert M. Frisby, *This Is Our War* (Baltimore: The Afro American, 1944), p. 169.

10. Jean Byers, *A Study of the Negro in Military Service* (Washington, D.C.: Department of Defense, 1947), p. 164.

11. Lt. Gen. John C.H. Lee, letter to commanders of colored troops, December 26, 1944, Truman Library, Independence, Mo.

12. Otis E. Lee to author, interview, April 22, 2007: "I fought in the Battle of the Bulge."

13. Henry Easter to author, interview, June 5, 2009.

14. Wansley Hill to author, interview, January 6, 2009: "I knew two or three from the 388th who volunteered."

15. Byers, *A Study of the Negro in Military Service*, p. 166.

16. Nat Brandt, *Harlem at War: The Black Experience in WWII* (Syracuse: Syracuse University Press, 1996), p. 107.

17. Joe W. Wilson, *The 761st "Black Panther" Tank Battalion in World War II* (Jefferson, NC: McFarland, 1999), p. 53.

18. *San Francisco Chronicle*, February 16, 1995.

19. *Philadelphia Inquirer*, June 22, 1997.

20. *Ibid*.

21. *Stars and Stripes*, March 29, 1945.

22. *Philadelphia Inquirer*, June 22, 1997.

23. Dir. Plans & Operations, Entry 118, Box 472, NA RG165.

24. Robert B. Edgerton, *Hidden Heroism: Black Soldiers in America's Wars* (Boulder, CO: Westview Press, 2002), p. 164.

25. Lael Morgan, "Writing Minorities Out of History," *Alaska History*, Vol. 7, No. 2 (Fall 1992).

26. Eddie Bernice Johnson to author, e-mail, April 28, 2010.

Bibliography

Astor, Gerald. *The Right to Fight: A History of African Americans in the Military*. Cambridge, MA: Da Capo Press, 1998.

Atwood, George H. *Along the Alcan*. New York: Pageant Press, 1960.

Bak, Richard. *Joe Louis: Great Black Hope*. Cambridge, MA: Da Capo Press, 1998.

Barry, P.S. *The Canol Project: An Adventure of the U.S. War Department in Canada's Northwest*. Edmonton, Alberta: Self-published, 1985.

Bartlett, Bruce. *Wrong on Race: The Democratic Party's Buried Past*. New York: Palgrave Macmillan, 2008.

Bellafaire, Judith L., ed. *The U.S. Army and World War II: Selected Papers from the Army's Commemorative Conferences*. Washington, D.C.: Center of Military History United States Army, 1998.

Berton, Pierre. *Klondike: The Life & Death of the Last Great Gold Rush*. Toronto: McClelland & Stewart, 1958.

_____. *Prisoners of the North: Portraits of Five Arctic Immortals*. New York: Carroll & Graf, 2004.

Blasor-Bernhardt, Donna. *Pioneer Road: Anthology of the Alaskan Highway*. Las Vegas: ArcheBooks, 2004.

Bolte, Charles G., and Louis Harris. *Our Negro Veterans*. New York: Public Affairs Committee, 1947.

Borneman, Walter R. *Alaska: Saga of a Bold Land*. New York: HarperCollins, 2003.

Bowman, Waldo G. *Bulldozers Come First: The Story of U.S. War Construction in Foreign Lands*. New York: McGraw-Hill, 1944.

Boyd, Robert Platt, Jr. *Me and Company "C."* Self-published, Library of Congress Catalog Card #92-90656, 1992.

Brandt, Nat. *Harlem at War: The Black Experience in WWII*. Syracuse: Syracuse University Press, 1996.

Brebner, Phyllis Lee. *The Alaska Highway: A Personal & Historical Account of the Building of the Alaska Highway*. Erin, Ontario: The Boston Mills Press, 1985.

Broadfoot, Barry. *Six War Years 1939–1945: Memories of Canadians at Home and Abroad*. Toronto: Doubleday Canada, 1974.

Brown, Earl, and George R. Leighton. *The Negro and the War*. New York: AMS Press, 1972.

Brown, Earl L. *Alcan Trail Blazers: Alaska Highway's Forgotten Heroes*. Fort Nelson, B.C.: Autumn Images, 2005.

Buchanan, A. Russell. *Black Americans in World War II*. Santa Barbara: Clio Books, 1977.

Buckley, Gail. *American Patriots: The Story of Blacks in the Military from the Revolution to Desert Storm*. New York: Random House, 2001.

Bush, James D. *Narrative Report of Alaska Construction, 1941–44*. Anchorage: U.S. Army Engineer District Alaska, 1984.

Byers, Jean. *A Study of the Negro in Military Service*. Washington, D.C.: Department of Defense, 1947.

Chandonnet, Fern, ed. *Alaska at War 1941–1945: The Forgotten War Remembered*. Fairbanks: University of Alaska Press, 2008.

Christy, Jim. *Rough Road to the North: Travels Along the Alaska Highway*. New York: Doubleday, 1980.

Coates, Kenneth. *The Alaska Highway: Papers of the 40th Anniversary Symposium*. Vancouver: University of British Columbia Press, 1985.

_____. *North to Alaska: Fifty Years on the World's Most Remarkable Highway*. Fairbanks: University of Alaska Press, 1992.

_____, and William R. Morrison. *The Alaska Highway in World War II: The U.S. Army of Occupation in Canada's Northwest*. Norman: University of Oklahoma Press, 1992.

Coe, Douglas. *Road to Alaska: The Story of the Alaska Highway*. New York: Julian Messner, 1943.

Cohen, Stan. *The Trail of '42: A Pictorial History of the Alaska Highway*. Missoula: Pictorial Histories, 1988.

Conn, Stetson, Rose C. Engelman, and Byron Fairchild. *The Western Hemisphere: Guarding the United States and its Outposts*. Washington, D.C.: Office of the Chief of Military History, 1964.

Dalfiume, Richard M. *Desegregation of the United States Armed Forces*. Columbia: University of Missouri Press, 1969.

Davis, Benjamin O., Jr. *Benjamin O. Davis, Jr.* Washington, D.C.: Smithsonian Institution Press, 1991.

Dawson, Carl A. *The New North-West*. Toronto: University of Toronto Press, 1947.

Driscoll, Joseph. *War Discovers Alaska*. New York: J.B. Lippincott, 1943.

Dod, Karl C. *The Corps of Engineers: The War Against*

Japan. Washington, D.C.: Office of the Chief of Military History, 1966.

Duesenberg, H. Milton. *Alaska Highway Expeditionary Force: A Roadbuilder's Story*. Clear Lake, IN: H&M Industries, 1994.

Dziuban, Stanley W. *Military Relations Between the United States and Canada, 1939–1945*. Washington, D.C.: Office of the Chief of Military History, 1959.

Edgerton, Robert B. *Hidden Heroism: Black Soldiers in America's Wars*. Boulder, CO: Westview Press, 2002.

Finkle, Lee. *Forum for Protest: The Black Press During World War II*. Cranbury, NJ: Associated University Presses, 1975.

Finnie, Richard. *Canol: The Sub-Arctic Pipeline and Refinery Project Constructed by Bechtel-Price-Callahan for the Corps of Engineers United States Army 1942–44*. San Francisco: Ryder & Ingram, 1945.

Frisby, Herbert M. *This Is Our War*. Baltimore: The Afro American, 1944.

Godsell, Philip H. *The Romance of the Alaska Highway*. Toronto: The Ryerson Press, 1944.

Grafe, Willis. *An Oregon Boy in the Yukon: A Story of the Alaska Highway*. Albany, OR: Chesnimus Press, 1992.

Grant, Shelagh D. *Sovereignty or Security? Government Policy in the Canadian North, 1936–1950*. Vancouver, B.C.: University of British Columbia Press, 1988.

Griffin, Harold. *Alaska and the Canadian Northwest: Our New Frontier*. New York: W.W. Norton, 1944.

Griggs, William E. *The World War II Black Regiment That Built the Alaska Military Highway*. Jackson: University Press of Mississippi, 2002.

Gruber, Ruth. *Inside of Time: My Journey From Alaska to Israel*. New York: Carroll & Graf, 2003.

Gruening, Ernest. *Many Battles: The Autobiography of Ernest Gruening*. New York: Liveright Press, 1973.

Haigh, Jane. *The Alaska Highway: A Historic Photographic Journey*. Whitehorse, Yukon: Wolf Creek Books, 2001.

Hamilton, John David. *Arctic Revolution: Social Change in the Northwest Territories 1935–1994*. Toronto: Dundurn Press, 1994.

Hesketh, Bob. *Three Northern Wartime Projects: Alaska Highway, Northwest Staging Route, Canol*. Edmonton, Alberta: University of Alberta and the District Historical Society, 1996.

Hill, Robert A. *The FBI's RACON: Racial Conditions in the United States During World War II*. Boston: Northeastern University Press, 1995.

Ickes, Harold L. *The Secret Diary of Harold L. Ickes: The Lowering Clouds 1939–1941*. New York: Simon & Schuster, 1954.

James, C.L.R., and George Breitman. *Fighting Racism in World War II*. New York: Monad Press, 1980.

Jenkins, Wilbert L. *Climbing Up to Glory: A Short History of African Americans During the Civil War and Reconstruction*. New York: Rowman & Littlefield, 2002.

Jones, Robert Huhn. *The Roads to Russia: United States Lend-lease to the Soviet Union*. Norman: University of Oklahoma Press, 1969.

Katznelson, Ira. *When Affirmative Action Was White: An Untold History of Racial Inequality in Twentieth-Century America*. New York: W.W. Norton, 2005.

Keith, Ronald A. *Bush Pilot with a Briefcase: The Happy-Go-Lucky Story of Grant McConachie*. Toronto: Doubleday Canada, 1972.

Kilian, Crawford. *Go Do Some Great Thing: The Black Pioneers of British Columbia*. Vancouver, B.C.: Douglas & McIntyre, 1978.

Klinkner, Philip A., and Rogers M. Smith. *The Unsteady March: The Rise and Decline of Racial Equality in America*. Chicago: University of Chicago Press, 1999.

Kryder, Daniel. *Divided Arsenal: Race and the American State During World War II*. New York: Cambridge University Press, 2000.

Lanks, Herbert C. *Highway to Alaska*. New York: D. Appleton-Century, 1944.

LaRocca, Joe. *Alaska Agonistes: The Age of Petroleum*. North East, PA: Rare Books, 2003.

Lee, Frank C. *Alaska Highway Poems*. Mason City, IA: Klipto, 1944.

Lee, Ulysses. *The Employment of Negro Troops*. Washington, D.C.: U.S. Government Printing Office, 1963.

Leising, William A. *Arctic Wings: The Breathtaking Adventures and Experiences of a Flying Missionary in the Trackless Wastes of the Frozen North*. Garden City, NY: Doubleday, 1959.

Leuchtenburg, William E. *The White House Looks South: Franklin D. Roosevelt, Harry S. Truman, Lyndon B. Johnson*. Baton Rouge: Louisiana State University, 2005.

MacDonald, Malcolm. *Down North: A View of Northwest Canada*. New York: Farrar & Rinehart, 1943.

MacGarrigle, George L. *Aleutian Islands*. Washington, D.C.: U.S. Army Center of Military History, 1992.

MacGregor, J.G. *The Land of Twelve-foot Davis: A History of the Peace River Country*. Edmonton, Alberta: Applied Art Products Limited, 1952.

MacGregor, Morris J., Jr. *Integration of the Armed Forces 1940–65*. Washington, D.C.: Center of Military History, 1985.

_____, and Bernard C. Nalty. *Blacks in the United States Armed Forces: Basic Documents*. Wilmington, DE: Scholarly Resources, 1977.

Massey, Vincent. *What's Past Is Prologue: The Memoirs of the Right Honourable Vincent Massey*. Toronto: University of Toronto Press, 1963.

McGuire, Phillip. *He, Too, Spoke for Democracy: Judge Hastie, World War II, and the Black Soldier.* New York: Greenwood Press, 1988.

———. *Taps for a Jim Crow Army: Letters From Black Soldiers in World War II.* Lexington: University of Kentucky Press, 1983.

Mead, Chris. *Joe Louis: Black Hero in White America.* New York: Penguin Books, 1986.

Menzies, Don. *The Alaska Highway.* Edmonton, Alberta: Stuart Douglas, 1943.

Miller, Boulton B. *A Hand on My Shoulder.* Self-published, 2001.

Moore, Christopher Paul. *Fighting for America: Black Soldiers—the Unsung Heroes of World War II.* New York: Random House, 2005.

Morehouse, Maggi M. *Fighting Jim Crow in the Army: Black Men and Women Remember World War II.* Lanham, MD: Rowman & Littlefield, 2000.

Morritt, Hope. *Land of the Fireweed: A Young Woman's Story of the Alaska Highway Construction Days.* Edmonds, Wash.: Alaska Northwest Publishing Company, 1985.

Motley, Mary Penick. *The Invisible Soldier: The Experience of the Black Soldier in World War II.* Detroit: Wayne State University Press, 1975.

Mullen, Robert W. *Blacks in America's Wars: The Shift in Attitudes from the Revolutionary War to Vietnam.* New York: Monad Press, 1973.

Murphy, Carl, ed. *This is Our War.* Baltimore, Md.: The Afro American, 1944.

Nalty, Bernard C. *Strength for the Fight: A History of Black Americans in the Military.* New York: The Free Press, 1986.

Navratil, Sid, John K. Lloyd, Helen Navratil, and Stan R. Caldwell. *Alcan Trail Blazers.* Pittsburgh: 648th Memorial Fund, 1992.

Nielson, Jonathan M. *Armed Forces on a Northern Frontier: The Military in Alaska's History, 1867–1987.* New York: Greenwood Press, 1988.

Nordman, Curtis R. *The Army of Occupation: Malcolm MacDonald and the U.S. Military Involvement in the Canadian Northwest.* Vancouver, B.C.: University of British Columbia Press, 1985.

Overstreet, Everett Louis. *Black on a Background of White: A Chronicle of Afro-Americans' Involvement in America's Last Frontier, Alaska.* Fairbanks: That New Publishing Co., 1988.

Plochmann, George Kimball. *The Last Bulldozer: For the Men of the United States Army who were stationed in Dawson Creek, 1942–44.* Edmonton, Alberta: The Hambly Press, 1944.

Potter, Jean. *Alaska Under Arms.* New York: Macmillan, 1942.

Remley, David A. *Crooked Road: The Story of the Alaska Highway.* New York: McGraw-Hill, 1976.

Roeder, George H. *The Censored War: American Visual Experience During World War Two.* New Haven: Yale University Press, 1993.

Rosten, Norman. *The Big Road.* New York: Rinehart, 1946.

Russell, Chester L. *Tales of a Catskinner: A Personal Account of Building the Alcan Highway, the Winter Trail, and Canol Pipeline Road in 1942–43.* Fort Nelson, B.C.: Autumn Images, 1999.

Schmidt, John. *This Was No — Picnic: 2.4 Years of Wild and Woolly Mayhem in Dawson Creek.* Hanna, Alberta: Gorman & Gorman, 1991.

Shogan, Robert, and Tom Craig. *The Detroit Race Riot: A Study in Violence.* Philadelphia: Chilton Books, 1964.

Sill, Van Rensselaer. *The American Miracle: The Story of War Construction Around the World.* New York: The Odyssey Press, 1947.

Sitkoff, Harvard. *A New Deal for Blacks: The Emergence of Civil Rights as a National Issue—The Depression Decade.* Oxford: Oxford University Press, 1978.

Stimson, Henry L., and McGeorge Bundy. *On Active Service in War and Peace.* New York: Harper & Brothers, 1947.

Stouffer, Samuel A., Edward A. Suchman, Leland C. DeVinney, Shirley A. Star and Robin M. Williams, Jr. *The American Soldier: Adjustment During Army Life*, Vol. 1. Princeton, N.J.: Princeton University Press, 1949.

Stursberg, Peter. *Journey Into Victory: Up the Alaska Highway and to Sicily and Italy.* London: George G. Harrap, 1944.

Sweeney, Michael S. *The Secrets of Victory: The Office of Censorship and the American Press and Radio in World War II.* Chapel Hill: University of North Carolina Press, 2001.

Takaki, Ronald. *A Different Mirror: A History of Multicultural America.* New York: Back Bay Books, 2008.

———. *Double Victory: A Multicultural History of America in World War II.* New York: Little, Brown, 2000.

Taylor, Quintard. *In Search of the Racial Frontier: African Americans in the American West, 1528–1990.* New York: W.W. Norton, 1998.

Tingley, Kenneth W., ed. *For King and Country: Alberta in the Second World War.* Edmonton, Alberta: Reidmore Books, 1995.

Twichell, Heath. *Northwest Epic: The Building of the Alaska Highway.* New York: St. Martin's Press, 1992.

Tynan, Thomas Martin. *The Role of the Arctic in Canadian-American Relations.* Ann Arbor: University Microfilms International, 1976.

Weil, Gordon W. *America Answers a Sneak Attack: Alcan and Al Qaeda.* Los Angeles: The Americas Group, 2005.

Williams, Albert E. *Black Warriors: The Legacy World War II.* Haverford, PA: Infinity, 2002.

Wilson, Joe W. *The 761st "Black Panther" Tank Battalion in World War II.* Jefferson, NC: McFarland, 1999.

Winks, Robin W. *The Blacks in Canada: A History*. Montreal: McGill-Queen's University Press, 1997.

Wolf, Donald E. *Big Dams and Other Dreams: The Six Companies Story*. Norman: University of Oklahoma Press, 1966.

Woodman, Lyman L. *Duty Station Northwest: The U.S. Army in Alaska and Western Canada, Volume Two 1918–1945*. Anchorage: The Alaska Historical Society, 1997.

Wright, Kai. *Soldiers of Freedom: An Illustrated History of African Americans in the Armed Forces*. New York: Black Dog & Leventhal, 2002.

Wynn, Neil A. *The Afro-American and the Second World War*. New York: Holmes & Meir, 1975.

Zaslow, Morris. *The Northward Expansion of Canada 1914–1967*. Toronto: McClelland and Stewart, 1988.

Articles

Andrews, G.S. "Alaska Highway Survey in British Columbia." *The Geographical Journal*, Vol. 100, No. 1, July 1942, pp. 5–21.

Armagnac, Alden P. "Six-Month's Miracle: How U.S. Army Engineers Conquered Bogs and Forests in One of the Greatest Road-Building Jobs of Our Day." *Popular Science*, February 1943, pp. 99–103.

Barry, P.S. "The Canol Project: An Adventure of the U.S. War Department." *NeWest Review*, Vol. 4, No. 8, April 1976.

_____. "The Canol Project, 1942–45." *The Arctic Institute of North America* Vol. 45, No. 4, 1992, pp. 401–403.

_____. "The Prolific Pipeline: Finding Oil for Canol." *Dalhousie Review*, No. 57 (2) 1977, pp. 205–223.

_____. "The Prolific Pipeline: Getting Canol Under Way." *Dalhousie Review*, No. 56 (2), 1976, pp. 252–267.

_____. "'Punch' Dickins and the Origin of Canol's Mackenzie Air Fields." *Arctic*, Vol. 32, No. 4, December 1977, pp. 366–373.

Bell, W. Y., Jr. "The Negro Warrior's Home Front." *Phylon*, Vol. 5, No. 3, 3rd Qtr. 1944, pp. 271–278.

Bergreen, Laurence. "Irving Berlin: This Is the Army." *Prologue*, Vol. 28, No. 2, Summer 1996.

Brebner, Elizabeth. "Sovereignty and the North: Canadian-American Cooperation 1939–45." *CCI Occasional Publication*, No. 38, 1996, 47–64.

Brown, Earl. "American Negroes and the War." *Harper's*, April 1942, pp. 545–552.

Bucksar, Richard G. "The Alaska Highway: Background to Decision." *The Arctic Institute of North America*, Vol. 21, No. 4, 1968, pp. 215–222.

Butler, John Sibley. "Affirmative Action in the Military." *Annals of the American Academy of Political and Social Science*, Vol. 523, September 1992, pp. 196–206.

Butow, R.J.C. "The FDR Tapes: Secret Recordings Made in the Oval office of the President in the Autumn of 1940." *American Heritage*, February/March 1982, pp. 23–4

Chappell, Kevin. "Blacks in World War II." *Ebony*, September 1, 1995.

Coates, Kenneth S., and William R. Morrison. "Soldier-Workers: The U.S. Army Corps of Engineers and the Northwest Defense Projects 1942–1946." *The Pacific Historical Review*, Vol. 62, No. 3, August 1993, pp. 273–304.

_____. "Wartime Boom Town: Fort St. John During World War II," *Journal of the West*, Vol. 36, Issue 4, 1997, pp. 36–42.

_____. "Whitehorse and the Building of the Alaska Highway." *Alaska History*, Vol. 4, issue 1, 1989, pp. 1–26.

_____, and Judith Powell, "Whitehorse and the Building of the Alaska Highway, 1942–1946." *The Alaska Historical Society*, Vol. 4, No. 1, Spring 1989, pp. 1–26.

Cocklin, Robert F. "Report on the Negro Soldier." *Infantry Journal*, December 1946.

Dalfiume, Richard M. "The 'Forgotten Years' of the Negro Revolution." *Journal of American History*, June 1968, pp. 90–106.

Deacon, Kenneth J. "Alcan: The Story of Black Engineers and the Road They Made Reality." *Engineer Update*, April 1986.

Diubaldo, Richard J. "The Canol Project and Canadian-American Relations." *Historical Papers*, Vol. 12, No. 1, 1977, pp. 178–195.

Drapeau, Raoul. "Pipe Dream: With Creative Engineering and Heroic Endurance, Beleaguered Workers Pushed the CANOL Pipeline Through the Brutal Arctic Wilderness During World War II." *American Heritage*, Vol. 17, Issue 3, Winter 2002.

Dwyer, Ellen. "Psychiatry and Race During World War II." *Journal of the History of Medicine and Allied Sciences*, No. 61 (2), 2006, pp. 117–143.

Eberhardt, Frank J. "Alaska Military Highway." *Alaska Life*, January 1944, pp. 38–40.

Eicher, George Jr. "'Cat Skiing' Hopeless Land." *Alaska Life*, September 1942, pp. 7–11.

Ells, S.C. "Alaska Highway." *Canadian Geographical Journal*, Vol. XXVIII, No. 3, March 1944, pp. 104–119.

Embree, Edwin R. *Julius Rosenwald Fund: Review for the Two-year Period 1942–1944*. Chicago, 1944.

Eminhizer, E.M. "An Alcan Scrapbook." *The Alaska Journal*, Vol. 8, Issue 4, 1978, pp. 344–5.

Evans, James C., and David A. Lane, Jr. "Integration in the Armed Services." *Annals of the American Academy of Political and Social Sciences*, Vol. 304, March 1956, pp. 78–85.

Fenderson, Lewis H. "The Negro Press as a Social Instrument." *The Journal of Negro Education*, Vol. 20, No. 2, Spring 1951, pp. 181–188.

Finkle, Lee. "The Conservative Aims of Militant

Rhetoric: Black Protest During World War II." *The Journal of American History*, Vol. 60, No. 3, December, 1973, pp. 692–713.

Finnie, Richard. "A Route to Alaska through the Northwest Territories." *Geographical Review*, Vol. 32, No. 3, July, 1942, pp. 403–416.

_____. "Canol Blitz." *Maclean's*, August 15, 1943, p. 36.

_____. "The Epic of Canol." *Canadian Geographical Journal*, March 1947.

_____. "The Evolution of Canol." *Polar Notes*, November 1959, pp. 28–35.

_____. "The Origin of Canol's Mackenzie Air Fields." *Arctic*, Vol. 33 No. 2, June 1980, pp. 273–279.

Forbes, Sherman. "The Canol." *Alaska Life*, May 1944, pp. 21–26.

Fradkin, Philip L. "The First and Forgotten Pipeline." *Audubon*, November 1, 1977, pp. 58–79.

Greenwood, John T. "Building the Road to Alaska." *Builders and Fighters: U.S. Army Engineers in World War II*, Barry W. Fowle, ed. Washington, D.C.: Office of History, U.S. Army Corps of Engineers, 1992, pp. 117–35.

Hancock, Lyn. "Canol Road Dilemma: Is Easy Access Spoiling Yukon's Old Pipeline Route?" *Canadian Geographic*, April/May 1982.

Harris, Edward A. "Canol: The War's Epic Blunder." *Nation*, May 5, 1945, pp. 513–14.

Hastie, William H. "The Negro in the Army Today." *Annals of the American Academy of Political and Social Science*, Vol. 223, September 1942, pp. 55–59.

Haulman, Daniel L. "The Northwest Staging Route." *CCI Occasional Publication*, No. 38, 1996, pp. 31–46.

Hendricks, Charles. "The Eskimos and the Defense of Alaska." *Pacific Historical Review*, Vol. 54, No. 3, 1985, p. 280.

Honigmann, J.J. "On the Alaska Highway." *Dalhousie Review*, Vol. 23 No. 4, January 1944, pp. 400–408.

Hopkins, Oliver B. "The 'Canol' Project: Canada Provides Oil for Allies." *Canadian Geographical Journal*, Vol. XXVII, No. 5, November 1943, pp. 238–249.

Johnson, Gregory A. "Strategic Necessity or Military Blunder? Another Look at the Decision to Build the Alaska Highway." *CCI Occasional Publication*, No. 38, 1996, pp. 5–22.

Karamanski, Theodore J. "The Canol Project: A Poorly Planned Pipeline." *The Alaska Journal*, Autumn 1997, pp. 17–21.

Krakauer, Jon. "Ice, Mosquitoes and Muskeg: Building the Road to Alaska," *Smithsonian*, Vol. 23, No. 4, July 1992, pp. 102–112.

Lawler, Pat. "Taking the Territory by Storm: Buckner and His Boys Invade Alaska!," *The Alaska Journal*. 1981, pp. 84–99.

Lloyd, Trevor. "Oil in the Mackenzie Valley." *Geographical Review*, Vol. 34, No. 2, April 1944, pp. 275–307.

Long, Howard H. "The Negro Soldier in the Army of the United States." *The Journal of Negro Education*, Vol. XII, No. 3, Summer 1943, pp. 307–15.

Ludington, Bryr. "Pioneer of the Alaska Highway." *Alaska* magazine, October 2008.

McCormack, Patricia A. "The Canol Project at Fort Chipewyan." *CCI Occasional Publication*, No. 38, 1996, pp. 183–199.

MacDonald, Donald. "Highway ... Hell!" *Alaska Life*, September 1942, pp. 3–12.

McGuire, Phillip. "Desegregation of the Armed Forces: Black Leadership, Protest and World War II." *The Journal of Negro History*, Vol. 68, No. 2, Spring 1988, pp. 147–158.

_____. "Judge Hastie, World War II, and Army Racism." *The Journal of Negro History*, Vol. 62, No. 4, October 1977, pp. 351–362.

_____. "Judge William H. Hastie and Army Recruitment, 1940–1942," *Military Affairs*, Vol. 42 No. 2, April 1978, pp. 75–79.

McLaughlin, Les. "North to Alaska." *Legion*, October 2002.

McMillion, Shelby A. "The Strategic Route to Alaska." *The Military Engineer*, November 1942.

Milner, Lucille B. "Jim Crow in the Army." *The New Republic*, Vol. 110, March 13, 1944, pp. 339–342.

Morgan, Lael. "Miles and Miles...: Remembering Black Troops Who Built the Alcan Highway." *CCI Occasional Publication*, No. 38, 1996, pp. 149–63.

_____. "Writing Minorities Out of History: Black Builders of the Alcan Highway," *Alaska History*. Fall 1992.

Morrison, William. "Uncle Sam's Warpath." *Horizon Canada*, Vol. 7, No. 76, 1986, pp. 1820–24.

Neuberger, Richard L. "Behind the Scenes at the Alcan Opening." *Alaska Life*, February 1943.

_____. "Highballing at Sixty Below." *Saturday Evening Post*, November 27, 1943.

_____. "Yukon Adventure." *Saturday Evening Post*, February 19, 1944.

Perras, Galen Roger. "Canada as a Military Partner: Alliance Politics and the Campaign to Recapture the Aleutian Island of Kiska." *The Journal of Military History*, Vol. 56, No. 3, July 1992, pp. 423–454.

Peterson, Audrey. "Northern Exposure." *American Legacy*, Fall 2005.

Pierce, J. Kingston. The Biggest and Hardest Job Since the Panama Canal." *American History*, Vol. 35, 2001.

Prattis, P.L. "The Morale of the Negro in the Armed Services of the United States." *The Journal of Negro Education*, Vol. XII, No. 3, Summer 1943, pp. 355–63.

_____. "The Role of the Negro Press in Race Relations." *Phylon*, Vol. 7, No. 3, 3rd Qtr. 1946, pp. 273–283.

Pride, Armistead S. "The Negro Press Re-examined." *The Journal of Negro History*, Vol. 45, No. 1, January 1960, pp. 51–53.

Quattlebaum, Charles B. "Military Highways." *Military Affairs*, Vol. 8, No. 3, Autumn 1944, pp. 225–238.

Rainey, Froelich. "Alaskan Highway an Engineering Feat." *National Geographic Magazine*, February 1943.

Richardson, Harold W. "Alcan-America's Glory Road: Part I — Strategy and Location." *Engineering News-Record*, December 17, 1942.

———. "Alcan-America's Glory Road: Part II — Supply, Equipment and Camps." *Engineering News-Record*, December 31, 1942.

———. "Alcan-America's Glory Road: Part III — Construction Tactics." *Engineering News-Record*, January 14, 1943.

Sabin, Paul. "Voices from the Hydrocarbon Frontier: Canada's Mackenzie Valley Pipeline Inquiry (1974–1977)." *Environmental History Review*, Vol. 19, No. 1, Spring 1995, pp. 17–48.

Schiffman, Joseph. "The Education of Negro Soldiers in World War II." *The Journal of Negro Education*, Vol. 18, No. 1, Winter 1949, pp. 22–28.

Seeber, Frances M. "'I Want You to Write to Me': The Papers of Anna Eleanor Roosevelt." *Prologue*, Summer 1987.

Sitkoff, Harvard. "Racial Militancy and Interracial Violence in the Second World War." *The Journal of American History*, Vol. 58, No. 3, December 1971, pp. 661–681.

Sklaroff, Lauren Rebecca. "Constructing G.I. Joe Louis: Cultural Solutions to the 'Negro Problem' During World War II." *The Journal of American History*, December 2002, pp. 958–83.

Smith, E. Valerie. "The Black Corps of Engineers and the Construction of the Alaska Highway." *Negro History Bulletin*, December 1993.

Snow, Edgar. "The Most Valuable Ground on Earth." *Saturday Evening Post*, July 4, 1942, pp. 9–10, 80.

Spellman, Charles C. "The Black Press: Setting the Political Agenda During World War II." *Negro History Bulletin*, December 1993.

Stillman, Richard II. "Negroes in the Armed Forces." *Phylon*, Vol. 30, No. 2, 1969, pp. 139–159.

Sturdevant, Brig.-Gen. Clarence L. "The Military Road to Alaska: Organization and Administrative Problem." *The Military Engineer*, January 1943, pp. 173–81.

———. "U.S. Army's First Official Story of the Alaska Highway." *Roads and Bridges*, March 1943.

Thompson, Charles H. "The American Negro in World War I and World War II." *The Journal of Negro Education*, Vol. XII, Summer 1943.

Thompson, Paul W. "ALCAN." *Infantry Journal*, October 1942.

Weil, Frank E.G. "The Negro in the Armed Forces." *Social Forces*, Vol. 26, No. 1, October 1947, pp. 95–98.

White, Walter. "Behind the Harlem Riot." *The Republic*, August 16, 1943, pp. 220–2.

———. "Race Relations in the Armed Services of the United States." *The Journal of Negro Education*, Vol. XII, No. 3, Summer, 1943, pp. 350–54.

———. "What the Negro Thinks of the Army." *Annals of the American Academy of Political and Social Sciences*, September 1942.

Williams, Charles. "Harlem at War." *Nation*, January 16, 1943, pp. 88.

Williams, G.A. "Winter-Maintenance Problems on the Alaska Highway." *Roads and Bridges*, November 1943, pp. 27–30, 58–90.

Williams, Griffith H. "Alaska's Connection: The Alcan Highway." *Pacific Northwest Quarterly*, Vol. 76, Issue 2, 1985, pp. 61–68.

Woodman, Lyman L. "Building the Alaska Highway: A Saga of the Northland." *The Northern Engineer*, Vol. 8, No. 2, pp. 11–28.

———. "CANOL: Pipeline of Brief Glory." *The Northern Engineer* Vol. 9, No. 2, pp. 14–28.

Yost, Harry. "Building the Alaska Highway." *The Alaska Journal*, Autumn 1985, pp. 23–27.

Interviews

Sgt. Jesse Balthazar
Sgt. Reginald Beverly
Lt. Floyd A. Bishop
Sgt. John A. Bollin
Winnie Boyd
Capt., later Lieut. Col. James C. Coleman
Helene Dobrowolsky
Sheila Dodds
Pvt. Nathaniel Dulin
Pvt. Henry Easter
George Ford
Sgt. William E. Griggs
Ruth Gruber
Pvt. Joseph Haskins
Spence Hill
Sgt. Wansley Hill
Representative Eddie Bernice Johnson
Pvt. James F. Jones
Sgt. Otis E. Lee
Casey McLaughlin
Ralph McManus
Sister Cecile Montpetit
Pvt. Anthony Mouton
Walter Muir
Lt., later Brig. Gen. Alton Post
Allen W. Sowden
Pvt. Fred Spencer
Thelma Tucker
Pvt. George Young
Sgt. Lee Young

Index

Afro American (Baltimore) 22, 29, 44, 172, 180, 182
Agattu, Aleutian Islands 72
Alaska Highway: approval 15; black and white regiments race to complete highway 102; black and white soldiers bet on bridge completion 92–95; construction begins 66; court-martial of ten black soldiers overturned 138–9; death by freezing 127, 134–5; initial study 11–13; name change 157; onsite visit 17–18; opening ceremony 105–8; route selection 16; soldiers help rebuild burned town 144–6; work of black soldiers praised 159–61
Albanati, Oscar 135
Alcan Highway *see* Alaska Highway
Alcohol use 150
Anderson, Joseph 33
Anderson, Marian 95
Army General Classification Tests 56, 177
Arnold, Maj. Thomas 168
Atkinson, Sgt. Nehemiah 40, 135, 189
Atlanta Daily World 48
Attu, Aleutian Islands 72, 86, 155
Attucks, Crispus 20

Baer, Buddy 41
Baker, Lt. Vernon 191
Balthazar, Sgt. Jesse 38, 131, 134, 136, 149, 168, 185, 189
Barclay, William W. 146
Barnett, Albert G. 183–4
Barnhardt, Glen 144
Bartlett, E.L. 105–6
Battle of the Bulge 187–8
Bear Island, N.W.T. 117
Beaver Creek, Yukon Territory 102, 137
Bechtel, Steven 163
Bechtel-Price-Callahan consortium 19, 111
Bennett, Charles 9
Berch, Insp. A.G. 114
Berlin, Irving 150

Berton, Pierre 164
Beverly, Sgt. Reginald 39, 51, 76, 130
Bishop, Lt. Floyd A. 168
Blondin, George 111
Bollin, Sgt. John E. 38, 45, 52–3, 63, 70, 84, 137, 143, 182, 189
Bond, Sgt. Thomas 93
Borden, Prime Minister Robert 58
Borders, Elden 12
Borneman, Walter R. 108
Bowe, Pvt. Robert 101, 107
Boyd, Lt. Robert Platt, Jr. 46, 52, 64, 79, 83–4, 121, 131 154
Boyer, Lt. Col. James W., Jr. 31
Brawley, Sgt. Gordon 92, 94
Brehon, Sgt. Franklin J. 115, 119–20, 128, 135
Bridges, Pvt. Sims 139
Brotherhood of Sleeping Car Porters 23
Brown, Matthew S. 188
Bryant, Sgt. Warren 43
Buckner, Brig. Gen. Simon Bolivar, Jr. 15, 56–8, 76, 83, 86, 96, 141, 155, 186
Buckner, Gen. Simon Bolivar, Sr. 57
Bull, Brig. Gen. H.R. 30
Burke, Sgt. George H. 60, 90–1, 128
Bush, Col. K.B. 76, 105
Bush, Pvt. Philip 105
Butler, Cpl. James J. 105, 147
Byers, Jean 170–1

Calhoun, Pvt. Willie B. 59
Call and Post, Cleveland 48
Calloway, Ernest 41
Calverley, Dorothea 144
Camp Butner, N.C. 104, 134
Camp Canol, N.W.T. 117
Camp Claiborne, La. 7, 50, 66, 109, 168, 185
Camp Forest, Ga. 182
Camp McCain, Miss. 43
Camp Prairie, Alta. 110–1, 119
Camp Shanks, N.Y. 186
Camp Shelby, Miss. 43

Camp Swift, Tex. 43
Camp Van Dorn, Miss. 43
Camsell, Dr. Charles 106
Canadian Bank of Commerce 143, 151
Canadian Broadcasting Corporation 107–8
Canadian Pacific Airlines 17
Canadian Steamship Lines 6
Canol Pipeline: airfields built 118; project accepted 19–20; refinery built 125; route determined 110–1; soldiers save officer from drowning 116; troops spend winter 122–4; Truman committee investigates project 161–65; winter road built 119; work begins 115; work regiment assembled 53
Carcross, Yukon Territory 83–4
Carmack, George 9
Carroll, Chaplain Edward G. 62, 89–90, 94–5, 97, 107, 152, 168–9, 188
Chambers, Harold 135
Chandler, Sgt. Augustus 132
Charlie Lake, B.C. 90, 142
Chicago Defender 29, 136, 168, 180, 183
Chinook 104
Christensen, Lt. Col. J.C. 30
Churchill, Winston 181
Civil War 20, 22, 24, 27, 35, 57
Clark, Sen. Bennett Champ 73
Clarke, Mel 135
Clinton, Pres. Bill 191
Coleman, Capt. James C. 98–9, 167–8
Coliva, Pvt. Joe 151
Command of Negro Troops 177
Confederate Army 20
Congressional Medal of Honor 20–1
Conley, Pvt. Howard G. 66, 121
Cook, Les 67
Couch, Orval 149
Coudert, Bishop Jean Louis 136
Crawford, Brig. Gen. Robert W. 136
Crosby, Bing 137

Index

Dade, Floyd 188
Dallas Morning News 43
Danielson, Maj. Gen. C.H. 139
Daugherty, James 9
Davis, Lt. Benjamin O., Jr. 21, 166
Davis, Brig. Gen. Benjamin O., Sr. 21, 25, 51, 166–7, 169
Davis, Wesley 136, 160
Dawson City, Yukon Territory 10–12, 17, 60, 67
Dawson Creek, B.C. 7, 18, 58, 60–2, 143, 149
Deacon, Kenneth J. 158
Deal, Lt. Clyde S. 158
Demetrovich, Pete 88
De Priest, Rep. Oscar S. 166
DeWitt, Lt. Gen. John L. 15, 56–7
Dighton, Maj. Samuel R. 143, 146
Dimond, Rep. Anthony J. 14, 157
diseases 82, 133
Dobrowolsky, Helene 75
Donald, Sgt. Edward 50
Donovan, William J. 16
Doolittle, Col. James H. 72
Dorset, George W. 189
Double V 181–2
Drew, Dr. Charles R. 28
Dudrow, Col. Walter 52, 78
Duesenberg, Warren 128
Dulin, Pvt. Nathaniel 37–8, 62, 92–4, 141, 151, 167
Dutch Harbor, Aleutian Islands 15, 72–3, 109–10

Early, Steven 24
Easter, Pvt. Henry 49, 89, 141, 187, 189
Edmonton, Alta. 11, 13, 16, 58–9, 144, 152
Edmonton Journal 60, 152
Eglin Field, Fla. 42
Eisenhower, Gen. Dwight D. 187, 189
Elliott, Peter 60
Emancipation Proclamation 20, 27
Embarras Portage, Alta. 117–8
Engineering News-Record 99, 102
English, Pvt. Charles 145
Evans, Cpl. Horace 44
ExxonMobil 19, 109

Fairbanks, Alaska 7, 11–14, 17, 97, 137
Federal Works Agency 156
Finnie, Richard 55, 122, 163–4
Fischer, Col. Donald H. 96, 108
Ford, George 130
Forrest, Helen 137
Fort Belvoir, Va. 17, 40, 51, 88
Fort Benning, Ga. 36, 44, 170

Fort Bliss, Tex. 51
Fort Bragg, N.C. 40, 44, 62
Fort Clark, Tex. 51
Fort Devens, Mass. 187
Fort Fitzgerald, Alta. 112–3
Fort Glen, Aleutian Islands 86
Fort Graham, B.C. 13, 16
Fort Huachuca, Ariz. 51
Fort McMurray, Alta. 111, 143
Fort Meade, Md. 39, 51
Fort Nelson, B.C. 14, 120, 128
Fort St. John, B.C. 18, 56, 67–8
Fort Simpson, N.W.T. 120
Fort Smith, N.W.T. 113–18, 121–2
Fortas, Abe 172
Fradkin, Philip L. 121
France, Sgt. Albert E. 143, 189
Francis, Paul W. 130–1, 142, 160
Frank, Richard 149
Franklin, John Hope 35
Freeman, Pvt. George 188
Freeman, Sgt. Linton 141
French Army 21
Fulks, Pvt. Eugene 139

Ganong, Maj. Gen. H.N. 106
Garber, Lt.-Col. Howard A. 100
Gardener, Charles 168
Gardener, Lt. Willis G. 116, 119
Germany 13–4, 19
Gibson, Truman K. 121
Gillen, Gen. Alvan C., Jr. 189
Gladwin, Eldson 159
Godsell, Philip H. 82
Goebbels, Joseph 55
Grafe, Willis R. 64
Graham, James H. 19, 109, 161
Grande Prairie, Alta. 14
Great Circle Route 13
Great Slave Lake 112
Greyhound Bus Line 158
Griggs, Thomas 77
Griggs, Sgt. William E. 42, 64, 78–9, 82, 97–8, 135, 143, 149–50, 160, 170, 188
Grimshaw, Alta. 119
Gronke, Cpl. Otto 101, 107
Gruber, Ruth 170–2
Gruening, Gov. Ernest 12, 57–8

Hale, Milton S. 188
Hamel, Charles 107
Hamilton, Nolan 38, 57
Handy, Maj. Gen. Thomas T. 172
Harlin, Norman 68
Haskin, Joseph 38, 45, 63, 88, 136, 141–2, 150, 166, 189
Haskins, Murphy 33
Hastie, Judge William H. 25–9, 31–2, 48, 121, 169
Hatfield, Sgt. Ernie 29
Hayes, Sgt. Robert 116–7, 122

Hayes, Roland 173
Hazelton, B.C. 12–3
Heard, Sgt. James M. 138–9
Henry, Lt. Andrew 97
Henry, Pvt. Walter 94
Henson, Matthew 10
Herron, Tec 4 Clemmie L. 134
Hickens, Allen 93
Hill, Pvt. Jus 48
Hill, Sgt. Wansley 39, 53–4, 66, 111, 122–4
Hitler, Adolf 37
Hoge, Brig. Gen. William M. 17, 54–5, 60, 66–8, 73–5, 77–9, 83, 89, 92, 96, 99, 106, 108, 110, 125, 187, 189
Ho-Lem, Dave 146
Hollingsworth, Pvt. James V. 139
homosexuality 143
Hoover, Pres. Herbert 11
Hoover, J. Edgar 180
Horne, Lena 147
House, Mate W. Charles 72
Householder, Col. Eugene R. 31
Howe, C.D. 118
Howell, Lt. Dewitt C. 138, 150
Howell, Pvt. Willie 189
Hudson's Bay Company 67, 82, 90, 110, 114–5
Hull, Sec. Cordell 157
Hunt, Lt. Ralph W. 102
Hunter, Charles 9
Hunter, Lucile 9

Ickes, Sec. Harold 16, 19, 55, 110, 162, 170–2
Imperial Oil 19, 109, 124, 162–3
Ingalls, Lt. Col. Robert D. 17, 74, 105
International Highway Commission 11, 55

Jackson, Pvt. Andrew 115
Jalufka, Pfc. Alfred 72, 104, 109
Japan 12–3, 18, 72, 104, 109
Jenness, Diamond 148
Jim Crow 24, 41, 49, 51
Johnson, Rep. Eddie Bernice 193
Johnson, Col. Frank M.S. 63, 83–4, 86
Johnson, Henry 21
Johnson, James 104
Johnston, George 55
Johnston, R.A.N. 68
Jones, Lt. G.H. 102
Jones, Pvt. James F. 39, 90, 167, 189

Keenan, Pearl 82
Keesler Field, Miss. 48–9
Keith, Homer 18
Keys, Ulysses S. 50

Index

King, Prime Minister Mackenzie 11–13, 18, 61, 106, 163–4
Kiska, Aleutian Islands 72, 86, 155
Klondike Gold Rush 9–10, 63, 67, 128, 133
Knowles, Pvt. Charlie 167
Knox, Sec. Frank 23, 27
Kodiak, Aleutian Islands 15
Ku Klux Klan 25

LaGuardia, Fiorello 27
Land, Lt. Samuel B. 151
Lane, Col. Albert L. 145–6, 152, 158, 169
Lanks, Herbert C. 159
Leadership and the Negro Soldier 177
Lee, Frank C. 128
Lee, Lt. Gen. John C.H. 187
Lee, Lt. Lloyd B. 92–4, 167
Lee, Sgt. Otis E. 38–9, 71, 76, 82, 90, 128, 134, 143, 150–1, 160, 165, 187, 189
Lee, Ulysses Grant, Jr. 22
Leising, Fr. William A. 114, 124
Leonard, Col. Joseph S. 29
Leval, Victor 117
Lewis, Gen. H.B. 29
Lewis, Lt. Col. James L. 36, 84, 131, 143, 166, 183
Lincoln, Abraham 20
Lindy, Pvt. Warren H. 139
Livengood, Alaska 137
Lockott, John 137
Logan, John 12
Logan, Pvt. William E. 124
London, Jack 84
Long, Sgt. Eugene 130
Lord Ha-Ha 144
Los Angeles Times 121
Loston, Wilbur W. 86
Louis, Sgt. Joe 41, 88, 150 86
Luckow, Maj. Dick 104
Lyles, Pvt. N. 48
Lynn, Winfred W. 40

MacDonald, Donald 12, 15
MacDonald, Malcolm 69, 115, 160, 165
MacDonald, Thomas 74
Mackenzie, Ian 106–7
Mackenzie River 112, 116–8
MacLeish, Archibald 182
MacNaughton, Gen. A.G.L. 189
Magee, Maj. Gen. James C. 29
Magnuson, Congressman Warren G. 12, 16
Malcom, Roger and Dorothy 189
Marshall, E.C. 160
Marshall, Gen. George C. 13, 31, 46, 56, 180, 187, 189

Marshall, Justice Thurgood 35, 48
Martin, Capt. Sydney A. 95
Mason, Skokum Jim 9
Mason, Lt. Walter 41, 58, 61, 65, 99, 101, 149–50
Massey, Vincent 165
Massie, Tec 5 Hubert 116–7, 122
May, Chaplain Irwin T. 107
McArthur, James 17–18
McCloy, John J. 24, 172–3
McConachie, Grant 14, 17, 110
McCutcheon, W.E. 61
McDill Field, Fla. 44
McKinley, James 90
McLaughlin, Casey 79
McManus, Ralph 151
McMeekin, Capt. Andrew 101
McNamara, Sec. Robert S. 190
McNarney, Lt. Gen. Joseph T. 58
Miller, Col. Boulton B. 128
Miller Construction Company 126
Mitchem, Maj. Charles 98, 101
Moffat, J. Pierrepont 18, 118
Monk, Sgt. Clifton Brant 78, 96, 98, 128, 136, 141, 185
Moore, Sen. Edward H. 162
Morgan, Lael 179–80, 162
Mouton, Anthony 33–4, 37, 50, 53, 62, 84, 88, 130, 134, 137, 168, 189
Mueller, Lt. Col. E.A. 17, 60
Munnikhuysen, Gen. Henry Dorsey 30
Munro, Maj. Ronald J. 95

National Association for the Advancement of Colored People (NAACP) 23, 47, 170, 181
National Negro Congress 23
Neuberger, Lt. Richard L. 95, 133, 135, 158
Neuman, Col. David L. 89, 92, 169
New York Amsterdam News 170
New York Herald Tribune 122, 158
New York Times 164
Newfoundland 8
Nielson, Jonathan M. 160
93rd Regiment 6–7, 33, 36, 38, 50–56, 62–3, 70–71, 74, 80, 83–8, 134, 137, 143
95th Regiment 6–7, 38–9, 40, 51, 54, 58, 62, 71, 74, 78, 88–95, 128, 130, 149
97th Regiment 6–7, 36, 38–9, 40, 42, 54, 56, 58, 61, 64, 74, 78, 96–108, 128, 130, 134, 137, 140, 143
Nix, Pvt. Willie 118
Noland, Donald W. 80
Norfolk Journal and Guide 29, 180

Norman Wells, N.W.T. 13, 16, 19–20, 109, 111, 115–19, 121, 124, 161
Northern Alberta Railway 17–8, 61–2, 122
Northern Transportation Company Limited 110
Northwest Service Command 75, 110, 128, 131, 133, 136, 138–9, 143, 157
Northwest Staging Route 14–6, 19, 59, 110, 156
Norwegian, Rose 148

O'Connor, Brig. Gen. James A. ("Patsy") 74–5, 86, 88, 94–5, 104–5, 107, 110, 143, 156, 160, 180, 187
Officer Cadet School 89, 166, 168–9
Oubre, Sgt. Hayward, Jr. 39, 65, 99, 128, 137, 141, 149–51, 188
Owens, Sgt. George A. 51, 188

Panama Canal 8
Parsons, Lt. Walter 36, 65, 82, 103, 128, 139
Patterson, Robert P. 23, 27, 122, 162–3
Patton, Gen. George 187
Pattullo, Premier Thomas J. 11–12
Paules, Col. Earl G. 75, 101, 105
Payne, Hazel Dixon 147
Peace River 18, 67–8, 119
Pearl Harbor 7, 15–7, 20, 35, 41, 44, 73, 109, 155, 182
Peary, Adm. Robert E. 10
Pegler, Westbrook 182
Pensacola, Fla. 7
Pittsburgh Courier 22, 29–30, 42–3, 48–9, 63, 180–3
Post, Lt. Alton 43
Pouce Coupé, B.C. 144
Powell, Pvt. Alexander 136, 160, 189
Powell, Gen. Colin 191–2
Powell, Pen 132
Prattis, Percival 63, 181
Prejean, Joseph 33–4, 189
Price, Sgt. James A. 92–4
Prince George, B.C. 13, 63
Prince Rupert, B.C. 6, 16, 125
Public Roads Administration 7, 18, 56, 64, 73–4, 84, 98–9, 101, 104, 156

Randolph, A. Philip 23, 25–7
Randolph Field, Tex. 48
Ratliff, Pvt. Lee I. 139
Raymond, Allen 158
Reagan, Nancy 171

219

Index

Reagan, Lt. Ronald 150
Rebouche, Cpl. James 74
Red Cross 28–9, 141, 146–7
Reilly, Pvt. John T. 105, 107
Reybold, Maj. Gen. Eugene 56, 75, 156
Richardson, Harold 99, 102
Richardson, Willie 141
Roberts, Sgt. Henry 51, 62, 167
Roberts, Needham 21
Robins, Maj. Gen. Thomas M. 162
Robinson, Jack Roosevelt 190
Robinson, Lt. Col. Lionel E. 99–101, 128, 137, 140
Robinson, Sugar Ray 41, 84
Robinson, Rep. Will 161
Romel, Field Marshal Erwin 19
Roosevelt, Eleanor 26, 172–3
Roosevelt, Pres. Franklin D. 11–13, 15–16, 19, 22–7, 37, 43, 49, 104, 161–2, 186
Roosevelt, Theodore 21
Ross, Sgt. John 91
Rosten, Norman 95
Roundtree, Pvt. Richard 93
Rowland, Bill 75
Royal Bank of Canada 151
Royal Canadian Mounted Police (RCMP) 8, 11, 67, 85, 105, 114, 155
Royall, Kenneth Claiborne 190
Rucker, Pvt. Robert M. 139
Rumble, J. Lance 159
Russell, Charles 135
Russia 11

St. Louis Post Dispatch 164
Sandiford, Paul E. 53
Saturday Evening Post 73
Saunders, Jack 148
Schmitt, Lt. Donald J. ("Smitty") 167
Schnurstein, Lt. Leslie ("Bud") 84
Schuyler, George 182
Seattle, Wash. 7, 109
Selective Service Act 34, 37, 40
Service, Robert 128
Sharp, Sgt. Alfred 105
Siddall, K.H. 68
Sikanni Chief River 92–4
Simmons, C.E. 59
Simon, Sgt. Walter 95
Sims, Cpl. Refines, Jr. 102–5, 183
Sincavage, Lt. Joseph J. 167

Skagway, Alaska 6, 9, 63, 75, 125
Skelton, Red 88
Slana, Alaska 98
Smarch, Virginia 78
Smith, Capt. Albert L. 137
Smith, Sgt. Benjamin 105
Smith, James 188
Smith, Lt. Sidney 118–9
Snow, Edgar 73
Soldier's Medal 116
Soldiers Summit 104
Somervell, Maj. Gen. Brehon B. 19, 74–5, 109, 119, 157, 161–2
Soviet Union 19
Sowden, Allen W. 142
Spencer, Fred 38, 71, 87–8, 137, 149, 160, 168, 186, 189
Spicely, Pvt. Booker T. 44
Stacey, C.P. 160
Standard Oil of California 109, 162
Standard Oil of New Jersey 109
Stefansson, Vilhjalmur 13, 16, 19
Stewart, Charles 19
Stimson, Sec. Henry L. 14, 19, 21, 25–6, 28, 31–2, 34, 36, 46, 48, 57, 101, 104, 106, 121
Stuart, Lt. Gen. Kenneth 58
Sturdevant, Brig. Gen. Clarence L. 17–8, 57, 86, 89, 99, 139
Stursberg, Peter 136, 149, 160
Styer, Maj.-Gen. W.D. 180
Suicide Hill, Yukon Territory 140
Sutton, Jim 135

Tatum, Capt. Walter 136
Taylor, Charlie 135
Taylor, Clifford 147
Taylor, James 40
Terlizzi, Capt. Carmelo 95
Teslin, Yukon Territory 84–5
388th Regiment 6–7, 53, 58, 66, 77, 109–128
Thurman, Ned 45
Toronto Star 157
Trent, Richard E. 40, 78, 81, 185
Truman, Sen. Harry S 161, 189–90
Tucker, Pvt. Clarence 124
Tucker, Sgt. Herbert 93, 169, 188
Tully, Col. James K. 16
Tuskegee Pilots 25, 108
Twichell, Lt. Col. Heath 92, 95, 169

Urquhart, Dr. J.A. 114

Valdez, Alaska 65, 96–7
Vancouver Sun 122
Von Zelinski, Col. Walter F. 131

Waldrum, Pvt. Otis 93
Walker, Sgt. Harvey 93
Walker, Tommie L. 40
Walker, Pvt. William 45
War of Independence 20
Washington, George 20
Waterways, Alta. 7, 13, 58, 111–3, 115, 119
Watson, Maj. Gen. Edwin M. 27
Watson Lake, B.C. 14, 67, 128
Weaver, Pvt. Josh 139
Weeke, Sgt. Jessie 160
Welch, Cpl. Jonathan 91
Welling, Maj. Alvin C. 68
Wheeler, Col. John W. 158
Whipple, Col. Stephen C. 96, 99
White, Walter 23, 25–6, 28, 181
White Pass and Yukon Railway 11, 63, 75–6, 125
Whitehorse, Yukon Territory 12–3, 19, 75, 84, 109, 125, 137, 158
Williams, Charles 137, 182
Williams, Clyde ("Slim") 12
Williams, Dan 90
Williamson, Lt. Buel A. 182
Willis, J. Frank 108
Willkie, Wendell 22
Wilmore, Don 93
Wilson, Charles 49, 190
Wilson, Sec. Charles E. 189
Wilson, Sgt. John 91
Wilson, Lt. Col. W.P. 76
Womack, Timothy 95
Woodman, Lt. Col. Lyman L. 108, 164
World War I 21
Worsham, Col. L.D. 119
Wyman, Col. Theodore, Jr. 110, 117, 119

Yakulic, George 61
Young, Pvt. Clyde, Jr. 61
Young, Sgt. George 129, 136
Young, Lee 36, 43, 98–9, 130, 135

www.ingramcontent.com/pod-product-compliance
Lightning Source LLC
Chambersburg PA
CBHW081554300426
44116CB00015B/2879